REBA MICHELS HILL, M.D.

℞:

A Doctor's Prescription for Gourmet Cooking

Sig: *Enjoy Daily*

Refill: yes ✔
no ____

Reba Michels Hill M.D.
Physician

Mercer Island, Washington

Back Cover Photograph: James De Leon, Jr.
Production Coordinator: Lee Shepard
Copy Editor: Heidi Oman
Design and Production: Carol Naumann
Production Assistant: Lisa Huffstutter
Typesetter: Compu/Systems

Copyright © 1984 by Peanut Butter Publishing, 2445 76th Ave. S.E., Mercer Island, Washington 98040. All rights reserved. No part of this book may be reproduced or transmitted in any form or by any means without written permission from the publisher.
Printed in the United States of America

ISBN 0-89716-135-1

TABLE OF CONTENTS

REFERRAL v

INTRODUCTION vii

PREFACE ix

ACKNOWLEDGEMENTS x

SUCCESSFUL MENUS xiii

APPETIZERS 1

BEVERAGES 27

BREADS 37

DESSERTS 49

EGGS AND STARCHES 93

MEATS 121

SALADS 163

SAUCES AND DRESSINGS 183

SEAFOODS 197

SOUPS 223

VEGETABLES 231

TABLES 256

INDEX 259

THE VICE PRESIDENT'S HOUSE
WASHINGTON, D.C. 20501

December 14, 1983

Dear Dr. Hill,

It was a special pleasure to learn about the great project you have undertaken: "A Doctor's Prescription For Gourmet Cooking"! Although to have become a gourmet cook through the years with your busy life and schedule is itself a feat; to share your knowledge and successes with others is the wonderful part!

I know to the many who use and enjoy this book -- put together so lovingly -- it will bring great joy and pleasure. They will also be delighted, as am I, in knowing that the proceeds will benefit the outstanding St. Luke's Episcopal Hospital Linda Fay Halbouty Newborn-Premature Research Center.

Happy eating to all and congratulations!

Warmly,

Barbara Bush

I am looking forward to trying some of your prescriptions... whoops -.. recipes!

INTRODUCTION

Dr. Reba Michels Hill is a pediatrician and a specialist in Neonatology (care of sick newborn infants). She is a full Professor of Pediatrics and Head of the Developmental Toxicology Section at Baylor College of Medicine, Houston, Texas. Dr. Hill is Chief of Newborn Research at the Linda Fay Halbouty Newborn Premature Research Center at St. Luke's Episcopal Hospital. She is married and the mother of three daughters.

In 1962, Dr. Hill began developing a newborn research program at St. Luke's Episcopal Hospital. Now, more than twenty years later, she remains actively involved in study of the effect of maternal drugs on the fetus, the transfer of maternal drugs into breast milk and the effect of intrauterine malnutrition on infant development. Her published works include over 90 articles which have appeared in the medical literature.

A love for cooking began for Dr. Hill as a child. It seemed logical that this interest in cooking also should support her driving interest in improving the quality of life for newborn infants by supporting research in the field. Therefore, proceeds from the sale of this cookbook will be used to further Newborn Research.

Pediatricians, especially those who limit their attention to the newborn infant, must combine clinical skills with imagination and possess an inherent love for children. We are justly proud of Dr. Hill's many accomplishments and gratefully acknowledge her life's devotion to the infants entrusted to our care.

Newell E. France
Executive Director
St. Luke's Episcopal and
Texas Children's Hospitals
Houston, Texas

PREFACE

This book is the result of my interest in cooking that has grown over the years. When I married, the pinnacle of my cooking ability was Mexican food which was limited to tacos and enchiladas. By the time I finished my Pediatric Residency and Neonatology Fellowship, I had mastered rock cornish hens. With the appointment to faculty level in the Department of Pediatrics at Baylor College of Medicine, I inherited a group of hungry young doctors in training on whom I practiced my culinary skills. Their numbers grew in rank from 30 to 90 housestaff physicians a year. As the years went by, a telephone ring at night was as frequently a request for the recipe for rum cream pie or directions for preparing the marinated beef tender as for instructions in the medical management of a critically ill patient.

This book then is dedicated to the past and present Pediatric Residents of Baylor College of Medicine who served as my gourmet guinea pigs over the last 20 years. They accepted by culinary failures as well as my triumphs with a smile.

Reba Michels Hill, M.D.
Chief of Newborn Research

Linda Fay Halbouty
Newborn-Premature Research Center
St. Luke's Episcopal Hospital
Chief of Developmental Toxicology
Professor of Pediatrics
Baylor College of Medicine

ACKNOWLEDGEMENTS

There are many people who contributed to this book. First and foremost is my mother, Bessie Michels who was an excellent cook but never measured an ingredient. It took me many years of experimenting to produce her cornbread dressing.

Additional influences from others are:

Marilyn Catchings, Baton Rouge, La.
Anne Cheney, Houston, Texas
Mary Cummings, Houston, Texas
Jeannine Curtis, Houston, Texas and Canada
Myrtyl Davidson, R.N., Houston, Texas
Vivian Dickson, Washington, D.C.
Bonnie Lees de Vries M.D., Reno, Nevada and Canada
Jean Hall, Jacksonville, Florida
Pat Helms, R.N., Amarillo, Texas
Courtney Hill, Houston, Texas
Doris Hill, Salt Lake City, Utah
Laurie Hill, Houston, Texas
Melanie Hill, Houston, Texas
Hermena Kelly, Houston, Texas
Lee McCulley, R.N., Houston, Texas
Dorothy Minor, Houston, Texas
Rev. Nicolas Notar, Stamford, Conn. and Florida
Margaret Northcutt, Houston, Texas
Francis Papacchia "Mama Poli', Houston, Texas
Paulene "Gabbio" Roberts, Gainesville, Texas
Roger Rashbach, Houston, Texas
Ann Rosenberg, Houston, Texas
June Wilson, Houston, Texas
Reba Wright, Dallas, Texas
Helen Savage, R.N., Houston, Texas

Others who had their own influence on my cooking skills:

J.R. "Bob" Michels (my father)
Velma Michels (my grandmother)
Jack Puddy (my grandfather)

My special thanks to Annette Sparks for the many hours spent typing the recipes and to Linda Tennyson, R.N. for her helpful suggestions and for proofing the book and to my husband, L. Leighton Hill, M.D. for allowing me this flight of fancy.

My favorite time to consolidate the recipes that I collected through the year was on summer vacation. The recipes would be stuffed into a large shopping bag and packed with the rest of our belongings that we took to Florida.

One year on such a trip the zipper on the carry-all packed on top of the station wagon broke. I suddenly saw little sheets of paper forming a trail behind the car. I hollered to my husband 'Stop, we're losing my recipes." He pulled the station wagon to a screeching halt by the side of Interstate 10. We locked the children in the car and frantically began gathering the tiny pieces of paper from the median. People slowed their cars to look at the unusual couple gathering litter off the busy highway.

Each year when we pass that spot en route to Florida, the children say "Do you remember when mamma lost her recipes here?" We were so embarrassed.

SUCCESSFUL MENUS FROM THE HUNDREDS OF RECIPES IN THIS BOOK

SPECIAL EVENTS

Christmas Dinner
    Holiday Cranberry Dessert
    Ambrosia
    Grandmother's Mashed Potato Salad
    Roast Turkey
    Turkey Gravy with Mushrooms
    Cornbread Dressing for an Army and a Few Others
    Green Beans Like Mother Makes
    Banana and Sweet Potato Muffins
    Mincemeat Crepes with Whiskey Sauce

Thanksgiving Dinner
    Gazpacho
    Glazed Ham with Ambrosia Sauce
    Spinach Salad with Chutney Dressing
    Sweet Potatoes Alexander
    Hermena's Asparagus Casserole
    Cheese Biscuits
    Mincemeat Upsidedown Cake with Rum Sauce and Mrs. Davidson's German Fruit Cake

Wedding Reception
    Wedding Reception Punch
    Warm Orange Spiced Tea
    Phyllo Appetizers
    Stuffed Mushrooms with Crabmeat
    Marinated Sausages
    Chicken Salad with Almonds and Grapes spread on Cheese Biscuits
    Leave the cakes up to the bakery.

Mexican Dinner	Mexican Cheese Dip Like Ninfa's
Special Chili Rellenos Dip with Tortilla Chips
Pinata Double Dip
Mexican relish tray (ripe tomatoes, jalapeño peppers, sliced avocados, and green onions.)
Chicken Enchiladas
Tacos you assemble yourself
Salsa
South of the Border Surprise
Favorite Sunday Dinner	Roast Beef with Gravy, with Mushrooms
Green Beans Like Mama Made
Macaroni and Cheese
Green salad, tomatoes, asparagus and celery with Fresh Lemon Dressing
Small Party Rolls
Pralines and Cream Ice Cream or Rum Cream Pie
Cocktail Buffet	Beef Tender in Sherry with Mushrooms
Meatballs with Spaghetti Sauce
Pickled Shrimp Hermena Kelly
Spinach Crepes with Wine-Cheese Sauce
Small Party Rolls
Hello Dollies
Cocktail Party	Cheese Sausage Balls
Salmon Appetizer
Grab-Bag Dip
Cheese with Mustard Sauce
Meatballs in Spaghetti Sauce
A tray containing:
Bird's Nests, Praline Crescents and Hello Dollies

Patio Party for 250	Molds of Philadelphia Cream Cheese topped with green Jalapeño jelly served with favorite crackers Green salad with plum tomatoes, sliced zucchini, purple onions, croutons and ripe olives with Simple Salad Dressing Beef Tender in Sherry with Mushrooms Copper Pennies Italian Potato Salad Quick Italian Rum Cake
Patio Supper	Smoked Beef Brisket 24 Hour Salad Italian Green Bean Casserole Ratatouille Stuffed Mushrooms Cheddar Cheese Pennies Custard and Fruit
Patio Buffet Supper	Mexican Cerviche Pork Roast with Avocado and Lemon Garlic Dressing German Potato Salad Marinated Peas or Beans Jalapeño Cornbread #2 Zabaglione Cream
Patio Party	Salmon Appetizer Squash Salad Barbecued Shrimp in Wine Sauce Spinach Stuffed Potatoes Jalapeño Cornbread #1 Frozen Cake
Brunch	Mexican Cerviche Mexican Breakfast Fiesta Banana Treats Breakfast Monkey Bread Praline Crescent Cookies and Ice Cream

Brunch	Mushroom Cheese Puff Breakfast Souffle Hot Fruit Casserole Carmel Breakfast Rolls Gingerbread with Brandy Custard Sauce
Brunch	Oysters in Sherry Sauce Italian Brunch Eggs on Italian Garlic Bread Fruit Salad with Angel Salad Dressing Amaretto Souffle
Brunch	Mexican Cheese Dip Like Ninfa's Gambler's Eggs Carmol Fruit Breakfast Rolls Bourbon Peaches Cherry Surprise
Brunch	Shrimp Dill Pâté Egg Omelette Sausage Squares Grits Souffle Mixed Fruits Nut Delight
Luncheon	Shrimp and Artichokes Chicken Salad with Almonds and Grapes Fruit Salad with La Martinique Poppyseed Dressing Ricotta Muffins Fruit with Cream
Luncheon	Cold Cream of Avocado Soup Fried Chicken Salad Guacamole and Shrimp Salad Mushrooms Supreme Cheese Biscuits Cheese Pie

Luncheon	Scallops in Green Sauce Spinach with Hot Bacon Dressing Shellfish Crepes in Wine Sauce Quick Asparagus Tomatoes Stuffed with Mushrooms Coconut Kahlúa Cream Pie
Luncheon	Seafood Mousse Artichoke Rings Spinach Salad with Chutney Dressing Bourbon Peaches Cheddar Cheese Pennies Amaretto Souffle
Luncheon	Lobster Bisque Italian Vegetable Salad Spinach Crepes Marinated Carrots Sweet Potato Muffins Eggnog Mousse with Apricot Sauce
Luncheon	Gazpacho Shellfish Crepes in Wine Sauce Holiday Cranberry Salad Puffed Broccoli Gabbio's Orange Bread Bourbon Street Cheesecake
Dinner	Escargots in Butter Green Salad with sliced, yellow squash, ripe marinated artichokes, olives, Feta cheese and Simple Salad Dressing Chicken Breasts and Tomato Sauce Italian Spinach Fettuccini, Zucchini and Mushrooms Party Rolls

Dinner
: Mock Turtle Soup
Hearts of Palm Salad
Shrimp Creole with Eggplant and Brown Rice
Mushroom Supreme
Jalapeño Cornbread #2
Brandy Alexander Pie

Dinner
: Italian Oysters
Green Salad with shrimp, Romano cheese, ripe olives, cherry tomatoes and Simple Salad Dressing
Veal Lasagna
Marinated Eggplant
Jean's Garlic Bread
Tortoni

Dinner
: Shrimp in Mustard Sauce
Spinach with Chutney Dressing
Chicken Florio
Wild Rice with Grapes and Almonds
Six Week Muffins
Raspberry Souffle with Anglaise Sauce and a Chocolate Cookie

Dinner
: Boiled Shrimp with Arnaud Sauce
Green Salad with purple onions, ripe olives, yellow squash, tomatoes, Mozzarella cheese and Simple Salad Dressing
Italian Chicken
Italian Vegetables
Garlic Bread-Vintage 1960
Amaretto Coconut Cream Pie

Dinner
- Spanish Fish Soup
- Green Salad with tomato slices, ripe olives, small boiled shrimp, sour pickles, boiled egg slices, and Fresh Lemon Dressing
- Veal Scallops
- Green and Red Bell Peppers in Spaghetti Sauce
- Italian White Beans
- Jean's Garlic Bread
- Rum Cream Pie

Dinner
- Tomatoes Camille
- Green Salad with Apples and Cheese
- Gourmet Fish in Cheese Sauce
- Peas and Lettuce
- Broccoli with Tomato Sauce
- Riccota Cheese Muffins
- Jeannine's Fruit Pizza

Dinner
- Beef Brisket Appetizer
- Green Bean Salad
- Marinated Chicken
- Holiday Potatoes
- Mexican Spoon Bread with Chilies
- Quick Asparagus with Asparagus Sauce
- Bourbon Pie

Dinner
- Cold Cream of Avocado Soup
- Green Salad with tomatoes, miniature corn-on-the-cob, ripe olives, cherry tomatoes, Romano cheese and Simple Salad Dressing
- Shrimp, Tomatoes, Wine and Feta Cheese
- Fettuccini, Mushrooms and Zucchini
- Italian Bread Vintage 1960
- Nesselrode Chiffon Pie

Dinner
    Lettuce Soup
    Green Salad with Hot Bacon Dressing
    Flounder with Ye Olde College Inn Stuffing
    Potato-Broccoli Cheese Bake
    Lenten Spinach
    Six Week Muffins
    Chocolate Chestnut Dessert

Dinner
    Shrimp with Rèmoulade Sauce
    Green Salad with Tangy French Dressing and Crabmeat
    Pork in Crust
    Tomatoes Bombay
    Broccoli with Lemon and Butter Sauce
    Marilyn's Crème de Cassis Pie

Dinner
    Oysters Daytona
    Cheese-Onion Marinade over Romaine
    Gutsey Shrimp
    Vermicelli with Spinach Pesto Sauce
    Quick Asparagus
    Italian Bread Vintage 1960
    German Chocolate Pie

Dinner
    Shrimp in Mustard Sauce
    Green Salad with avocados, tomatoes, croutons, Romano cheese and Golden Simple Salad Dressing
    Mother's Ritz Cracker Chicken
    Italian Vegetables
    Monkey Bread
    Bourbon Pie

Dinner   Spanish Fish Soup
                  Green Salad with Feta cheese,
                     Artichokes, red onions, olives and
                     Simple Salad Dressing
                  Crabmeat Landry
                  Potatoes with Spiced Cheese,
                     Tomatoes and Onions
                  Fancy Peas
                  Tavern Spoon Bread
                  Rum Cream Pie

Dinner   Pickled Shrimp Hermena Kelly
                  Hearts of Palm Salad
                  Easy Gourmet Chicken
                  Bourbon Peaches
                  Italian Spinach
                  Cheese Biscuits
                  Mississippi Fudge Cake

Dinner   Italian Oysters
                  Eggplant Salad
                  Easy Gourmet Pork Casserole
                  Broccoli with Butter and Lemon
                     Sauce
                  Mexican Spoon Bread with Chilies
                  Trifle

Date: *Today*

For Those Who Enjoy Eating
Patient's name

℞: APPETIZERS

Dispense: *Small Nibbles*

Sig: *Use Small Serving Spoons*

Refill: yes _____
no ✓

Reba Michile Hill MD.
Physician
DEA Number AH 0000000

APPETIZERS

BEEF BRISKET APPETIZER LIKE TUJAQUE'S IN NEW ORLEANS

2 pound brisket of beef, trimmed	⅓ cup celery
2 cups cold water	⅛ teaspoon pepper
½ onion	1 bay leaf
1 clove garlic, minced	2-3 whole peppercorns
	1 teaspoon salt

Place meat in pan and add remaining ingredients except salt. Bring water to boil then simmer for 2 hours until meat is fork tender. Add more water as necessary so that meat is always covered. Salt when cooked. Serve with warm Red Sauce (See Index) or Tujaque's Boiled Beef Sauce (See Index). Serve only about 1 ounce portions as an appetizer.

MARINATED SAUSAGE

3 dozen small cocktail smoky sausages	⅛ teaspoon crushed dried thyme
¼ cup soy sauce	¼ teaspoon dry mustard
¼ cup ketchup	⅛ teaspoon garlic
2 tablespoons salad oil	1 ounce sherry
2 tablespoons cider vinegar	

Prick sausages with toothpick. Combine all ingredients and pour over sausage. Allow to stand 2 hours or overnight. Place in 350° oven and bake until sausages are just cooked. DO NOT OVERCOOK. Good served on toothpicks. You can also cut refrigerator crescent rolls in strips, roll a slender piece around sausage and bake until dough is light brown. Makes 36.

For many years my children thought that having a party meant you had to roll up the rug in the family room, clean the floor and replace the rug so the floor was clean when the residents rolled it back to dance. One day my oldest returned home to report critically that Susan's mother didn't clean under the rug for her party.

APPETIZERS

MINIATURE CHALUPAS

1 avocado
1 teaspoon lemon juice
salt and pepper
miniature round tortilla chips for nachos
refried beans
Monterey Jack cheese, shredded
jalapeño pepper
lettuce, shredded
tomatoes, finely chopped
sour cream

Take pulp of avocado and mash with lemon juice. Add salt and pepper. Layer tortilla chips with refried beans, Monterey Jack cheese, avocado, jalapeño pepper, lettuce, tomato and sour cream.

PAN FRIED BRIE CHEESE

1 pound French Brie, cut into bite-sized pieces
2 cups flour
1 teaspoon cayenne
1 teaspoon black pepper
1 teaspoon salt
1 cup buttermilk
¼ pound margarine

Season flour with salt, pepper and cayenne. Add to buttermilk. Batter cheese twice and place in freezer. Pan fry cheese in margarine until golden brown. Serves 4-6.

SPICED SUGAR PECANS

1 cup sugar
½ teaspoon ground cinnamon
½ cup evaporated milk
1 teaspoon vanilla
2 cups pecan halves

Combine sugar, cinnamon and milk in saucepan and cook to soft ball stage. Add vanilla. With slotted spoon, add pecans to mixture to coat them. Put on wax paper to cool. Makes 2 cups.

APPETIZERS

MRS. DAVIDSON'S CHEESE SAUSAGE BALLS

- 1 pound Owens Hot Sausage, broken up
- 2 cups Bisquick
- 1 teaspoon salt
- 10 ounces sharp cheddar cheese, grated

Sauté sausage briefly to remove fat. Drain. Combine all ingredients and roll into balls. Put on cookie sheet and bake at 350° for 10 minutes.

STUFFED JALAPEÑOS

- 15-20 mild fresh jalapeños
- 4 ounces Muenster cheese, grated
- ½ cup cornmeal
- ½ cup flour
- 1 egg, beaten
- ¾ cup milk
- cooking oil

Wear rubber gloves to cut peppers in half but leave stems on. Remove seeds and rinse peppers. Drain and dry. Stuff with Muenster cheese. Combine cornmeal and flour. Mix egg with milk. Dip pepper in cornmeal/flour mixture and then in egg/milk mixture. Fry in 1 inch hot fat and drain. Makes 15-20 pieces.

MARINATED EGGPLANT - MAMA POLI

- 1 small narrow eggplant
- red wine vinegar
- garlic powder
- crushed red pepper
- oregano
- olive oil

Cut eggplant so that each slice contains part of skin. Put vinegar in pan and layer slices of eggplant in it. Place saucer on top of eggplant to keep it from breaking up. Bring vinegar to boil. Do not overcook. Eggplant should remain semi-firm. Drain and cool. Layer eggplant in container. After each layer, sprinkle heavily with garlic powder, red pepper and oregano. Fill container with equal parts of vinegar mixture and olive oil. Seal and allow 48 hours to marinate. Good as appetizer or in salads.

APPETIZERS

SEAFOOD SAINT-JACQUES

2 cups white sauce
2 eggs, beaten
¾ cup Swiss cheese, grated
2-3 dashes Tabasco
salt and pepper
¼ cup white wine
1 cup whipping cream, whipped
1 cup fresh mushrooms, sliced, sautéed
1 pound crabmeat
1 pound shrimp, peeled and deveined
1 cup cooked mashed potatoes

Add eggs and cheese to cool white sauce. Correct seasoning with salt, pepper and Tabasco. When cheese melts, add wine. Take ½ of cheese sauce and mix with crabmeat, shrimp and mushrooms. Divide into 12 buttered seashells. Spread with thin layer of whipped cream. Cover with sauce. Pipe edges with mashed potatoes to keep sauce from running off shells. Serves 10-12.

ITALIAN OYSTERS

24 oysters
4 tablespoons olive oil, divided
4 ounces white wine
4 green onions, chopped
¼ cup parsley, minced
salt and pepper
Tabasco
1 teaspoon garlic powder
juice of 1 lemon
½ cup seasoned bread crumbs (Pepperidge Farm seasoned croutons with cheese whirled in food processor)
½ cup Parmesan cheese, grated
2 tablespoons margarine

Put 2 tablespoons of oil in baking dish. Arrange oysters in dish. Sprinkle rest of oil over oysters. Add wine, green onions, parsley, salt, pepper, Tabasco, garlic powder and lemon juice. Cover with seasoned bread crumbs and Parmesan cheese. Dot with margarine. Bake at 400° until crumbs brown. Serves 4-6.

APPETIZERS

OYSTERS ROCKEFELLER
LIKE ANTOINES, NEW ORLEANS

	fresh oysters on half shell	3	tablespoons minced green onions, bottom and tops
9	tablespoons minced iceberg lettuce	3	teaspoons margarine
3	tablespoons minced romaine lettuce	1½	cups water
		¾	teaspoon Pernod
3	tablespoons minced celery hearts with some dark green leaves		black pepper
		4-8	drops Tabasco
			French bread

Mince iceberg, romaine, celery and onions individually using metal blade of food processor. Put into pan with margarine and cook for about 10 minutes. Add water to keep from cooking dry and cook for 1 hour. This smells like you are cooking for rabbits until you get to the end of the cooking period and then it smells like spinach. The sauce should look like a puree at this point. Add Pernod, Tabasco and pepper and cook 10 minutes more. Salt cautiously because romaine and celery give a salt flavor. Drain oysters. Place oyster on shell in flat pan filled with rock salt. Put spoonful of sauce on oysters and place under broiler until oysters are cooked and sauce bubbly (about 5 minutes). Serve at once with french bread for dunking.

There are many stories told about Oysters Rockefeller. Some say they are made with spinach, but to native cooks around New Orleans, no spinach is added to the dish.

APPETIZERS

ARTICHOKES AND SHRIMP

3	pounds cooked shrimp, shelled and deveined	2-3	(8 ounce) jars horseradish sauce, Tulkoffs Tiger Sauce
30	ounces marinated artichoke hearts		juice of 3 limes
1	teaspoon garlic powder	12	shakes Tabasco

Cut shrimp and artichoke hearts into bite size pieces. Mix shrimp, garlic powder, artichokes including liquid, horseradish sauce, lime juice and Tabasco. Marinate several hours before serving. Serve on small seashells. Size of shells determines how many people this will serve. I receive the most compliments on this dish. Serves 25-30.

Most commercial horseradish sauces are too mild and taste floury. If Tiger Sauce not available, use My Rendition of Tiger Sauce (See Index).

CALIFORNIA AVOCADO ESCABECHE

2	pounds fish filet	1	tomato, chopped
1	cup lime juice	¼	teaspoon oregano
1	large onion, sliced and separated into rings		salt and pepper
		4-5	dashes Tabasco
¼	cup chopped green pepper	2	avocados, cubed
	garlic powder	1	basket cherry tomatoes, halved
½	cup olive oil		

Allow raw fish to marinate in lime juice for 24 hours. The meat will turn white. Sauté onion and green pepper in olive oil, seasoned with garlic powder. Cook only until vegetables begin to soften. Combine with fish; add oregano, salt, pepper and Tabasco. Refrigerate. Before serving, add avocados and cherry tomatoes. Serves 10-12.

APPETIZERS

MEXICAN CERVICHE

2	pounds fish filet cut in bite size pieces	¼	cup Rotel tomato juice
1	cup lime juice or mixture lime and lemon	1	small onion, minced
		1	teaspoon cilantro
		1	teaspoon cumin
2	jalapeño peppers, seeded and chopped	2	teaspoons chili powder
			salt and pepper
1	(10 ounce) can Rotel tomatoes (tomatoes with green chilies) strained and chopped		garlic powder

Place fish in lime juice and marinate overnight. Stir fish at least once. Add remaining ingredients about 2 hours before serving. Serves 8.

STUFFED OYSTERS

12	large oysters in shells	4	tablespoons mayonnaise
½	pound margarine, softened	4	tablespoons drained capers
1	cup green onion, finely chopped	3	tablespoons lemon juice
1	cup parsley, minced	1	cup seasoned bread crumbs
6	large garlic cloves, minced		Parmesan cheese
	Tabasco		olive oil
	salt and pepper		

Mix green onions, parsley, garlic with margarine. Add Tabasco, salt, pepper, mayonnaise, capers and lemon juice. Spread over oysters in shell or in individual casserole. Cover with bread crumbs and Parmesan cheese. If mixture too thick to spread, thin with small amount of olive oil. Bake in 400° oven until bread crumbs are just golden. Makes 12 servings. These taste similar to escargots.

APPETIZERS

℞

OYSTERS IN SHERRY SAUCE

24 raw oysters	2 tablespoons Worcestershire sauce
flour	
margarine	
¼ cup lemon juice	2 ounces pale dry sherry
1 cup A-1 Steak Sauce	3 tablespoons water
	2 tablespoons flour

Dredge oysters in flour and fry in margarine. Cook until brown and crisp. Remove. Combine lemon juice, steak sauce, Worcestershire sauce and sherry. Heat but do not boil. Blend 2 tablespoons flour into 3 tablespoons water and add to sauce. Cook until thickened. Serve oysters with heated sauce. Must serve at once. Good as a pass around dish at cocktail party. Serves 24. Do not substitute broiled oysters.

OYSTERS DAYTONA

2 dozen raw oysters and liquid	½ pound margarine
	¼ cup flour
1 pound uncooked shrimp, peeled and deveined	¼ cup tomato puree
	½ cup dry red wine
	4 teaspoons garlic, minced
½ pound fresh mushrooms, chopped	
	1½ teaspoons hot red pepper
1 cup chopped onions	1 teaspoon salt
1 cup green onions, chopped including green tops	

Drain oysters. Add enough water to liquid to make ½ cup and reserve. Mince shrimp, mushrooms, onions, green onions with metal blade of food processor. Sauté 4-5 minutes in margarine. Add flour, tomato puree, wine, garlic and oyster/water to sauce. Cook until thickened. Stir in red peppers and salt. Puree mixture in blender and spoon sauce over oysters in individual ramekins. Bake oysters for 15 minutes in 350° oven until edges curl. Serves 8-10.

APPETIZERS

ESCARGOTS IN BUTTER

1 (7½ ounce) can snails	6 large garlic cloves, finely chopped
6 tablespoons butter, divided	1 teaspoon salt
2 tablespoons parsley, finely chopped	¼ teaspoon pepper
2 teaspoons finely chopped green onion	6-8 large fresh mushroom caps

Drain and wash snails. Mix all ingredients together except 2 tablespoons butter and mushrooms and pour over snails. Sauté mushrooms in 2 tablespoons butter. Place snail mixture in mushroom caps in greased pan. Heat in oven until oil begins to bubble. Serves 4-6.

CLAMS IN MARINER SAUCE

2 pounds fresh clams	1 cup white wine
3 tablespoons olive oil	3 tablespoons parsley, finely chopped
1 large onion, minced	salt and pepper to taste
4 medium tomatoes, peeled, seeded and chopped	French bread
1 teaspoon sweet paprika	

Scrub clams well. In large skillet, heat oil and fry onions. Add tomatoes and sweet paprika and cook a few minutes. Add clams, wine, parsley, salt and pepper. Cover and cook until clams open. Serve with French bread for dipping. Discard any clam that does not open. Serves 6. Shelled, uncooked shrimp with tails left on may be substituted for clams.

APPETIZERS

PICKLED SHRIMP HERMENA KELLY

10 pounds cooked shrimp, peeled and deveined
¾ cup water
2 cups white vinegar
2½ cups salad oil
3 (2¾ ounce) bottles capers and juice
5 teaspoons celery seed
3 teaspoons salt
several dashes Tabasco
1-2 cloves garlic or equivalent garlic powder
1 tablespoon sugar
8-10 bay leaves, broken
4 cups onion rings
2 tablespoons pickling spices
8 whole cloves

Heat vinegar and water until boiling. Add rest of ingredients except shrimp. Let marinade cool. Add cooked shrimp. Refrigerate at least 24 hours before serving. Serves 30-40 people. I first had these 25 years ago when Mrs. Kelly gave a dinner party honoring my husband and me at the time of our marriage.

SALMON APPETIZER

1 (8 ounce) can refrigerated crescent rolls
4 ounces salmon roe
1 (4 ounce) carton sour cream
1 (2¾ ounce) jar capers
1 small onion, chopped
1 egg, beaten
2 tablespoons water

Separate crescent rolls so that you have 4 rectangles. Layer ¼ of salmon, sour cream, capers and onions on each crescent rectangle. Fold pastry forward like an envelope to cover. Glaze with egg mixture made of water and egg. Bake at 350° for 25 minutes until light brown. Do not overcook. Cut in ½ inch slices and serve immediately. Serves 10-12. Excellent with sliced fruit and cheese.

APPETIZERS

℞

SCALLOPS IN GREEN SAUCE

1	pound scallops	¾ to 1	cup cider vinegar
	juice of 2 limes	¼	teaspoon garlic powder
1	teaspoon salt		
1	bunch watercress	¼	cup cream
		1	bunch parsley, stems removed

Sprinkle lime juice and salt over scallops. Cover with water and marinate overnight. Mince watercress and parsley in food processor. Add vinegar and garlic. Add cream. Drain scallops and toss with green sauce. Serves 4.

SHRIMP DE JONG

2	pounds shrimp, uncooked	1	teaspoon salt
		1	teaspoon Worcestershire sauce
½	pound margarine		
1	cup bread crumbs	1	teaspoon A-1 Sauce
¼	cup sour cream		juice of ½ lemon
¼	cup parsley, minced		cracked pepper
2	garlic cloves, minced		

Peel and devein uncooked shrimp, leaving the tails on. Cream margarine and mix with bread crumbs and sour cream. Add parsley, garlic, salt, Worcestershire sauce, A-1 Sauce, lemon juice and pepper. Arrange shrimp in individual ramekins and cover with mixture. Bake at 400° until tails are brown. Serves 6-8.

APPETIZERS

℞

SHRIMP IN MUSTARD SAUCE #1

- 2 pounds unshelled shrimp
- 1½ cups beer
- 2 sprigs dill
- 4 stems parsley
- 1 bay leaf
- 1 teaspoon crushed red pepper
- ¼ teaspoon ground allspice
- 2 cloves garlic, crushed

Add seasoning to beer and bring to boil. Add shrimp and cook 3 minutes. Drain and cool. Shell.

Sauce:

- 1 cup mayonnaise
- 3 tablespoons sour cream
- 1 tablespoon Dijon mustard
- 1 tablespoon stone ground mustard
- 1 tablespoon white wine vinegar

Combine ingredients and let stand 1 hour. Serve over shrimp.

Only walking, sleep-deprived bodies called housestaff physicians can inhale food by merely passing the table.

SHRIMP IN MUSTARD SAUCE #2

- 2½ pounds shrimp, cooked
- ¼ cup parsley, chopped
- ¼ cup white tarragon vinegar
- ¼ cup white wine vinegar
- ½ cup olive oil
- 4 tablespoons Dijon mustard
- 2 teaspoons crushed red pepper
- 2 teaspoons salt cracked pepper

Combine all ingredients except shrimp in blender and mix well. Pour over shrimp and refrigerate overnight. Serves 10.

APPETIZERS

℞

SHRIMP AND SCALLOP DELIGHT

- ½ pound shrimp
- ¼ pound scallops, cut in ¼ inch slices
- ¼ cup lime juice
- 1 green onion, sliced
- 1 tablespoon fresh coriander, minced
- 1 tablespoon green pepper, minced
- 1 tablespoon olive oil
- dash of Tabasco
- salt and pepper

Cook shrimp for 3 minutes in boiling water. Drain and shell. Refrigerate overnight. Place scallops in lime juice and marinate overnight. Combine green onion, coriander, green pepper, olive oil and Tabasco. Pour over shrimp and drained scallops. Salt and pepper to taste. Serve on individual seashells. Serves 4-6.

BALLS OF FIRE

- instant mashed potatoes for 4 servings
- ¼ teaspoon salt
- 20 drops Tabasco sauce
- 1 egg yolk, lightly beaten
- 2 tablespoons green onion, chopped
- 1 tablespoon parsley, chopped
- 1 tablespoon pimento, chopped
- 2 tablespoons Dijon mustard
- ⅓ cup grated Parmesan cheese
- 18-20 small squares Monterey Jack cheese
- 18-20 small squares canned green chilies
- 1 egg
- 1 tablespoon milk
- ¾ cup enriched cereal flake crumbs
- oil for deep frying

Prepare mashed potatoes as package directs, reducing water by 2 tablespoons and adding an additional ¼ teaspoon salt. Combine with Tabasco, egg yolk, green onion, parsley, pimento, mustard and Parmesan cheese. Shape into tiny balls, about 1 inch in diameter, embedding a square of Monterey Jack cheese and/or a square of

APPETIZERS

℞

green chili in center of each. Beat egg with milk. Dip balls in egg mixture, then roll in crumbs. Fry balls in oil until golden brown. Drain. Makes 36-40 balls.

SPINACH-CHEESE APPETIZERS

½	cup green onions, sliced	¼	teaspoon baking powder
½	teaspoon dillweed	2	eggs, beaten
1	tablespoon oil	1	cup cottage or Ricotta cheese
1	(10 ounce) package frozen spinach, thawed and drained	½	cup Feta cheese, crumbled
4	tablespoons margarine	14	leaves phyllo pastry
¼	cup flour	½	pound margarine, melted
½	teaspoon salt		

Sauté onion and dillweed in oil. Add spinach. Melt margarine and add flour, salt and baking powder. Then add eggs and cheeses. Combine with spinach mixture. Put phyllo leaf in pan. Coat with melted margarine. Place second phyllo leaf on top of first and coat. Cut into 5 sections and place 1 tablespoon of filling in center of each section. Fold ends over to make square. Seal edges with margarine. Repeat with rest of phyllos and spinach mixture. May freeze. If baked after freezing, bake in 400° oven unthawed for 15-20 minutes. If baked unfrozen, bake at 350° for 15-20 minutes. Makes 35 pieces.

APPETIZERS

℞

REDFISH APPETIZER

5	pounds of redfish fillet	½	medium onion, grated
1	package Zatarian Crab boil (in bag)	½	teaspoon dry mustard
4	carrots	1	teaspoon Worcestershire sauce
	salt and pepper		Tabasco sauce
1	pint yogurt mayonnaise		
½	(4 ounce) jar horseradish		

Poach fish in water with crab boil and carrots until meat is falling from the bone. Remove bones. Chop carrots fine. Combine fish and carrots with rest of ingredients and place into lightly buttered fish mold. Refrigerate several hours to let season. Unmold on plate and surround with parsley and plum tomatoes. Serve with favorite crackers or on tomato halves. Serves 20-25 people.

CHEESE PUFF

6	eggs	10	ounces Monterey Jack cheese, grated
1	(20 ounce) package biscuit mix	6	ounces mild cheddar cheese, grated
2½	cups milk		
8	ounces cottage cheese	1	pound plain or hot sausage, cooked and crumbled
1	(3 ounce) package cream cheese, softened		

In a large bowl, beat eggs. Add biscuit mix and milk. Stir in cheeses and sausage. Pour into 3 quart greased casserole. Bake at 350° for 45 minutes. Serves 12.

APPETIZERS

CHEDDAR CHEESE PENNIES

- 1 cup shredded cheddar cheese
- ½ cup all-purpose flour
- ¼ cup butter or margarine, softened
- ⅛ teaspoon dry mustard

Combine ingredients well. Form into 1 inch balls and place 1 inch apart on ungreased pan. Bake for 10-12 minutes at 425°. Serve warm. Makes 2 dozen appetizers.

PHYLLO APPETIZERS

- 1 box phyllo sheets
- ½ cup margarine, melted

Take layer of phyllo and spread with margarine. Cover with second phyllo sheet and repeat. Layer 4 sheets. Cut sheets into 2 inch strips lengthwise. Add 1 teaspoon of mushroom, shrimp or lamb filling at one corner of strip. Fold over to make triangle. Cut and seal edges. Place under damp towel. Continue to make triangles until filling is used. Brush with margarine. Keep unused phyllo sheets under damp towel while not using to keep from drying out.

Bake in a 375° oven for 15-18 minutes or until lightly browned. They are best served at once. Once assembled, the appetizers can be frozen for baking later or covered and refrigerated and baked the next day.

Mushroom Filling

- 1 pound fresh mushrooms, finely chopped
- ⅔ cup green onion, finely chopped
- 3 tablespoons margarine
- ½ cup sour cream or yogurt
- ¼ teaspoon thyme
- ¼ teaspoon oregano
- salt to taste

Sauté mushrooms and onions in margarine. Drain. Cool to lukewarm. Add sour cream, herbs and salt. Fill phyllo strips to make triangles. Makes about 4 dozen pastries.

APPETIZERS

℞

Shrimp Filling

- 2 cups minced shrimp
- 2 tablespoons minced parsley
- 2 tablespoons minced chives or green onion tops
- 1 cup grated Monterey Jack cheese
- ½ teaspoon oregano
- ½ teaspoon salt

Combine all ingredients. Season to taste. Fill phyllo pastry as directed above. Makes 4 dozen pastries.

Spicy Lamb Filling

- ½ cup finely chopped onion
- 2 cloves garlic, minced
- 2 teaspoons olive oil
- ⅔ pound ground lamb
- 1 teaspoon curry powder
- ¼ teaspoon cayenne pepper
- 1 cup crumbled Feta cheese
- salt

Sauté onion and garlic in oil. Remove from pan. Add lamb to oil and brown. Drain excess drippings and return onions and garlic to pan. Add spices and Feta cheese. Salt to taste. Fill and make phyllo triangles. Makes about 4 dozen pastries.

SPECIAL BLEU CHEESE DRESSING OR DIP

- 1 cup mayonnaise
- ¾ cup buttermilk
- 1 (6 ounce) package Bleu cheese, crumbled
- 1 teaspoon Worcestershire sauce
- 7 drops hot sauce
- 1 tablespoon Italian seasoning
- 1 tablespoon parsley flakes
- 1 clove garlic, pressed

Combine all ingredients. Chill in covered container. Serve on tossed salad or with assorted raw vegetables. Yield: About 2½ cups.

APPETIZERS

℞

FETA CHEESE GREEK PUFFS

2	medium onions, minced	1	(13 ounce) can evaporated milk
1	pound raw spinach, washed and chopped fine	¼	cup each oil and sherry
4	tablespoons margarine	⅛	teaspoon salt
1	pound Feta or farmer's cheese	⅛	teaspoon pepper
¼	teaspoon dill	⅛	teaspoon nutmeg
¼	teaspoon ground fennel	2	containers unbaked crescent rolls
4	eggs	1	egg
		2	tablespoons water

Sauté onions in margarine. Add spinach and cook until wilted. In bowl, blend spinach mixture, cheese, dill, fennel and eggs. Add milk, oil, sherry and remaining seasonings. Blend until mixture is smooth. Roll out crescent roll dough to ⅛ inch thickness and cut into 4 inch squares. Center 2 tablespoons filling on each square and fold edges over like an envelope. Pinch seams to secure and set seam-side down on a buttered baking sheet. Glaze with egg/water mixture. Bake in a 375° oven 35 minutes or until puffed and golden brown. Serves 12.

CAVIAR DIP

1	(8 ounce) carton sour cream	1	package cream of leek soup
1	cup caviar		

Mix and let season; refrigerate overnight. Serve with melba toast.

APPETIZERS

℞

GRAB-BAG DIP (WARM OR COLD)

Warm Ingredients

- 2 jars pickled mushrooms, drained
- 2 jars pickled onions, drained
- 1 can ripe olives, drained
- 1 box frozen crab or fish meat balls, cooked by directions on box
- 1 box frozen scallops (cut in half) cooked by directions on box

Serve in chafing dish with sauce.

Cold Ingredients

- ½ pound raw scallops, cut in half (soak in milk and drain)
- 1 box cherry tomatoes
- ½ pound cooked shrimp
- 1 can ripe olives, drained
- 2 (8½ ounce) cans water chestnuts or raw vegetables: sliced zucchini, summer squash, carrots, cucumber

Cover with sauce.

Sauce

- 2 cups mayonnaise
- ½ cup horseradish
- 2 teaspoons hot dry mustard
- 2 teaspoons lemon juice
- ½ teaspoon salt

Sauce may be made ahead by adding mayonnaise, horseradish, mustard, lemon juice and salt. Heat. Pour over above ingredients. Serves 15-20 people. This is an unusual dip in that each time you taste it you get a different piece of food. That's why it's called Grab-Bag.

APPETIZERS

MEXICAN CHEESE DIP LIKE NINFA'S

- 2 pounds Monterey Jack cheese, grated
- 1 green bell pepper, sliced
- 1 onion, cut in rings
- ½ pound fresh mushrooms, sliced
- 1 tablespoon margarine
- salt and pepper
- 1 teaspoon garlic powder

Melt cheese in double boiler. Sauté green peppers, onion and mushrooms in margarine until just cooked. Add vegetables to cheese mixture. Season with garlic powder, salt and pepper. Serve with flour tortillas or fried cornmeal tortillas. Serves 8-10.

LIVERWURST DIP

- 2 (4¾ ounce) cans liverwurst
- 1 cup sour cream
- ½ cup red onion, chopped
- ½ cup sweet relish
- bacon bits
- 1 cup canned french fried onion rings, crushed
- melba toast
- zucchini or carrot sticks

Mix liverwurst with sour cream, onion and relish. Chill. Sprinkle with bacon bits and 1 cup coarse crushed french fried onion rings. Serve with melba toast, zucchini or carrot sticks.

BANANA TREATS

Coat bananas with yogurt and honey. Then roll in toasted sliced almonds or grated coconut.

APPETIZERS

STUFFED MUSHROOMS

12	large mushroom caps	½	pound crabmeat
6	tablespoons butter, divided	¼	cup bread crumbs
		4	ounces Tiger Sauce
¼	teaspoon garlic powder, divided		Tabasco
			salt and pepper
4	green onions		
2	teaspoons parsley, chopped		

Sauce

4	tablespoons butter	3	(1 ounce) triangles Gruyère cheese
1	tablespoon flour		
2	cups milk	1	ounce vermouth

Sauté mushroom caps in 4 tablespoons butter. Sprinkle with ⅛ teaspoon garlic powder. Place in greased casserole dish. Sauté green onion and parsley in 2 tablespoons butter. Add crabmeat, bread crumbs and sprinkle with ⅛ teaspoon garlic powder. Add Tiger Sauce (see Index.) and a couple dashes Tabasco sauce. Salt and pepper to taste.

Make sauce with butter, flour and milk. Add Gruyère cheese and vermouth. Place crabmeat in mushrooms and cover with cheese sauce. Bake in 350° oven for 15-20 minutes. Serves 6-12.

MUSHROOM AND CHEESE PUFF

1	pound fresh mushrooms, sliced	2	tablespoons grated Parmesan cheese
4	tablespoons oil, divided	2	tablespoons flour
		1	teaspoon salt
½	cup onion, chopped	⅛	teaspoon ground black pepper
6	eggs, separated		
6	ounces cheddar cheese, grated		

APPETIZERS

℞

Sauté half the mushrooms in oil and remove. Add onions and remaining mushrooms. Sauté until golden. Spread evenly on the bottom of the skillet and set aside. To egg yolks, add cheeses, flour, salt and black pepper. Beat whites until stiff. Fold whites into cheese mixture. Spread on top of mushrooms and onions in skillet. Top with reserved sautéed mushrooms. Bake at 350° until puffy and firm, about 20 minutes. Serves 4 to 6.

INDIA CHEESE BALL

- 1 (10 ounce) package sharp cheddar cheese, softened
- 1 (3 ounce) package cream cheese, softened
- ¼ cup shredded coconut
- 1 tablespoon cream sherry
- 1 tablespoon chopped chutney
- 1 teaspoon curry powder
- ¼ teaspoon salt
- 1 cup Brazil nuts or almonds, sliced or chopped

Combine cheddar cheese, cream cheese, shredded coconut, cream sherry, chopped chutney, curry powder and salt. Mix well. Chill until mixture is pliable (about 20 minutes). Form into ball and garnish with nuts. Serve with crackers. Makes 1 ball. Serves 8.

CHEESE-ONION MARINADE

- 3 ounces Bleu cheese, crumbled
- ½ cup salad oil
- 2 tablespoons lemon juice
- 1 teaspoon salt
- ½ teaspoon sugar pepper paprika
- 4 onions, sliced and separated into rings

Mix all ingredients and pour over onion rings. Marinate onions overnight.

APPETIZERS

PINATA DOUBLE DIP

- 1 (16 ounce) can refried beans (2 cups)
- 1 (10 ounce) can Rotel tomatoes with green chilies, drained (1¼ cups)
- ¼ cup Rotel juice
- ½ pound cheddar or Monterey Jack cheese, grated
- ¼ teaspoon onion powder
- ¼ teaspoon garlic powder
- ¼ teaspoon salt

Mix all ingredients together well. Heat on low until cheese melts. Put in warmer or chafing dish. Serve with Fritos or fried tortillas.

CHEESE WITH MUSTARD SAUCE

- 2 cups vinegar
- 1 cup dry mustard (Colemans)
- 1 cup sugar
- ⅛ teaspoon salt
- 2 eggs, beaten
- Monterey Jack or Swiss cheese, sliced

Blend mustard and vinegar and let sit for 2 hours. Add sugar, salt and eggs and cook over low heat until thick. Serve with Monterey Jack or Swiss cheese slices for dunking. Serves 12.

CONFETTI DIP

- 1 (10½ ounce) can bean dip
- 1 (4 ounce) can green chilies
- 1 (8 ounce) can frozen avocado dip, thawed
- 1 (4½ ounce) can ripe olives
- 3 hard boiled eggs, chopped
- 1 red tomato, chopped (may substitute tomato salsa)
- 1 cup cheddar cheese tortilla chips

Layer bean dip, green chilies, avocado dip, ripe olives, eggs, tomatoes

APPETIZERS

and cheddar cheese. Put in refrigerator and allow flavors to mellow. Serve with tortilla chips. Serves 8.

COQUILLES SAINT-JACQUES

2 tablespoons butter	2 cups Mornay sauce
2 green onions, chopped	salt and pepper
1 tablespoon parsley, chopped	½ cup whipped cream
1 pound scallops	Parmesan or Swiss cheese, grated
6-8 mushrooms, sliced	½ cup mashed potatoes
½ cup white wine	
12 shrimp, cut into bite size pieces	

Sauté green onions, parsley, scallops and mushrooms in butter. Add wine and simmer. Add shrimp. Remove seafood and mushrooms. Reduce liquid to 2-3 tablespoons. Combine liquid and 1⅓ cups Mornay sauce with seafood. Season with salt and pepper. Place seafood mixture in ramekins or shells. Spread whipped cream over seafood and top with Mornay sauce and Parmesan cheese. Heat in 350° oven. Pipe mashed potatoes around seafood. Serves 6.

SHRIMP DILL PÂTÉ (DIP)

½ cup cold tomato juice	½ teaspoon salt
2 envelopes unflavored gelatin	½ teaspoon Worcestershire sauce
1 cup boiling tomato juice	4 or 5 ounce can shrimp, drained, or ¾ cup fresh boiled shrimp, chopped
2 cups sour cream	
1 tablespoon dried dillweed	
2 tablespoons lemon juice	

Combine tomato juice and gelatin in blender. Blend until gelatin is softened. Add boiling tomato juice to dissolve. Add remaining ingredients except shrimp, continue blending until smooth. Add shrimp. Pour into 5 cup mold and chill 4 hours. Serves 8.

Date: *Occasionally*

For Those Who Enjoy Eating
Patient's name

℞: BEVERAGES

Dispense: *Conservative Amounts*

Sig: *Moderation*

Refill: yes _____
        no ✔︎

Reba Michele Hill M.D.
Physician
DEA Number AH 0000000

BEVERAGES

RICE FIELD PUNCH

1 (6 ounce) can frozen lemonade concentrate, thawed
1 (6 ounce) can frozen orange juice concentrate, thawed
1 (46 ounce) can pineapple juice, chilled
1 (24 ounce) bottle ginger ale, chilled
fresh mint leaves

Combine lemonade and orange concentrates, pineapple juice and ginger ale. Serve over ice. Garnish with mint leaves. For a cocktail party, substitute champagne for ginger ale. Makes about 3 quarts.

CRANBERRY MIST

1¼ cups cranberry juice
4 ounces Southern Comfort
1 tablespoon lime juice
1 teaspoon sugar
1 egg white
6 ounces crushed ice

Blend ingredients in blender. May store in refrigerator in blender container and re-blend to foamy state before serving. Makes 4 drinks.

McCULLEY'S PUNCH

2 (12 ounce) cans lime concentrate
block of ice
4 (33.8 ounce) bottles of quinine water
1 fifth vodka
1 lemon, sliced
1 lime, sliced

Combine all ingredients and pour over ice before serving. Makes 45 (4 ounce) drinks.

HOLIDAY PUNCH

¼ cup lemon juice
¼ cup sugar
1 cup cranberry juice
1 cup orange juice
1 cup strong tea
1 fifth rum
12 cloves
ice cubes
lemon slices

BEVERAGES

℞

Combine all ingredients and serve hot or cold. Makes 12 (4-5 ounce) drinks.

MILK PUNCH FREEZE

8 pints light cream	6½ ounces powdered
6½ cups brandy	sugar
5 tablespoons vanilla	nutmeg
3 pints vanilla ice cream	

Combine light cream, brandy and vanilla. Add ice cream and sugar. Blend. Refrigerate overnight. Makes 60 (4 ounce) drinks. Serve with sprinkle of nutmeg.

DADDY'S EGGNOG

1 cup sugar	1 quart milk
6 eggs, separated	1 pint whipping cream
½ fifth bourbon	nutmeg
1 quart commercial eggnog, refrigerated	

Blend egg yolks and sugar. Add bourbon slowly and stir constantly to keep eggs from curdling. Add eggnog and milk. Beat egg whites and fold into mixture. Beat whipping cream to stiff peaks. Fold into mixture. Lightly sprinkle with nutmeg to serve. Makes 25 (4 ounce) drinks. Freezes well.

On Christmas morning I would help my father make eggnog for our annual open house. People came especially to drink Bob's eggnog. Bob, by the way, was a tea-totaller.

BLOODY MARY

4 ounces tomato juice	Tabasco to desired
1 ounce vodka	hotness
salt and pepper	ice
dash Worcestershire sauce	1 teaspoon vinegar
	squeeze of lime juice

Combine all ingredients and serve over ice. Makes 1 drink.

BEVERAGES

℞

NEW ORLEANS GIN FIZZ

juice of ½ lemon	1 cup crushed ice
juice of ½ lime	1 tablespoon egg white
1 teaspoon sugar	1½ ounces gin
1½ ounces cream	2 ounces club soda
¼ teaspoon orange flavored water	1 orange slice or cherry

Combine all ingredients and whirl in crushed ice. Garnish with orange slice or cherry. Serves 1.

MANGO DAIQUIRI

½ cup mango puree	3 ounces light rum
2 tablespoons lime juice	1 ounce Curacao
2 tablespoons sugar	1 cup crushed ice

Put canned mangoes and juice in blender. Puree. Combine ½ cup puree with remaining ingredients and blend. Serves 2.

STRAWBERRY DAIQUIRIS

1 (6 ounce) can frozen pink lemonade concentrate	4 ice cubes light rum fresh strawberries
1 (10 ounce) package frozen strawberries	

Combine lemonade concentrate and strawberries in blender. Add ice cubes, one at a time, blending until smooth. Add rum to taste. When blended, pour into champagne glasses. Top with fresh strawberries. Serves 4.

BEVERAGES

PINEAPPLE BRANDY FROST

1½ ounces brandy	½ cup crushed ice
2 tablespoons undiluted frozen pineapple juice concentrate	2 scoops (⅔ cup) lemon sherbet

Combine brandy, pineapple juice and ice in blender. Mix until smooth. Add sherbet and blend. Makes 2 (6 ounce) servings.

We had 40 people coming to the party at a time when our budget was low so I had to have good old faithful husband tend bar. The telephone rang - 15 minutes before guests were to arrive - husband had an emergency. I tended bar and served the food. Hubby arrived as I said farewell to our last guest. The joy of entertaining.

SPICED COFFEE PUNCH

2 cups strong coffee	1 quart milk
1½ sticks cinnamon, broken	1 tablespoon vanilla
6 whole cloves	1 cup brandy
6 whole allspice	1 quart coffee ice cream
	2 cups club soda

Combine coffee, cinnamon, cloves, allspice in saucepan. Cook over low heat 15 minutes. Strain and chill. Combine milk, vanilla, brandy and coffee mixture. Pour coffee and milk mixture over ice cream. Add club soda. Makes 24 (4 ounce) cups.

CHOCOLATE SMOOTHIE

3 cups half and half	½ cup brandy
1 (6 ounce) package semisweet chocolate chips	1 quart mocha ice cream

Heat half and half. Put chocolate chips in blender and pour in heated half and half. Blend on high speed until smooth. Add brandy. Put scoop of ice cream in a mug and add chocolate mixture. Makes 6-8 servings.

BEVERAGES

WEDDING RECEPTION PUNCH

¾	cup sugar	1½	cups orange juice
	juice of 3 lemons	1⅓	cups Cointreau
2	quarts fresh straw-berries, sliced	3	bottles champagne
		1½	quarts sparkling water

Dissolve sugar in lemon juice and add strawberries. Add orange juice and Cointreau. Chill for 1-2 hours. Pour into punch bowl and add champagne and sparkling water. Serves 50. This is a beautiful punch.

POWDERED CAFE AU LAIT MIX

¼	cup brown sugar	¼	cup instant nonfat dry milk powder
¾	teaspoon vanilla		
¾	cup instant coffee powder	¼	cup non-dairy creamer

Put vanilla in sugar and stir until moisture gone. Add remaining ingredients. Sift to blend. Store in air tight container. To use add 2-3 teaspoons of mix to boiling water. Makes 1¼ to 1½ cups of mix.

ORANGE SPICED TEA MIX

2	cups powdered orange concentrate breakfast drink	½	cup and 2 teaspoons of lemon flavored instant tea
2	cups sugar	1	teaspoon cloves
1	teaspoon cinnamon		

Mix ingredients together and seal in jar.

To use:
Add 1 teaspoon to 1 cup of boiling water. Refreshing to serve at receptions or teas.

Quick version: Make tea with Constant Comment tea seasoned with orange and sweet spice. Add 1 teaspoon of orange concentrate to each cup of tea.

BEVERAGES

℞

Doctors, like school teachers, are recipients of cherished gifts and sayings from children. One of my favorite patients, Susie, age 5, gave me a coffee mug with the picture of a cow grazing in the field. The inscription said "Someone Outstanding in the Field." As she handed it to me she said, "Here, Dr. Hill, to someone standing out in the field."

LIME AND STRAWBERRY CHAMPAGNE PUNCH

½ cup sugar
2 tablespoons water
2 cups strawberry nectar
⅔ cup Persian lime juice
½ cup brandy
1 bottle champagne
lime slices or strawberries for garnish

Dissolve sugar in water over low heat. Add strawberry nectar, lime juice and brandy. Divide mixture between 6 (12 ounce) glasses filled with ice. Add champagne. Garnish with strawberry and a lime slice. Serves 6.

TEQUILA ALLMENDRADA

1 ounce Tequila Allmendrada (you can only buy this in Mexico)
4-5 ounces Sprite
juice of ¼ to ½ lime
1 cup ice

Place ingredients in blender and blend. Makes 8 ounces. This drink can be made with golden tequila and ⅛ teaspoon almond extract for each ounce of tequila. Do not use regular white tequila. Serves 1.

Adage - Never serve more than 2 tequila drinks to a guest.

BEVERAGES

MILK PUNCH

1½	gallons vanilla mellorine (not ice cream), divided	2	fifths bourbon
		1	fifth rum
1	gallon milk	1	cup white Crème de Cocoa

Thaw 1 gallon of mellorine until mushy. Add milk, bourbon, rum, Crème de Cocoa and mix. Freeze. Allow 2 hours to thaw before serving. Put remaining ½ gallon mellorine into punch bowl and pour thawed punch over it.

This can be made several days ahead. Any leftover may be refrozen. Makes 50 cups.

FISH HOUSE PUNCH

1	pound brown sugar	2	quarts Jamaican rum
2	quarts water	1	quart cognac
1	quart lemon juice	4	ounces peach brandy

Put sugar and water in punch bowl; when dissolved, add lemon juice. Combine remaining ingredients, keeping sugar mixture and liquor in separate containers for 2 hours before serving. Combine sugar mixture and liquor in punch bowl with mold of ice; let chill to acquire proper dilution. Yield: 1½ gallons.

CRANBERRY RUM DELIGHT

1½	ounces light rum	juice of ¼ lime
3	ounces cranberry juice	sugar to taste

Mix rum, cranberry juice and lime juice. Add sugar if desired. Serve over ice. Serves 1.

BEVERAGES

LINDA'S SMOOTHIE

- 3 bananas
- 1 cup orange juice
- ½ cup pecans
- 3 eggs
- ½ cup honey
- ⅛ teaspoon cinnamon
- ⅛ teaspoon allspice
- ⅛ teaspoon spearmint extract

Place all ingredients into blender and whirl. Pour over ice. Serves 4.

Date: *Today*

For Those Who Enjoy Eating
Patient's name

℞: **BREADS**

Dispense: *Small Servings*

Sig: *Do Not Over Indulge*

Refill: yes _____
        no ✓

Physician
DEA Number AH 0000000

BREADS

CARAMEL FRUIT BREAKFAST ROLLS

2	(10 ounce) cans refrigerator biscuits	½	cup raisins, plumped
1	cup brown sugar	½	cup maraschino cherries, sliced and drained
1	(5½ ounce) regular vanilla pudding mix	1	cup crushed pineapple, drained and squeezed
½	cup margarine, melted		
¼	cup half and half		
½	cup toasted pecans, chopped		

Quarter biscuits and place ½ in bottom of 3 quart, greased baking dish. Combine sugar, pudding mix, margarine and half and half. Drizzle ½ of the mixture over dough. Sprinkle pecans, raisins, cherries and pineapple over dough. Add remaining dough and drizzle with remaining sugar mixture. Bake at 325° for 50-60 minutes. Serves 8.

CHEESE BISCUITS

4	ounces cheddar cheese	½	teaspoon salt
¼	pound margarine	¼	teaspoon red pepper
½	cup cool water	½	teaspoon baking powder
1½	cups flour	¼	teaspoon paprika

Cream cheese and margarine. Add water. Sift dry ingredients together and add to cheese mixture. Chill dough for 2 hours. Roll out and cut into small biscuits. Bake at 450° for 10-12 minutes. Makes 20 small biscuits.

BREADS

℞

RICOTTA CHEESE MUFFINS

Shells

12	tablespoons margarine	1	teaspoon double acting baking powder
1	cup sugar		
2	eggs, beaten	½	teaspoon salt
1½	teaspoons vanilla	½	teaspoon nutmeg
3½	cups all purpose flour, sifted		

Filling

3	pounds Ricotta cheese	4	eggs, beaten
1	cup sugar	1¾	teaspoons cinnamon

To make shells: Cream margarine and sugar until fluffy. Add eggs and vanilla. Combine flour, baking powder, salt and nutmeg. Sift. Add to butter-egg mixture, ¼ at a time. Cover dough loosely and chill for 1 hour. Take walnut sized amounts of dough and roll out on floured surface. Cut each into rounds with 3 inch cutter. Press into buttered muffin tins.

To make filling: Combine Ricotta, sugar, eggs, and cinnamon. Spoon into shells and bake for 30 minutes at 400°. Bake 5 minutes less if Teflon tin is used. Cool 15 minutes before removing. Makes 48 cupcakes. Great with chicken or fruit salad. These may be made ahead of time and frozen. Place in oven to re-warm.

Resident asked Dr. Hill after one of her dinner parties, "Do you give doggie bags?"

EASY PRALINE BISCUITS

2	(10 ounce) cans refrigerator biscuits	1	cup toasted pecans
		1	cup margarine, melted
1	cup brown sugar		

Cut biscuits into quarters and place in well greased 3 quart pan or dish. Pour sugar and nuts over biscuits. Pour margarine over biscuits. Bake at 400° for 20-25 minutes. Serves 8.

BREADS

MEXICAN SPOON BREAD WITH CHILIES

- 1 cup evaporated milk
- 1 cup water
- 1 cup cornmeal
- 1 tablespoon sugar
- 1 teaspoon salt
- 2 tablespoons margarine
- 4 eggs, separated
- ½ cup (2 ounces) shredded cheddar cheese
- 1 cup mild green chilies, chopped

Cook milk, water and cornmeal until thickened. Mix in sugar, salt, and margarine. Cool. Stir in egg yolks, cheese and green chilies. Fold in beaten egg whites. Pour into greased 1½ quart baking dish and bake at 350° for 40-45 minutes. Serves 8. Good with pork.

JALAPEÑO CORNBREAD #1

- 2 cups cream style corn
- 2 cups cornbread mix
- 1 cup vegetable oil
- 4 eggs, beaten
- 2 cups sour cream
- 1½ cups grated cheddar cheese
- 1 (4 ounce) can jalapeño or fresh peppers, minced
- 1 cup chopped onion

Combine ingredients and put into 3 quart greased cooking pan. Bake at 350° for 1 hour. Serves 12.

JALAPEÑO CORNBREAD #2

- 1 cup cornmeal
- 1 tablespoon sugar
- ½ tablespoon baking powder
- 1 teaspoon salt
- 2 eggs, beaten
- ½ cup bacon drippings
- 1 (#2) can cream style corn (2½ cups)
- 1 large onion, diced
- ¾ pound cheddar cheese, grated
- ¼ cup jalapeño peppers, chopped
- ⅛ cup chopped pimento
- 1 clove garlic, squeezed
- 1 tablespoon picante sauce

BREADS

℞

Mix cornmeal, sugar, baking powder and salt. Add eggs, bacon drippings, corn, onion, cheese, peppers, pimento, garlic and picante sauce. Pour into greased pan and bake at 400° for 35 minutes. Serves 6-8.

HOT WATER CORNBREAD

2	cups white cornmeal		boiling water
1	teaspoon salt	1	tablespoon bacon grease
	pinch sugar		

Mix cornmeal, salt, and sugar. Add enough water to make consistency of mush. Add bacon grease. Drop 2 tablespoons dough into hot grease and fry. These should look like thin pancakes. You may add chips of bacon to dough. Good with vegetables or fish. Serves 6.

MONKEY BREAD

1	cup milk, scalded	1	cake yeast
1	cup cooked, unsalted potatoes, mashed	½	cup lukewarm water
⅔	cup shortening	2	eggs, beaten
⅔	cup sugar	6	cups flour
1-1½	teaspoons salt		margarine, melted

Combine scalded milk, potatoes, shortening, sugar and salt. Add yeast to lukewarm water to dissolve. To potato mixture, add eggs and 1½ cups flour and beat well. Add dissolved yeast. Add flour to make stiff dough. Put on floured board and knead. Return to mixing bowl and grease top of dough. Cover, let rise until doubled. Punch down, cover and refrigerate to chill. Roll dough out on pastry cloth to ½ inch thickness. Cut into 1 inch circles, dip in margarine and place in ring mold or monkey bread pot. Recipe will make 4 layers in ring mold. Let rise for 1 hour. Bake at 400° for 30 minutes. Invert on plate. Pull apart to eat. Serves 8.

This is the best recipe I have found to duplicate the Monkey Bread served at the Neiman-Marcus restaurant in Houston.

BREADS

BREAKFAST MONKEY BREAD

- 3 (10 ounce) cans Hungry Jack buttermilk biscuits
- ½ cup toasted nuts, chopped
- 1 cup melted margarine
- 1 teaspoon cinnamon
- ½ cup sugar
- 1 cup brown sugar

Cut biscuits into quarters. Pour nuts into greased bundt pan or monkey bread pot. Dip dough in ½ cup margarine to coat. Combine cinnamon and sugars. Roll dough in sugar/cinnamon mixture. Layer dough in pan over nuts. Combine remaining margarine and sugar and pour over dough. Bake at 350° for 30-40 minutes. Serves 8.

HOLIDAY NUT BREAD

- 1 egg, beaten
- 1½ cups commercial eggnog mix
- ¼ cup sugar
- ¼ teaspoon nutmeg
- 1 teaspoon salt
- 3 cups biscuit mix
- 1 cup toasted pecans, chopped
- ½ cup candied cherries, chopped

Mix eggs, eggnog mix, sugar, nutmeg and salt. Stir in biscuit mix. Add nuts and cherries. Mix. Turn into greased loaf pan. Bake at 350° for 45 minutes. Let stand 5 minutes before turning out. Serves 6-8.

GINGERBREAD

- 3 large eggs
- 1 cup sugar
- 1 cup molasses
- 1 cup vegetable oil
- 2 cups flour, sifted
- 1 teaspoon ground cloves
- 1 teaspoon ginger
- 1 teaspoon cinnamon
- 2 teaspoons baking soda
- 2 tablespoons hot water
- 1 cup boiling water

Mix eggs, sugar, molasses, oil. Sift together flour and spices. Dissolve

BREADS

℞

baking soda in hot water and add to egg mixture. Stir in dry ingredients. Add 1 cup boiling water. Beat lightly and pour into greased buttered pan. Bake at 350° for 45 minutes. Serves 6. Serve with Brandied Peach Sauce (see Index).

LOUISE'S BLUEBERRY MUFFINS
THE GRAND HOTEL AT MACKINAC ISLAND

⅓ cup sugar	½ teaspoon salt
¼ cup soft butter	1 cup milk
1 egg	1 teaspoon vanilla
2⅓ cups flour or 2½ cups cake flour	1½ cups canned or frozen blueberries, drained
4 teaspoons baking powder	

Topping

½ cup sugar	⅓ cup flour
½ teaspoon cinnamon	¼ cup butter

Cream sugar and butter. Add egg. Combine and sift together flour, baking powder and salt. Add alternately with milk to butter mixture. Add vanilla. Fold in blueberries. For topping, combine sugar, cinnamon, flour and butter. Mix until size of small peas. Pour blueberry batter into cupcake tins lined with cupcake papers. Cover with topping. Bake at 375° for 20-25 minutes.

CRANBERRY ORANGE MUFFINS

2 cups all purpose flour, unsifted	1 cup milk
3 teaspoons baking powder	¼ cup salad oil
	½ cup cranberry-orange relish
½ teaspoon salt	½ cup margarine, melted
2 tablespoons sugar	1 cup sugar
1 egg	2 teaspoons cinnamon

Mix flour, baking powder, salt and sugar. Stir in egg, milk and oil. Blend well. Fold in cranberry-orange relish. Spoon into greased, tea size, muffin pans. Fill to ⅔ full. Bake at 425° for 12-15 minutes. Brush muffins with melted margarine and roll in cinnamon sugar mixture. Makes 36 tea size muffins.

BREADS

GABBIO'S ORANGE BREAD

peel of 2 large oranges
½ cup water
2 cups sugar, divided
1 egg, beaten
1 tablespoon melted butter

pinch salt
1 cup milk
2½ cups flour
2 teaspoons baking powder

Cut orange peel into small bits and boil, covered, in water until tender. Add 1 cup sugar and cook until thick. Mix egg, remaining sugar, butter, salt, milk, flour, baking powder and add candied orange peel. Cook in slow oven in greased and floured coffee cans. Makes 3 tubular cakes.

Coffee cans were frequently used to bake breads during World War II. The author of this recipe was 80 years old.

SIX WEEK MUFFINS

½ pound margarine
1 cup sugar
4 eggs
1 cup molasses
4 cups all purpose flour, sifted

2 teaspoons cinnamon
2 teaspoons soda
1 cup buttermilk
1 cup chopped, toasted nuts

Cream sugar and margarine. Add eggs and molasses. Sift flour, soda and cinnamon together. Add to egg/butter mixture alternately with buttermilk. Add nuts. Bake at 350° for 15 minutes in greased muffin tins. Muffin mix keeps in covered container in refrigerator for 6 weeks.

BREADS

SWEET POTATO MUFFINS

- ⅔ cup fresh canned sweet potatoes, drained and pureed
- 4 tablespoons margarine
- ½ cup sugar
- 1 egg
- ¾ cup all purpose flour
- 2 tablespoons baking powder
- ½ teaspoon salt
- ½ teaspoon cinnamon
- ¼ teaspoon nutmeg
- ½ cup milk
- 4 tablespoons toasted pecans
- 4 tablespoons raisins

Cream margarine, sugar and egg; add pureed sweet potatoes. Sift flour with baking powder, salt, cinnamon and nutmeg. Add dry ingredients and milk alternately to potato mixture. Fold in nuts and raisins. Pour into greased muffin tins and bake at 400° for 25 minutes. Makes 12 muffins.

SPOON BREAD SOUFFLE

- 2 cups milk
- ½ cup white cornmeal
- ¼ pound margarine
- 4 eggs, separated
- 1 teaspoon baking powder
- 1 teaspoon sugar
- 1 teaspoon salt

Combine milk and cornmeal in pan. Cook until consistency of cream gravy. Add margarine. Cool. Add beaten egg yolks, baking powder, sugar and salt. Beat egg whites to stiff peaks. Fold gently into egg mixture. Bake in a well greased 2 quart souffle dish at 350° for 45-50 minutes until top puffed and golden. Serves 4-6.

BREADS

HUSH PUPPIES

- 2 cups cornmeal
- 1 tablespoon flour
- 1 teaspoon baking powder
- 1 teaspoon baking soda
- 2 teaspoons salt
- 1 teaspoon garlic powder
- ½ teaspoon pepper
- 4 tablespoons chopped green onion tops
- 1 large egg
- 1 cup buttermilk
- ½ cup cream style corn (optional)

Mix dry ingredients then add onion. Mix egg with buttermilk and add to dry ingredients. Add corn if desired. Drop a teaspoonful into deep hot oil and cook until light brown. Makes 40 pups.

BANANA SWEET POTATO MUFFINS

- ½ cup margarine
- 1 cup sugar
- 2 eggs
- 1 cup mashed banana (3 medium bananas)
- 1 (#300) can of sweet potatoes, rinsed and mashed (1¾ cups)
- 1½ cups flour
- 2 teaspoons baking powder
- ½ teaspoon cinnamon
- ¼ teaspoon salt
- ⅛ teaspoon nutmeg
- ⅓ cup milk
- ½ cup toasted pecans

Cream margarine and sugar. Beat in eggs. Add mashed bananas and sweet potatoes. Sift flour, baking powder, cinnamon, salt and nutmeg together. Stir into cream mix alternately with milk. Add pecans. Spoon into greased and floured muffin cups and bake at 400° for 20-25 minutes. Makes 12 muffins.

GARLIC BREAD - VINTAGE 1960

- 1 loaf coarse grain Italian bread, halved
- ¼ pound margarine
- 1 teaspoon garlic powder
- ½ cup red wine vinegar
- oregano
- parsley
- Parmesan cheese grated
- red, coarse ground pepper

BREADS

℞

Melt margarine. Add garlic powder and then vinegar. Spoon mixture over bread. Sprinkle oregano, parsley, Parmesan cheese and red pepper on bread. Warm bread in 350° oven about 10 minutes. Slice before serving. Serves 10-12.

JEAN'S GARLIC BREAD

1 loaf Italian bread, halved	8 ounces Mozzarella cheese, grated
1 bowl whipped margarine	2 small red onions, sliced in rings
2 teaspoons garlic powder	1 can ripe olives, sliced
	1/8 cup parsley

Mix garlic powder and whipped margarine. Let sit for at least 30 minutes. Spread on bread. Add Mozarrella cheese, onion, ripe olives and parsley. Heat in 350° oven for 10 minutes. Serves 10-12.

ZUCCHINI FRUIT LOAF

3½ cups all purpose flour	1 teaspoon vanilla
1 teaspoon baking soda	2 cups nuts, coarsely chopped
1 teaspoon salt	
1 teaspoon cinnamon	1 cup chopped candied pineapple
3 eggs, beaten	
2 cups unpeeled zucchini, grated	½ cup chopped candied orange rind
1½ cups sugar	¼ cup chopped candied lemon rind
1 cup corn oil	
½ cup dark corn syrup	

Combine flour, baking soda, salt and cinnamon. In separate bowl, combine eggs, zucchini, sugar, oil, syrup and vanilla. Add to flour mixture. Stir in nuts and fruit. Turn into 2 greased and floured 8½ x 4½ x 2½ inch loaf pans. Bake at 350° for 1½ hours.

Date: *Only on Sunday*

For Those Who Enjoy Eating
Patient's name

℞: **DESSERTS**

Dispense: *Small Servings*

Sig: *Be Conservative*

Refill: yes _____
      no ✔

Reta Michils Hill MD
Physician
DEA Number AH 0000000

DESSERTS

℞

MINCEMEAT UPSIDE DOWN CAKE WITH RUM SAUCE

Prepare Pan

- ¼ pound margarine
- ¼ cup rum, brandy, whiskey or equivalent amount of flavoring
- 1 pound jar mincemeat
- ½ cup brown sugar
- 1 cup toasted pecans, chopped

Cake

- 1/4 pound margarine
- 1 cup white sugar
- 2 eggs
- 1 teaspoon vanilla
- 2 cups flour
- ⅛ teaspoon salt
- 2 teaspoons baking powder
- 1 cup milk

Sauce

- ¼ pound margarine
- ¼ cup flour
- ¾ cup sugar
- ⅛ teaspoon salt
- 1 pint whipping cream
- ½ cup rum

Prepare heavy iron skillet by melting ¼ pound margarine. Season mincemeat with rum and pour into skillet. Sprinkle brown sugar and nuts over mincemeat.

Cream white sugar and margarine. Add eggs and vanilla. Sift flour, salt and baking powder together and add alternately with milk to margarine/egg mixture. Pour batter into skillet over mincemeat. Bake in oven at 350° until cake pulls away from edge of pan.

To make sauce, combine melted margarine, flour, sugar, salt, whipping cream and cook until thickened. Add rum. Invert cake on plate and pour rum sauce over it. This cake does not stay around very long. Serves 8.

DESSERTS

℞

APRICOT BRANDY POUND CAKE

½ pound margarine
3 cups sugar
6 eggs
1 cup sour cream
½ cup apricot brandy
1 teaspoon vanilla
1 teaspoon orange extract
1 teaspoon rum extract
3 cups flour, sifted
½ teaspoon salt
¼ teaspoon baking powder

Cream margarine and sugar. Add eggs, sour cream, apricot brandy, vanilla, orange and rum extracts. Stir flour, salt and baking powder together and add to margarine/sugar mixture. Butter and flour a 2½ quart bundt pan. Bake at 325° for 1 hour. Cool on rack 1 hour before removing from pan. Cover with Orange Glaze (see Index).

ICE CREAM CAKE

white or yellow cake, baked
12 almond Hershey bars
36 full size marshmallows
1 pint whipping cream
½ gallon vanilla, chocolate or pralines and cream ice cream, slightly softened
slivered almonds or pecans, toasted
maraschino cherries
whipped cream

Place almond bars and marshmallows in double boiler and cook until melted. Stir frequently. Cool. Whip cream and fold into chocolate mixture. Turn heat off but let pot sit in hot water. Spread chocolate mixture over cake. Spread slightly softened ice cream over cake and return to freezer. Top with toasted nuts. Serve with cherries and whipped cream. Serves 8.

I sent out 75 invitations and had a call from a guest on June 23rd, wanting to know if the event is June 25th or 26th? He stated that his invitation says the 25th but some other residents' invitations say the 26th. I wondered, on how many invitations did I put the wrong date?

DESSERTS

HUMMINGBIRD CAKE WITH BRANDY SAUCE

3	cups flour	1	(8¼ ounce) can crushed pineapple, undrained
2	cups sugar		
1	teaspoon salt	2	cups mashed bananas
1	teaspoon baking soda	1	cup toasted pecans, chopped
1	teaspoon cinnamon		
1½	cups vegetable oil		Brandy Sauce
1½	teaspoons vanilla		
3	eggs		

Sift flour, sugar, salt, baking soda, and cinnamon together. Add vegetable oil, vanilla, eggs and pineapple. Fold in bananas and nuts. Turn into greased, floured 10 inch tube or bundt pan. Bake at 350° for 60-70 minutes. Cool for 15 minutes before inverting on plate. Serve with Brandy Sauce (see Index). Makes 12-16 servings.

CHOCOLATE DELIGHTS

3	ounces unsweetened chocolate	4	eggs separated
			pinch salt
¾	cup butter	½	cup all purpose flour, sifted
½	cup sugar		

Filling

1½	cups heavy cream	4	tablespoons dark rum
10	ounces semi-sweet chocolate	1	teaspoon vanilla extract

Melt chocolate in double boiler. Cool. Cream butter with sugar and add to chocolate. Add egg yolks. Beat egg whites and add salt. Combine with chocolate mixture. Fold in flour. Bake in buttered and floured jelly roll pan at 350° for 15-18 minutes.

For filling, combine cream and chocolate and cook until cream becomes thick. Refrigerate until cold. Add rum and vanilla. Beat until creamy. Cut cake in 2 layers. Spread ½ of filling on lower layer and ½ on the top layer. Cut into 1 inch squares. Makes 35 (1-inch) delights.

DESSERTS

FRUITED RUM CAKE

3 cups unsifted flour	1½ cups vegetable oil
2 cups sugar	¼ cup dark rum
1 teaspoon salt	2 cups chopped bananas
1 teaspoon baking soda	1 (8 ounce) can crushed pineapple, drained
1 teaspoon ground cinnamon	1 cup toasted pecans, chopped
3 eggs, slightly beaten	

Cream Cheese Icing

1 (8 ounce) package cream cheese, softened	1 (16 ounce) package powdered sugar
½ cup margarine, softened	2 teaspoons vanilla

Sift flour, sugar, salt, soda and cinnamon together. Add eggs, oil and rum and mix. Do not beat. Stir in bananas, pineapple and pecans. Pour into greased 10 inch tube pan. Bake at 325° for 1 hour 20 minutes. Cool before frosting with Cream Cheese Icing. Cream the cheese and margarine. Add sugar and vanilla. Mix until smooth. Ice cake. Refrigerate until ready to serve.

WHISKEY CAKE

1 pound white raisins	6 eggs, separated
1 quart pecans, chopped	¾ cup whiskey
3¾ cups all purpose flour	1 tablespoon nutmeg
½ pound margarine	1 tablespoon vanilla
2¼ cups sugar	

Mix raisins and pecans with flour to coat. Cream margarine and sugar. Add egg yolks and whiskey. Add nutmeg and vanilla. Fold in beaten egg whites. Pour into greased and floured 10 inch tube pan and bake 2 hours at 300°. Brush occasionally with whiskey as it bakes.

DESSERTS

CHERRY SPICE CAKE

¾	cup vegetable shortening	½	teaspoon salt
1¾	cups sugar	¾	cup buttermilk
3	eggs	1	cup applesauce
3	cups cake flour	1	(8 ounce) bottle maraschino cherries, halved, reserve juice
1	teaspoon baking soda		
1	teaspoon cinnamon		
1	teaspoon allspice		
1	teaspoon nutmeg	1	cup nuts, chopped

Cream shortening and sugar. Beat in eggs. Sift flour, soda, cinnamon, allspice, nutmeg and salt together. Combine buttermilk and ¼ cup maraschino cherry juice. Alternate adding buttermilk, applesauce and flour to shortening/egg mixture. Add cherries and nuts. Bake in greased and floured tube pan at 350° for 50 minutes. Ice with Confectioner's Sugar Icing (see Index) or leave plain.

CREAM CHERRY CAKE

1	(8 ounce) package cream cheese	½	cup maraschino cherries, quartered
1	cup margarine	½	cup raisins
1½	cups sugar	½	cup pecans, chopped
1½	teaspoons vanilla		Orange Glaze
4	eggs		
2¼	cups flour, sifted		
1½	teaspoons baking powder		

Combine cream cheese, margarine, sugar and vanilla. Add eggs. Sift flour with baking powder and add to cheese/butter mixture. Fold cherries, raisins and pecans into batter. Pour into 10 inch tube pan. Bake at 325° for 1 hour, 20 minutes. Cool before frosting with Orange Glaze.

DESSERTS

℞

Orange Glaze

1⅓	cups powdered sugar, sifted	1	teaspoon grated orange rind
5	tablespoons orange juice		dash salt

Combine ingredients and pour over cake. May substitute Cointreau for orange juice.

DOTTY'S CHOCOLATE TORTE

2	cups flour, sifted	1	teaspoon vanilla
½	cup cocoa, sifted	1⅔	cups sugar
½	teaspoon baking powder	3	eggs, beaten
	few grains salt	1	cup buttermilk
½	cup butter		chocolate, shaved

Sift flour, cocoa, baking powder and salt together. Cream butter, vanilla, and sugar. Add eggs. Add dry ingredients alternately with buttermilk. Blend until smooth. Grease bottom of three 9 inch round cake pans. Line with greased waxpaper. Pour batter into pans and bake at 350° for 18 minutes. Cool. Divide each cake into 2 layers and ice each layer with Venetian Cream Icing. Decorate with shaved chocolate.

Venetian Cream Icing

½	cup flour	1	cup butter
½	cup sugar	1	teaspoon vanilla
½	teaspoon salt	1½	cups confectioner's sugar, sifted
1⅔	cups milk		
1	cup cream		

In saucepan combine flour, sugar and salt. Add milk gradually. Stir in cream. Cook over medium heat, stirring constantly. Bring to boil for 1 minute. Chill. Cream butter, vanilla and half confectioner's sugar and beat until fluffy. Combine chilled cream mixture with butter mixture and add rest of confectioner's sugar.

DESSERTS

℞

MRS. DAVIDSON'S GERMAN FRUIT CAKE

2	cups sugar	1	teaspoon baking soda
10	tablespoons margarine	1	teaspoon vanilla
4	eggs	⅔	cup apricot preserves
3	cups flour	⅔	cup pineapple preserves
1	teaspoon cinnamon		
1	teaspoon nutmeg	⅔	cup cherry preserves
1	teaspoon allspice	1	cup pecans
1	cup buttermilk		

Mix sugar and margarine. Add eggs. Sift flour, cinnamon, nutmeg and allspice together. Add soda to buttermilk. Add dry ingredients to egg mixture alternately with buttermilk mixture. Fold in vanilla, preserves and pecans. Do not add more than the stated amount of preserves. Bake 1½ hours at 325° in greased and floured tube pan. Let cool in pan. A Christmas favorite. Keeps well if not eaten up immediately.

MISSISSIPPI FUDGE CAKE

Cake

½	pound margarine	⅛	teaspoon salt
⅓	cup cocoa	1½	cups pecans, toasted
2	cups sugar	1	large jar marshmallow cream
4	eggs		
1½	cups flour		

Icing

4	tablespoons margarine	1	box confectioner's sugar
⅓	cup cocoa		
1	teaspoon vanilla	⅓	cup milk

DESSERTS

℞

Melt margarine and add cocoa. In separate bowl, cream sugar and eggs. Add flour and salt. Blend in margarine and cocoa mixture. Add pecans. Bake in shallow greased pan at 375° for 20 minutes. Cover with marshmallow cream and return to oven to carmelize marshmallow cream. Remove and let cool.

To make icing, melt margarine and add cocoa. Add vanilla, sugar and milk. Ice cake. Cake must set 1 day before serving. This cake is very rich. Plan to serve small slices.

JOHN'S PUDDING CAKE

¼	pound margarine	1	(4½ ounce) package instant chocolate pudding
1	cup flour		
1	cup pecans, chopped		
1	(8 ounce) package cream cheese	1	(4½ ounce) package instant vanilla pudding
1	cup powdered sugar		
1	(9 ounce) carton Cool Whip, divided	2	cups cold milk

Combine margarine, flour and pecans for crust and press into 9 × 13 inch pan. Bake at 350° for 20 minutes. Cool completely.

Filling

Blend cream cheese, sugar and 1 cup Cool Whip. Spread over cool crust. Blend instant pudding mixes with milk until thick. Pour over cream cheese filling. Top with remaining Cool Whip. Chill until serving time.

DESSERTS

℞

QUICK ITALIAN CAKE

1 box cake mix	1 jar Smuckers Red Raspberry Jam (seedless)
1 small box instant vanilla custard	
1 teaspoon rum or rum flavoring	1½ cups toasted almonds, sliced

Bake cake according to instructions. Cool. Mix custard according to instructions for stiffer custard. Add rum. Let set. Slice cake in 2 layers. Place lower layer of cake on serving dish. Cover with jam, custard and almonds. Place second half of cake on lower layer. Ice with Confectioner's Sugar Icing and top with toasted almonds. Serves 8-10. Triple recipe for cake to fill 9 x 13 pan.

Confectioner's Sugar Icing

1 cup confectioner's sugar	2 tablespoons milk
	1 teaspoon vanilla
2 tablespoons margarine	

Cream sugar and margarine. Add milk and vanilla. Ice cake.

Custards I could never make; like the two dozen eggs lost in an effort to make a custard for this Italian cake. It was replaced by instant custard, seasoned with rum and no one knew the difference.

FROZEN CAKE

1 sponge cake	1 pint raspberry sherbet, softened
½ cup currant jelly	
½ cup sherry	1 cup whipped cream
2 pints vanilla ice cream, softened	½ cup almonds or pecans, toasted

Zabaglione Sauce

5 egg yolks	¼ cup sherry
¼ cup sugar	

DESSERTS

℞

Split cake in 3 layers. Spread one layer with jelly and one layer with sherry. Freeze. While still frozen, spread one layer with vanilla ice cream and one with sherbet. Put layer with raspberry sherbet on top of layer with vanilla ice cream. Top with third layer. Wrap with plastic wrap and freeze. Serve with whipped cream, nuts and Zabaglione Sauce.

To make sauce, combine egg yolks, sugar and sherry and cook on low heat until thickened. Refrigerate. Serves 12-16.

MELANIE'S RUM CAKE

Cake

½	pound margarine	2	cups plus 3 table-
2	cups sugar		spoons flour,
6	eggs		sifted
⅛	teaspoon salt	¼	cup dark rum

Rum Sauce

1½	cups sugar	2	tablespoons white
¼	cup water		corn syrup
½	cup dark rum		

Cream margarine, sugar and eggs. Add flour, salt and rum. Bake in greased and floured tube pan for 45 minutes at 300°. To make sauce, bring sugar and water to boil. Add corn syrup and rum. Pour over warm cake.

DESSERTS

MELANIE'S ANGEL CAKE SURPRISE

	angel food cake
1	cup whipped cream
3	tablespoons sugar
½	teaspoon vanilla
¼	cup drained, crushed pineapple
¼	cup maraschino cherries
¼	cup small marshmallows
½	cup toasted pecans, chopped
1½	cups whipping cream, flavored with 1 teaspoon confectioner's sugar, whipped

Cut 1 inch slice from top of angel food cake. Cut out well 2 inches wide and 2 inches deep in cake. Combine 1 cup whipped cream, sugar, vanilla, fruit, marshmallows and nuts and chill. Spoon chilled filling into well cut in cake. Replace slice cut from top. Frost with 1½ cups whipped cream. Chill. Serves 12.

One of Melanie's first birthday cakes. Although rich in calories, it is a light and refreshing cake.

DUNDEE CAKE

2½	cups self rising flour
¾	teaspoon allspice
½	cup margarine, softened
½	cup sugar
⅔	cup orange marmalade
1	teaspoon vanilla
2	eggs
¾	cup milk
½	cup currants
½	cup golden raisins
¼	cup almonds, chopped, reserve 1 tablespoon

Sift flour and allspice together. Combine margarine, sugar, marmalade, vanilla and eggs. Add flour and milk, alternately. Add currants, raisins and almonds. Pour into well greased 9 x 5 loaf pan. Sprinkle remaining almonds on top. Bake in 350° oven for 50-60 minutes. Cool before removing from pan.

DESSERTS

QUICK COFFEE CAKE

1	cup margarine	½	cup toasted pecans, chopped, divided
1	cup brown sugar		
¼	teaspoon cinnamon	1	can refrigerated biscuits
¼	teaspoon nutmeg		

Heat margarine, sugar and spices. Pour ½ of the mixture into greased ring mold pan. Add ½ of pecans. Cut biscuit dough in half and arrange in mold. Pour rest of margarine, pecans and sugar mixture on biscuits. Bake at 375° for 25 minutes.

COOKIES AND CANDIES

FRENCH CANADIAN FUDGE

5	cups white sugar	1	cup white corn syrup
1	can Eagle Brand milk	¾	cup milk
½	pound butter (no substitute)	16	large marshmallows

Combine all ingredients except marshmallows and cook over low heat exactly 25 minutes. Add marshmallows. Stir constantly. Cook for 5 minutes. Take off heat and whip until firm. Pour into buttered pan.

CHOCOLATE INDULGENCE

16	(1 ounce) squares semi-sweet chocolate	1	tablespoon flour
		4	eggs, separated
		1	teaspoon vanilla extract
¾	cup butter		
¾	cup powdered sugar	8	ounces sour cream

Melt chocolate and butter and gradually add sugar and flour. Remove from heat. With rotary beater, blend in egg yolks; then vanilla. In separate bowl, beat egg whites. Fold into chocolate mixture. Remove 1 cup of chocolate mixture and blend with sour cream. Pour remaining chocolate into greased 8 inch baking pan and top with sour cream/chocolate mixture. Bake 25 minutes at 375°. The center will be soft. Cool. Chill for 4 hours before serving. Makes 16 (2 inch) servings. To freeze, wrap in individual servings.

DESSERTS

℞

BUNUELOS

1	cup sugar	¼	teaspoon ground nutmeg
1	teaspoon ground cinnamon	12	(8 inch) flour tortillas

Mix first 3 ingredients in plastic bag. Cut tortillas in 3 x 2 inch strips. Fry in hot oil until crisp and golden brown. Do not overcook. Drain. While still warm shake in bag containing cinnamon/sugar mixture. Makes 5 dozen.

LOUISIANA PECAN LASSIES

Crust

¼	pound margarine	1	(3 ounce) package cream cheese, softened
1	cup flour		

Filling

2	eggs	2	tablespoons margarine
	dash of salt	1	teaspoon vanilla
1½	cups brown sugar		pecans chopped

Combine margarine and cream cheese. Add flour. Take 1 teaspoon full of crust and mash into each cup of miniature muffin tins. Mix all ingredients for filling and pour into crusts. Sprinkle with chopped pecans. Bake at 350° for 30 minutes.

GOLDEN TASSIES

¼	pound margarine, room temperature	½	teaspoon lemon rind
1	(3 ounce) package cream cheese, softened	1	cup flour
			pineapple or preferred preserves
½	teaspoon orange rind, grated		pecans, chopped

DESSERTS

℞

Mix margarine, cream cheese, orange and lemon rind. Add flour and blend; chill. Take small pinch of dough and press into each cup of small Teflon muffin tins to form shell. Place ¼ teaspoon chopped nuts and ¼ teaspoon pineapple preserves on the crusts. Sprinkle with chopped nuts. Bake at 400° for 10-15 minutes. Makes 3 dozen.

COCONUT MACAROONS

2	egg whites	2	cups cornflakes
1	cup sugar		almond extract
½	can Baker's shredded coconut	½	cup pecans, chopped

Beat egg whites until stiff. Add sugar, coconut, cornflakes, almond extract and pecans. Drop by teaspoonsful on buttered cookie sheet. Bake in 350° oven until golden, then turn oven down to 250° and watch carefully until they are as dry as you like. Cool on rack before removing. Recipe doubles.

PRALINE CRESCENT COOKIES

½	pound butter	1	tablespoon cold milk
¾	cup confectioner's sugar	2	cups toasted pecans, finely chopped
2	cups flour, sifted		flour
1½	tablespoons praline flavored liqueur		confectioner's sugar for coating (optional)

Cream butter and sugar. Add flour, liqueur and milk. Stir in pecans. Flour fingers. Shape batter into crescents (about 1 teaspoon per cookie). Bake at 350° for 10-15 minutes. Sprinkle with confectioner's sugar while warm and allow to sit in baking pan to cool. Makes 4 dozen cookies.

These are as addictive as popcorn and peanuts!

DESSERTS

PEACHES AND CREAM

1 (8 ounce) can refrigerated crescent dinner rolls	½ cup all purpose self-rising flour
1 (8 ounce) package cream cheese, softened	¼ cup brown sugar
	3 tablespoons margarine
½ cup sugar	½ cup almonds, toasted and sliced
½ teaspoon almond extract	
1 (21 ounce) can prepared peach fruit filling (2½ cups)	

Separate and form crescent dough into 2 long rectangles. Press into bottom of ungreased 13 x 9 inch pan. Blend cream cheese, sugar and almond extract. Spread over dough followed by fruit filling. Mix flour, brown sugar and margarine until crumbly. Stir in almonds and sprinkle over fruit filling. Bake at 375° for 25-30 minutes. Makes 12-15 squares.

HELLO DOLLIES

¼ pound margarine, melted	1 cup coconut
1½ cups graham cracker crumbs	1 (12 ounce) package toll house chocolate chips
½ teaspoon cinnamon	1 cup pecans
½ teaspoon nutmeg	1 can condensed milk

Mix margarine, graham cracker crumbs, cinnamon and nutmeg. Pat down in a Pyrex dish to make crust. Layer coconut, chocolate chips and pecans. Pour condensed milk on top. Bake at 350° for 30 minutes.

These are great to serve as a dessert at buffet parties and go well with bourbon. Men adore these. They are addictive.

DESSERTS

BIRD'S NESTS

1 cup all purpose flour	2 eggs, separated
¼ teaspoon salt	1 cup pecans, chopped
½ cup butter	2 tablespoons raspberry jelly
¼ cup brown sugar	

Sift flour and salt together. Cream butter, sugar and egg yolks. Add dry ingredients. Shape dough into small balls. Dip in beaten egg whites and roll in chopped pecans. Place on greased baking sheet. Make indentation in center of cookies. Bake at 350° for 8 minutes. Place ¼ teaspoon jelly in indentation of each cookie. Bake about 15 minutes longer. Makes 2 dozen cookies.

FRUIT

BOURBON PEACHES

½ cup butter	2 teaspoons lemon juice
8 fresh peaches, halved	4 tablespoons light brown sugar
1½ tablespoons grated orange peel	4 ounces bourbon

Melt butter. Add peaches and sauté until slightly brown. Add orange peel, lemon juice and sugar. Cook until sugar thoroughly melted. Add bourbon and ignite. Serve hot or with ice cream. This is an excellent dessert served with Sauce Anglaise (see Index).

MINCEMEAT PEACHES

canned peach halves	cheddar cheese, grated
brandied mincemeat	

Fill peaches with mincemeat. Cover with cheddar cheese and pass under broiler. A quick dessert or nice fruit to serve with ham or poultry.

DESSERTS

PINEAPPLE AU GRATIN

¾ cup sugar	½ cup Ritz cracker crumbs
3 tablespoons flour	
1 cup cheddar cheese, grated	4 tablespoons margarine, melted
1 cup pineapple chunks, drained (reserve liquid)	

Combine sugar, flour and cheese. Add pineapple and place in casserole. Pour ½ pineapple juice over pineapple/cheese mixture. Top with Ritz cracker crumbs. Combine rest of pineapple juice with margarine and drizzle over top. Bake at 350° for 30 minutes. May serve cold or warm. Good with ham or poultry.

SPICY STUFFED PEACHES

1 (28 ounce) can cling peach halves (3½ cups)	⅛ teaspoon nutmeg dash ground cloves
½ cup peach juice	1 (8 ounce) can crushed pineapple, non-sweetened
½ cup pear juice, non-sweetened	
2 tablespoons honey	3 tablespoons toasted pecans, chopped
1 tablespoon cornstarch	2 tablespoons raisins, plumped
½ teaspoon cinnamon	

Place peach halves in baking dish, flat side up. To make glaze, in a pan combine peach and pear juice with honey, cornstarch, cinnamon, nutmeg and cloves. Cook until thickened. Combine pineapple, pecans and raisins with ⅓ of glaze. Put mixture into pit indentations, dividing mixture equally among peach halves. Pour rest of glaze over peaches. Bake at 350° for 30 minutes. Serves 6-8. Good as dessert or accompanying ham or poultry.

DESSERTS

HOT FRUIT CASSEROLE

1 (28 ounce) can peach halves (3½ cups)
1 (28 ounce) can peach slices (3½ cups)
1 (28 ounce) can pear halves (3½ cups)
1 (15¼ ounce) can pineapple chunks (1¾ cups)
1 (28 ounce) can apricot halves (3½ cups)
1 (16 ounce) can dark Bing cherries (1¾ cups)
2-3 bananas
lemon juice
2 dozen macaroons
1 cup brown sugar
1 can toasted almonds
⅓ cup banana liqueur
4 tablespoons margarine

Day before serving, place all fruits except bananas in colandor to drain. The day of serving, slice bananas and sprinkle with lemon juice. In 2 quart casserole, layer fruit, macaroons, brown sugar and sprinkle with almonds and banana liqueur. Dot with margarine. Bake at 300° for 20-30 minutes. Serves 10-12. May be served as dessert or with ham or poultry.

TRIFLE

1 (8 inch) sponge cake
1 cup raspberry or strawberry jam
¼ cup sherry
½ cup juice from frozen raspberries or strawberries
2 cups instant vanilla custard
fruits: peaches, bananas, raspberries
1 cup whipping cream, whipped

Cut sponge cake into 3 layers. Line an 8 inch bowl with 1 layer of cake. Spread this layer with ⅓ cup raspberry jam. Combine sherry and raspberry juice. Pour ⅓ mixture over the layer then spread with ⅓ of the custard. Add layer of fruit. Repeat layers, ending with a third layer of custard. Top with whipped cream. Rum may be substituted for sherry. Serves 8.

DESSERTS

CUSTARD AND FRUITS

½ cup plus 2 tablespoons sugar
⅓ cup cornstarch
¼ teaspoon salt
3 cups milk
1 egg yolk, beaten
1 teaspoon vanilla
1 pint strawberries or preferred fruit
½ cup toasted almonds, sliced

Combine ½ cup sugar, cornstarch and salt in saucepan. Add milk slowly stirring constantly. Cook until thickened. Combine some of mixture to beaten egg yolk and return yolk mixture to custard sauce. Add vanilla. Cook for 3-4 minutes, but do not boil. Chill. Sprinkle remaining sugar over sliced fruit. Combine fruit with custard sauce. Sprinkle toasted almonds on top. Serves 6.

STRAWBERRIES AND CREAM

2 cups heavy cream
1 cup sugar
1 envelope gelatin
1 pint sour cream
1 teaspoon vanilla
2 pints fresh strawberries

Heat cream and sugar. Do not boil. Dissolve gelatin into cream mixture and cook until thickened. Cool and stir in sour cream and vanilla. Serve over strawberries. Serves 10.

CHERRY SURPRISE

3 cups cold water
1 cup sugar
1 cinnamon stick
4 cups sour cherries, drained
1 teaspoon arrowroot
1 teaspoon water
¼ cup heavy cream, chilled
¾ cup dry red wine

Combine water, sugar and cinnamon stick in pan and bring to boil. Add cherries and cook 35-40 minutes. Remove cinnamon stick. Combine arrowroot with water and add to cherry mixture. Simmer until clear and thickened. Chill. Fold in cream and wine. Serves 6.

DESSERTS

RASPBERRY BAVARIA

1	cup milk	¼	cup water
1	cup sugar	¼	cup sweet sherry
3	eggs, separated	2	cups raspberries
⅛	teaspoon nutmeg	2	tablespoons sugar
⅛	teaspoon salt	⅔	cup heavy cream, whipped
1	envelope unflavored gelatin		

Combine milk, sugar, egg yolks, nutmeg and salt in top of double boiler. Simmer until thickened. Remove from heat. Dissolve gelatin in water and sherry. Combine with milk/egg mixture. Put custard in blender and add berries; mix thoroughly. Chill mixture until it begins to gel. Beat egg whites with sugar. Add whipped cream. Combine with berry mixture. Pour into 2 quart bowl and chill. Serves 8.

ICE CREAM

SOUTH OF THE BORDER SURPRISE

12	flour tortillas	pralines and cream ice cream for 12
1	stick butter	chocolate syrup or chocolate liqueur
1	cup sugar	
½	teaspoon cinnamon	
½	teaspoon allspice	

Fry tortillas in butter until light brown. Do not overcook. Drain. Combine sugar, cinnamon and allspice in bag and shake tortillas in mixture while hot. Top with ice cream and add chocolate sauce. Serves 12.

DESSERTS

℞

TORTONI

2½	cups heavy whipping cream, divided	¼	cup dark rum
½	cup confectioner's sugar	1½	teaspoons vanilla
	pinch of salt	¼	cup toasted almonds, sliced
5-8	stale macaroons, crushed in blender	6	candied cherries

Line muffin tins with paper muffin liner. Combine 1½ cups heavy cream, sugar, salt, macaroons and chill for 30 minutes. Beat remaining cream to form soft peaks. Fold rum and vanilla into macaroon mixture. Fill the muffin cups with the cream mixture. Sprinkle with almonds and top with cherry halves. Freeze for 2 hours before serving. Serves 12 (2 x 2½ muffins).

After a dinner party an intern asked Dr. Hill, "May I return tomorrow for leftovers?"

MOUSSE

EGGNOG MOUSSE

4	cups milk	½	cup water
1	cup sugar	¼	cup bourbon
8	egg yolks	2	cups heavy cream, whipped
1½	teaspoons vanilla extract		
3	envelopes unflavored gelatin		

Bring milk to a boil. Add sugar and egg yolks to milk and cook until custard consistency. Do not boil. Add vanilla extract. Place gelatin in water and warm to dissolve. Add bourbon. Let cool. Add gelatin to whipped cream and combine with custard. Pour into wet ring mold coated with sugar. Refrigerate several hours. Serves 8. Make the day you serve. Serve with Apricot Sauce (see Index).

DESSERTS

CHOCOLATE CHESTNUT DESSERT

1⅓	cups semisweet chocolate	½	pound softened butter
¼	cup Kirsch, rum, or port wine	12	finger shaped sugar cookies
1	tablespoon vanilla	2-3	cups whipped cream
3	tablespoons strong coffee	¼	cup pistachio nuts, chopped
⅛	teaspoon salt		chocolate shavings
½-¾	cups sugar		
2	(1 pound 5 ounce) cans pureed unflavored chestnuts		

Melt chocolate with Kirsch and vanilla. Combine coffee with salt and sugar and heat to melt. Combine pureed chestnuts, butter, melted chocolate and sugar/coffee syrup. Line bottom of round soufflé dish with wax paper. Turn in 1 inch layer of chestnut mixture. Line sides of dish with upright sugar cookies. Fill the dish with the remaining chestnut mixture. Cover with wax paper and chill overnight. Top with whipped cream, chopped pistachio nuts and chocolate shavings.

MINCEMEAT MOUSSE

1	envelope unflavored gelatin	½	cup sugar
2	tablespoons cold water	4	cups heavy cream, whipped
⅓	cup boiling water	½	cup mincemeat
4	egg yolks	2	ounces rum

Sprinkle gelatin over cold water. Pour into boiling water and stir to dissolve. Beat egg yolks and sugar. Stir into gelatin mixture. Fold in whipped cream, mincemeat and rum. Pour into 6 cup mold. Chill for 2 hours.

DESSERTS

MINCEMEAT CREPES WITH BOURBON SAUCE

Crepes

6 eggs	2 tablespoons sugar
2 cups milk	½ teaspoon salt
2 tablespoons margarine, melted	oil
1½ cups all purpose flour, sifted	

Beat eggs; stir in milk and margarine. Sift in flour, sugar, salt and beat until smooth. Cover bowl and refrigerate 2 hours.

To make crepes, pour just enough crepe mixture in a lightly oiled 7 inch Teflon frying pan to cover bottom. Cook long enough that crepes separate from edge of pan and shake when the pan is moved. Pour onto wax paper squares. Do not overcook. Should be light brown on one side. Makes 12.

Mincemeat Filling

1 (18 ounce) jar prepared mincemeat	1 tablespoon lemon juice
1 cup chunky style applesauce	1 teaspoon vanilla
	1 teaspoon grated lemon peel

Combine all ingredients. Place mincemeat filling on lateral ⅓ of crepe and roll in cigar fashion. Place in pan with seam down. When ready to serve, put crepes in oven at 250° to warm. Cover container with damp cloth. Serve with warm Bourbon Sauce.

Bourbon Sauce

¼ pound butter	1 egg, beaten
1 cup sugar	½ cup bourbon
½ cup water	

Melt butter, stir in sugar and water. Let stand 10 minutes off heat. Beat in egg and add bourbon.

DESSERTS

℞

PIE AND PIE CRUST

JUNE'S PIE CRUST

2 cups enriched flour, sifted	¾ cup shortening
1 teaspoon salt	2-3 tablespoons ice water (must be ice water)

Sift flour and salt together. Cut in shortening until of cornmeal consistency. Add ice cold water a tablespoon at a time until dough cleans the bowl. Roll between wax paper. Do not flour paper. Remove paper and place in pie pan. Put holes in dough with fork to keep dough from puffing. Bake at 450° for 12-15 minutes. Makes 2 (8 inch) or 1 double pie crust.

VINEGAR CRUST

3 cups flour, sifted	1 egg, well beaten
1 teaspoon salt	5 tablespoons water
1¼ cups vegetable shortening	1 tablespoon vinegar

Sift flour and salt together. Cut ½ of the shortening into the mixture. Blend in remaining shortening so that mixture is size of small peas. Combine egg, water and vinegar. Blend into flour mixture. Divide evenly into 3 portions. Put in plastic bag and refrigerate. Keeps in refrigerator 3 weeks. Makes 3 (9 inch) crusts. Bake at 425° for 15 minutes.

GRAHAM CRACKER CRUST

¼ pound margarine, melted	1 tablespoon sugar
1½-2 cups graham cracker crumbs	¼ teaspoon cinnamon
	¼ teaspoon nutmeg

Mix melted margarine, cracker crumbs, sugar, cinnamon and nutmeg and pat down in a 9 x 13 or 2 (9 inch) pie pans. Bake at 350° about 10-15 minutes.

DESSERTS

CHOCOLATE NUT CRUST

1	box chocolate snaps (about 20 cookies)	⅛	teaspoon nutmeg
		⅛	teaspoon cinnamon
½	cup toasted pecans	½	cup margarine, melted

Whirl chocolate snaps and pecans in food processor. Combine with nutmeg and cinnamon. Mix with melted margarine. Mash into 9 inch pie plate. Chocolate Oreos may be used. If so, omit nutmeg and cinnamon.

BRANDY ALEXANDER PIE

2	envelopes unflavored gelatin	3	tablespoons Crème de Cocoa
2	cups cold water, divided	3	tablespoons brandy
1	cup sugar, divided	½	pint heavy cream, whipped
4	eggs, separated		pecans, toasted
8	ounces cream cheese, softened		chocolate shavings

Add gelatin to 1 cup water and heat to dissolve. Add rest of water and ¾ cup sugar. Cool. Add egg yolks. Cook until thickened. Beat cream cheese and fold into egg/sugar mixture. Add Crème de Cocoa and brandy. Chill. Fold in beaten egg whites, ¼ cup sugar and whipped cream. Chill until firm. Pour into refrigerated Chocolate Nut Crust. Top with pecans and chocolate shavings. Serves 14.

CHOCOLATE PECAN PIE

2	squares (2 ounces) unsweetened chocolate	½	teaspoon salt
		3	eggs, beaten
		1	teaspoon vanilla
6	tablespoons margarine	1½	cups pecans, toasted, chopped and divided
1	(14 ounce) can sweetened condensed milk	2	(9 inch) uncooked pie shells
½	cup sugar		

DESSERTS

℞

Melt chocolate with margarine. Combine condensed milk, sugar, salt, and eggs. Add to chocolate mixture and beat well. Add vanilla and 1¼ cups pecans. Put remaining pecans in bottom of uncooked pastry shells. Pour mixture into shell. Bake 10 minutes at 400°. Reduce heat to 300° and bake 45 minutes. Must be stored in refrigerator. This dessert is extremely sweet so serve small portions. Serves 8.

"Dr. Hill, the food's good," stated the resident. "I'm on my 5th helping" — a hostess' delight or horror.

AMARETTO COCONUT CREAM PIE

4	eggs	1	quart whipped cream, reserve 4 tablespoons
1¼	cups sugar		
½	cup water		
3	envelopes unflavored gelatin	1¼	cup shredded coconut, toasted (reserve 2 tablespoons)
4	ounces Amaretto liqueur		fresh strawberries, with stems
1	dash almond extract		

Combine eggs, and sugar. Mix gelatin in water and dissolve over low heat. Blend together gelatin, Amaretto, almond extract and egg/sugar mixture. Fold in whipped cream and coconut. Pour into 13 x 9 x 2 pan with Graham Cracker Crust (see Index). Spread pie with thin layer of whipped cream and coconut. Place a fresh strawberry with stem at the center of each proposed slice so that each person has a strawberry. Sprinkle top with remaining toasted coconut. Serves 12-16 depending on slices. Everybody loves this.

DESSERTS

GERMAN CHOCOLATE PIE

1	unbaked 9 inch deep pie shell	1½	cups sugar
1	package (4 ounce) German sweet chocolate	3	tablespoons cornstarch
		⅛	teaspoon salt
		2	eggs, beaten
¼	cup butter	1	teaspoon vanilla
1⅓	cups evaporated milk (14½ ounces)	1½	cups coconut
		½	cup pecans, chopped

Melt chocolate and butter. Remove from heat and stir in milk. Combine sugar, cornstarch and salt. Add beaten eggs and vanilla. Blend into chocolate mixture. Pour into unbaked pie shell. Combine coconut and pecans and sprinkle over top of pie. Bake at 375° for 45 minutes. Cool 4 hours before cutting.

NUT DELIGHT – A FOOTBALL RECIPE

3	egg whites	½	cup whipped cream, whipped
1	cup sugar		
1	teaspoon baking soda	2	tablespoons powdered sugar
1	teaspoon vanilla		
¾	cup pecans, chopped	1	teaspoon vanilla
1¼	cups Waverly Wafers, crumbled		

Beat egg whites. Add sugar, baking soda and blend well. Stir in vanilla, pecans and wafers. Pour into 9 inch pie pan and bake at 325° for 18-20 minutes. Let cool. Top with whipped cream flavored with powdered sugar and vanilla. Refrigerate for several hours so that moisture from the whipping cream penetrates pie. As this pie cooks, it makes its own crust.

Good dessert for football game dinners. You can eat it on the way to the stadium. This was one of the original no crust pies. Circa 1960.

DESSERTS

RUM CREAM PIE

2	(9 inch) Graham Cracker Crusts (see Index)	½	cup dark rum chocolate shavings pistachio nuts, chopped
6	eggs		
1	cup sugar		
2	envelopes gelatin		
½	cup water		
1	pint whipped cream, reserve 2 tablespoons		

Beat eggs and combine with sugar. Place gelatin into water and warm over low flame to dissolve. Cool. Pour gelatin mixture into the sugar/egg mixture. Whip cream until stiff and fold into mixture. Flavor with ½ cup of dark rum (do not use light rum). Cool and pour into Graham Cracker Crust (see Index). Garnish with thin layer of whipping cream, chocolate shavings and chopped pistachio nuts. Refrigerate. Recipe makes enough filling for 2 pies. Always a winner. May use cream mixture alone as dessert.

My secretary said this was the only dessert she ever served to her guests that made them drunk. She had inadvertently doubled the amount of rum.

CANDY BAR PIE

1	(9 inch) Graham Cracker Crust, reserve 2 tablespoons crumbs	20	marshmallows, cut in pieces
		½	cup milk
		1	teaspoon vanilla
6	small Hershey bars with nuts	½	pint whipped cream, divided

Melt chocolate bars and marshmallows in double boiler with milk. Cool and add vanilla. Add ½ of the whipped cream to the mixture and cool. Pour into Graham Cracker Crust (see Index). Top with remaining whipped cream and sprinkle with seasoned Graham Cracker Crust crumbs.

DESSERTS

COLLEGE INN'S PUMPKIN BOURBON PIE

- 1 (9 inch) unbaked pie crust
- 1 can mashed pumpkin
- 1 cup sugar
- 1½ cups canned evaporated milk
- ¼ cup bourbon
- 3 eggs, separated
- 1 teaspoon cinnamon
- 1 teaspoon mace
- ½ teaspoon nutmeg
- pecans, chopped

Combine pumpkin, sugar, milk, bourbon, egg yolks, and spices. Mix well. Fold in beaten egg whites and pour into pie pan. Sprinkle pecans on top. Bake at 450° for 15 minutes. Reduce heat to 300° and bake 20 minutes longer.

MINCEMEAT CREAM PIE

- 1 (9 inch) pie shell, baked and cooled
- 1 (4 ounce) package vanilla pie filling
- 1½ cups milk
- 1 cup whipped cream, divided
- ¾ cup mincemeat
- ¼ teaspoon rum extract
- ½ cup toasted, chopped pecans

Combine pie filling, milk and ¾ cup whipped cream. Fold in mincemeat and rum extract. Pour into shell and top with rest of whipped cream and pecans. Chill.

JEANNINE'S FRUIT PIZZA

- 1 box yellow cake mix
- ¼ cup water
- ¼ cup margarine
- 2 eggs
- ¼ cup brown sugar
- ½ cup pecans, finely chopped
- 8 ounces cream cheese at room temperature
- 1 pint whipped cream
- sliced strawberries, blueberries, bananas, chunked pineapple, sliced in half
- 1 small jar apricot preserves
- 1½ tablespoons water

DESSERTS

℞

Combine cake mix, water, margarine, eggs, brown sugar and pecans. Press into 2 pizza pans which have been greased and floured. Bake at 375° until brown. Whip cream cheese and fold into whipped cream. This takes awhile. Spread over cake crust. Drain fruit several hours before using. Soak bananas in pineapple juice and drain. Arrange fruit on crust in pie wedge design or in rows. Combine apricot preserves with water. Glaze fruit. This is a beautiful dessert; looks like a stained glass window.

CHEESE PIE
(Not to be confused with Cheese Cake)

8 ounces cream cheese	favorite fresh fruit, sliced, drained and sweetened with sugar
1 cup sugar	
1 tablespoon vanilla	
3 eggs, separated	
1 pint whipped cream	1 (9 inch) pie crust, baked

Cream the cheese and sugar until fluffy. Add vanilla and egg yolks. Whip the cream and fold into mixture. Whip the egg whites until stiff. Fold in gently. Pour into baked 9 inch pie crust. Top with fruits. Fruits may be flamed in brandy. Serve immediately. If serving later, mix pie contents and refrigerate then add to pie crust just before serving so crust will not be soggy.

This is a take off on a dessert served at Tortoricis in New Orleans.

DESSERTS

℞

EDELWEISS FUDGE NO CRUST PIE

4	ounces German sweet chocolate	½	cup flour
½	cup butter	1	teaspoon vanilla
3	large eggs	½	cup pecans, toasted
½	cup sugar		whipped cream or ice cream
½	cup packed brown sugar		

Melt chocolate with butter and cool. Beat eggs and add both sugars. Blend in flour, chocolate mixture, vanilla and nuts. Pour into well greased 9 inch pie pan. Bake at 325° for 40 minutes. Pie is puffy while baking and settles down to fudgy texture when cool. Serve with whipped cream or ice cream.

WHISKEY APPLE PIE

1	(10 inch) pastry crust, unbaked, plus pastry for topping	1½	cups sugar
		½	teaspoon salt
		1	teaspoon nutmeg
8	Granny Smith apples, pared and diced	½	teaspoon cinnamon
		1	tablespoon butter
	juice of 1 lemon	1½	ounces bourbon
	juice of 1 orange	2	tablespoons flour
	juice of ½ lime		

Combine apples, fruit juices, sugar, salt, spices, and butter. Cook slowly until juices become transparent. Add bourbon. Spoon apples into pastry crust. Sprinkle with flour. Add juice/spice mixture. Make lattice crust top. Sprinkle with sugar. Bake at 450° for 15 minutes. Reduce heat to 350° and bake an additional 30 minutes.

DESSERTS

APPLE CUSTARD PIE

Crust

1¾	cups flour	½	teaspoon salt
¼	cup sugar	1	teaspoon cinnamon
12	tablespoons butter	3	tablespoons apple juice

Mix and roll out for 10 inch crust. If you use your favorite pie crust, add cinnamon and substitute apple juice for water.

Filling

1½	cups sour cream	½	teaspoon salt
1	egg	6	large Rome or Jonathan apples, peeled, cored and sliced
1	cup sugar		
¼	cup flour		
2	teaspoons vanilla		

Combine above ingredients well and coat apples. Pour into crust. Bake at 450° for 10 minutes. Reduce heat to 350° and bake for 35-40 minutes. Add topping.

Topping

½	cup butter	¼	teaspoon salt
½	cup flour	⅓	cup sugar
½	cup pecans, chopped	½	cup brown sugar
1	teaspoon cinnamon		

Combine ingredients and top pie. Cook an additional 10 minutes at 350°.

DESSERTS

COTTAGE CHEESE APPLE PIE

1	(9 inch) pie crust, unbaked	1	teaspoon grated lemon rind
2	eggs	1½	cups peeled, thinly sliced Granny Smith apples
½	cup cottage cheese		
¾	cup sugar, divided		
½	cup cream	½	teaspoon cinnamon
⅛	teaspoon salt	½	teaspoon nutmeg

Beat eggs with cottage cheese, ½ cup sugar, cream, salt and lemon rind. Place apples in pastry crust. Pour cottage cheese mixture on apples. Combine remaining sugar, cinnamon and nutmeg and sprinkle on top of apples. Bake at 425° for 10 minutes. Reduce heat to 350° and bake 30 minutes longer.

COCONUT KAHLÚA CREAM PIE

Crust

⅓	cup coconut	¾	cup graham cracker crumbs
½	ounce butter, melted		

Filling

1	pint whipping cream	1	tablespoon vanilla extract
1	envelope unflavored gelatin	3	ounces Kahlúa
½	cup water	⅔	cup shredded coconut, toasted, divided
3	eggs		
1	cup sugar		

Lay coconut on a pan and brown in the oven. Mix coconut with crumbs and butter to make a "sticky" crust. Spread evenly on bottom of 9 inch springform pie pan.

Beat whipping cream until thick; set aside. Mix gelatin with water and warm to dissolve; set aside. Beat eggs and add sugar, vanilla, Kahlua and ⅓ cup of coconut. Fold in whipping cream and add gelatin. Pour into pie form. Sprinkle with remaining coconut. Chill in refrigerator for 3 hours. Before serving, pour some Kahlúa over the top of each piece of pie.

DESSERTS

MARILYN'S CRÈME DE CASSIS PIE

1 (10 inch) Graham Cracker Crust (see Index)	1 envelope unflavored gelatin
6 egg yolks	½ cup cold water
¾ cup sugar	1 pint whipped cream
¼ teaspoon salt	½ cup Crème de Cassis
	fresh nutmeg

Cream egg yolks, sugar and salt. Soften gelatin in cold water and heat to dissolve. Pour gelatin mixture into egg mixture. After mixture thickens, add whipped cream and Crème de Cassis. Turn into Graham Cracker Crust. Refrigerate overnight. Sprinkle with nutmeg before serving. Serves 8.

NESSELRODE CHIFFON PIE

1 Graham Cracker Crust or baked pie shell	¼ cup cold water
⅓ cup rum or brandy	4 eggs, separated
¾ cup chopped chestnuts in vanilla syrup	⅔ cup sugar, divided
	¼ teaspoon salt
4 tablespoons chopped, candied orange peel	2 tablespoons maraschino cherry juice
4 tablespoons raisins, chopped	1½ cups heavy cream, whipped and divided
¾ cup maraschino cherries, quartered	
1 envelope unflavored gelatin	

Marinate chestnuts, orange peel, raisins, and cherries in rum or brandy. Place gelatin in water and heat to dissolve. Combine egg yolks, ¼ cup sugar and salt. Add cherry juice to gelatin and pour into the egg yolk mixture. Chill. Fold in chestnuts/fruit mixture and remaining marinade. Chill. Beat egg whites and combine with 1¼ cups whipped cream. Fold into egg/fruit mixture. Chill for at least 4 hours or overnight. Pour into a baked pie shell or a Graham Cracker Crust. Garnish with remaining whipped cream.

DESSERTS

BOURBON PIE

Chocolate Nut Crust (see Index)
21 marshmallows (large)
1 cup evaporated milk
½ pint whipping cream
3 tablespoons bourbon
½ cup toasted pecans
¼ cup whipped cream, reserve for garnish

Melt marshmallows in undiluted milk. Do not boil. Chill. Whip cream and fold into marshmallow mixture. Add bourbon and pour into chocolate nut crust. Refrigerate overnight and top with toasted pecans and whipped cream. Serves 8.

BOURBON STREET CHEESECAKE

Graham Cracker Crust (see Index)
3 (8 ounce) packages cream cheese at room temperature
1¼ cups dark brown sugar
2 tablespoons all purpose flour
3 eggs
1½ teaspoons vanilla extract
½ cup toasted pecans, chopped
2 tablespoons liquid brown sugar
12 pecan halves, toasted

Combine cream cheese, dark brown sugar and flour until blended. Add eggs and vanilla. Pour into crust. Bake for 50-55 minutes at 350°. Refrigerate at least 2 hours. Cover with toasted pecans that have been coated in liquid brown sugar. Decorate with pecan halves.

A slogan among the Housestaff: "Don't eat for a week when you're invited to the Hill's."

BALKAN YOGURT PIE

3 eggs
½ cup plain yogurt
2 tablespoons honey
½ teaspoon vanilla
2 cups crumbled Feta cheese
18 phyllo leaves
½ cup margarine, melted
3 tablespoons lemon juice
3 tablespoons honey

DESSERTS

℞

Beat eggs with yogurt, honey and vanilla. If honey is too stiff, heat to soften. Stir in Feta cheese. In a casserole, layer 6 phyllo leaves, coating each with margarine. Place ½ of the filling on top of the 6th layer. Repeat with 6 more phyllo leaves and filling. Top with remaining 6 leaves which are coated with margarine. Make a couple slashes on the top of pie. Bake at 375° for 20-25 minutes. Cool and cut into squares. Before serving, heat lemon juice with honey and pour lightly over serving pieces. Serves 6.

CHOCOLATE MERINGUE

Meringue

4	egg whites	1	cup sugar
¼	teaspoon cream of tartar		

Filling

2	cups miniature marshmallows	4	egg yolks, beaten
¾	cup milk	3	tablespoons rum
1	(12 ounce) package semi-sweet chocolate chips	1	cup whipping cream, whipped
			shaved chocolate

Beat egg whites and cream of tartar until frothy. Add sugar and beat until stiff peaks form. Put egg white mixture in pastry tube. Cover cookie sheet with brown paper. Form meringue into shells on cookie sheet. Place in preheated oven at 275° and bake for 1 hour. Let meringues cool in oven for 1½ to 2 hours.

Combine marshmallows and milk and cook until marshmallows are melted. Add chocolate and stir until smooth. Add small amount of mixture to egg yolks and then return to chocolate mixture, stirring constantly. Cook until thickened. Add rum. Chill and fold in whipped cream. Pour into meringue shells. Sprinkle with shaved chocolate. Makes 12 shells or 1 (9-inch) meringue.

DESSERTS

PUDDINGS AND CREAMS

ZABAGLIONE CREAM

6	tablespoons sugar, divided	1	teaspoon vanilla
1	teaspoon unflavored gelatin	1	cup whipping cream
		3	egg whites
½	cup Marsala or dry sherry	⅛	teaspoon salt
		⅛	teaspoon cream of tartar
6	egg yolks	½	ounce semi-sweet chocolate, cut in curls
1	tablespoon brandy or ¼ teaspoon brandy flavoring		

In top of double boiler, mix 4 tablespoons sugar and gelatin. Stir in wine. Beat egg yolks and stir into gelatin/wine mixture. Remove from heat and stir in brandy and vanilla. Chill until cool but not set. Whip cream and stir into egg mixture. Beat egg whites with salt, cream of tartar and 2 tablespoons sugar. Fold egg whites into cream mixture. Spoon into parfait or champagne glasses. Garnish with chocolate curls. Serves 6-8.

BREAD PUDDING

10	slices day old bread, broken into pieces	1	teaspoon cinnamon
		½	teaspoon nutmeg
4	cups milk	¼	cup butter, melted
1	cup cream	½	cup seedless raisins
4	eggs, beaten	1	cup pecan halves, toasted
1	cup sugar		
1	teaspoon vanilla		

Combine bread, milk and cream. Add eggs and sugar. Add vanilla, cinnamon and nutmeg. Stir in butter and raisins and pecan halves. Put in pan. Place pan in container of water and bake at 350° for 1 hour. Serve with Lemon Sauce (see Index) or Whiskey Sauce (see Index). Serves 8.

DESSERTS

℞

Some of the favorite dishes are those which were created out of need. I can just imagine that bread pudding originated when a mother had nothing in the pantry but some stale bread, one egg, a cup of milk and she added the sugar and cinnamon to make it palatable. Voila! A classic creation.

BREAD PUDDING
BON TON RESTAURANT

1	loaf French bread	1	tablespoon vanilla
1	quart milk	1	cup raisins
3	eggs	2	tablespoons margarine, melted
2	cups sugar		

Soak bread in milk and crush with hands. Add eggs, sugar, vanilla and raisins. Melt margarine and add to bread/egg mixture. Put in pan. Place pan in container of hot water and bake at 350° until firm. Cut pudding into squares. To reheat, pass under broiler and serve with Whiskey Sauce (see Index).

SOUFFLE

AMARETTO SOUFFLE

5	eggs	2	pints whipping cream
¾	cup sugar	1	sponge cake, cut into ¼ inch cubes
⅓	cup water		
2	ounces Amaretto liqueur		

Beat eggs until lemon color. Combine sugar and water and cook to make candy syrup. Cool. Pour syrup into egg mixture. Beat at low speed until cool. Add Amaretto and refrigerate 15 minutes. Whip cream and fold into mixture. Put cake cubes into mold. Pour custard over cake cubes. Freeze 8 hours. Serve with Sauce Anglaise (see Index).

DESSERTS

℞

RASPBERRY SOUFFLE

5	eggs	1	box frozen raspberries
¾	cup sugar	2	pints whipping cream
⅓	cup water		

Beat eggs. Combine sugar and water and cook to form syrup. Cool. Add to egg mixture. Whirl raspberries in blender and add to egg/sugar mixture. Whip cream and fold into mixture. Freeze. Serve with Sauce Anglaise (see Index).

SWEET SAUCES FOR DESSERTS

BRANDY SAUCE

3	egg yolks, beaten	1	tablespoon cornstarch
1	cup sugar	¼	cup water
1	teaspoon vanilla	3	tablespoons brandy
1½	cups milk		

Combine eggs, sugar, vanilla and milk. Cook until it begins to boil, stirring constantly. Dissolve cornstarch in water and add to milk mixture. Cook until thickened. Add brandy. Makes 2 cups.

APRICOT SAUCE

1½	cups apricot preserves	2	tablespoons rum or other liqueur
1	tablespoon water		

Combine preserves with water and cook until smooth. Stir in rum. Serve with Eggnog Mousse.

DESSERTS

RUM SAUCE

1 cup evaporated milk	1½ tablespoons cornstarch
1 cup milk	¼ cup water
1 cup sugar	2 ounces rum
3 tablespoons butter	

In double boiler, combine milks, sugar and butter. Mix cornstarch in water and heat. When hot, stir into milk/egg mixture. Cook until thickened. Remove from fire and add rum. Yields 2 cups. Serves 12. Serve over gingerbread or bread pudding.

WHISKEY SAUCE

¼ pound butter or margarine	1 egg, well beaten
1 cup sugar	2 ounces bourbon

Cook butter and sugar in double boiler. Cool. Add well beaten egg, stirring so egg doesn't curdle. Cool. Add bourbon to taste. Serve over bread pudding or gingerbread. Serves 8-10.

SAUCE ANGLAISE

1 tablespoon vanilla	½ teaspoon cornstarch
3 egg yolks	1 pint coffee cream
3 tablespoons sugar	

Combine vanilla, eggs, sugar, cornstarch in double boiler. Heat cream separately and then combine to egg/sugar mixture. Cook until custard thickens. Cool. Serve over Amaretto or Raspberry Souffle.

DESSERTS

℞

BRANDY CUSTARD SAUCE

3	egg yolks	⅛	teaspoon salt
1¼	cups half and half	2	tablespoons brandy
3	tablespoons sugar	½	teaspoon vanilla
1	teaspoon cornstarch		

In top of double boiler beat 3 egg yolks. Stir in half and half, sugar, cornstarch and salt and cook until it thickens. Remove from heat and stir in brandy and vanilla. Makes 1½ cups. Good on gingerbread.

PRALINE SAUCE

1	cup brown sugar	⅛	teaspoon salt
1	cup whipping cream	¼	cup corn syrup
½	cup unsalted butter	1	cup toasted pecan halves, chopped
1	teaspoon vanilla extract		

Mix all ingredients together except pecan halves. Cook over medium heat for 10-15 minutes. Add pecans. Refrigerate. Makes 2½ cups. Use over ice cream, gingerbread, or bread pudding.

LEMON SAUCE

2	cups sugar	3-4	tablespoons lemon juice
3	tablespoons cornstarch		
½	cup water	1	teaspoon lemon rind
2	eggs, beaten	¼	cup butter

Combine sugar and cornstarch. Add water, eggs, lemon juice and rind and cook. Add butter and stir until thickens. Spoon over gingerbread or bread pudding. Makes 1 cup.

BRANDIED PEACH SAUCE

| 1 | cup peach nectar | 1 | level tablespoon cornstarch |
| 2 | tablespoons brandy | | |

DESSERTS

℞

Cook nectar, brandy and cornstarch over low heat until thick. Spoon over slices of gingerbread or ice cream.

FUDGE SAUCE FOR ICE CREAM
THE GRAND HOTEL AT MACKINAC ISLAND

¼	pound butter	½	pound unsweetened chocolate
1	pound powdered sugar		
1	can evaporated milk or	⅛	teaspoon salt
1¼	cups cream	1	teaspoon vanilla

Combine all ingredients, except vanilla, in top of double boiler and cook for 30 minutes. Cool and beat in vanilla. Store in refrigerator.

Date: *Once Daily*

For Those Who Enjoy Eating
Patient's name

℞: **EGGS AND STARCHES**

Dispense: *Small Servings*

Sig: *Moderation Unless You Are Twiggy*

Refill: yes _____
       no ✓

[signature]
Physician
DEA Number AH 0000000

EGGS & STARCHES

ITALIAN BRUNCH EGGS

½	pound Italian sweet sausage	8	eggs
2	tablespoons olive oil	¼	cup cream
1	cup raw potatoes, diced		salt and pepper Italian or French bread
½	cup onion, thinly sliced		garlic powder margarine
¼	cup green pepper, chopped	⅛	teaspoon oregano
1	cup tomatoes, peeled and diced	4	ounces Romano cheese

Sauté sausage in olive oil. Add potatoes, onion and green peppers. Cook until potatoes are brown and vegetables just limp. Add tomatoes. Beat eggs with cream. Season with salt and pepper. Stir eggs into sausage mixture. Cook until just set. Serve on warmed slices of French or Italian bread that have been spread with margarine and seasoned with garlic powder. Sprinkle eggs with oregano and fresh Romano cheese. Serves 8.

GAMBLER'S EGGS

12	tablespoons margarine	1	can (medium) mushrooms, stems and pieces
4	potatoes, boiled and cut into small pieces		
1	large slice ham, cut into small pieces	10	eggs
1	medium onion, finely chopped	1	large green pepper, chopped fine
4	average size fresh tomatoes, diced		

Sauté potatoes, ham, onion, tomatoes and mushrooms in margarine in a large skillet. Beat eggs well and pour over all. Add green pepper while cooking. Serves 8-10.

EGGS & STARCHES

MUSHROOM AND CHEESE PUFF

- 1 pound fresh mushrooms, sliced
- ½ cup onion, chopped
- 4 tablespoons oil
- 6 eggs, separated
- 6 ounces cheddar cheese, grated
- 2 tablespoons grated Parmesan cheese
- 2 tablespoons flour
- 1 teaspoon salt
- ⅛ teaspoon ground black pepper

Sauté mushrooms and onions in oil. In a separate container combine egg yolks, cheeses, flour, salt and pepper. Beat egg whites and fold into cheese mixture. Pour over mushrooms and onions and bake at 350° for 20 minutes until puffy. Serves 4-6.

BREAKFAST POTATO CASSEROLE

- 1 (6 ounce) box dehydrated hash browns with onions
- 5 eggs
- ½ cup cottage cheese
- 1 cup shredded Monterey Jack or Swiss cheese
- 1 green onion, chopped
- 1 teaspoon salt
- ⅛ teaspoon pepper
- 4 drops Tabasco
- 6 slices bacon, cooked and diced

Reconstitute hash browns by directions on box. Add remaining ingredients and bake at 350° for 25 minutes. Top with cooked bacon. Serves 4. Good with barbeque or as breakfast dish.

EGGS & STARCHES

℞

BREAKFAST SOUFFLE

- 1½ pounds bulk pork sausage, mild or hot
- 9 eggs, beaten
- 3 cups milk
- 1½ teaspoons dry mustard
- 1 teaspoon salt
- 3 slices bread, cut into ¼ inch cubes
- 1½ cups shredded cheddar cheese

Cook sausage until done but not hard. Crumble into pea size pieces. Drain. Combine sausage with other ingredients and turn into a well greased 9 x 13 x 2 baking dish. Refrigerate overnight. Bake for 1 hour at 350°. Serves 8-10.

BREAKFAST SUNNYSIDE SPECIAL

- ½ English muffin, lightly toasted
- 1 tablespoon melted butter
- 1 slice Canadian bacon, cooked
- 1 pineapple ring
- 1 teaspoon orange marmalade
- 1 egg, separated
- 1 tablespoon grated cheddar cheese

Butter both sides of muffin. Place Canadian bacon on muffin. Top with pineapple ring. Put marmalade in hole of pineapple ring. Beat egg white and cover sandwich. Sprinkle on cheese. Make indentation in center and place egg yolk. Bake at 400° for 12-17 minutes to brown. Serve immediately. Makes 1 serving.

SAUSAGE SQUARES

- 1 pound sausage, hot or mild
- ½ cup onion, chopped
- ¼ cup grated Parmesan cheese
- ½ cup grated Swiss cheese
- 1 egg, beaten
- ¼ teaspoon Tabasco
- 1½ teaspoons salt
- 2 tablespoons parsley
- 2 cups buttermilk biscuit baking mix
- ⅔ cup milk
- ¼ cup mayonnaise
- 1 egg yolk in 2 tablespoons water

EGGS & STARCHES

℞

Cook sausage and drain. Add onions, cheeses, whole egg, Tabasco, salt and parsley. Make dough of buttermilk biscuit mix, milk and mayonnaise. Spread ½ dough in bottom of a greased 8 inch square pan. Add sausage mixture. Top with remaining dough. Glaze with beaten egg yolk/water mixture. Bake at 400° for 25-30 minutes. Makes 16 squares. Recipe doubles well. Good for brunch. Taste depends on quality of sausage used. Serves 4-6.

CHILAQUILES

6	strips bacon	6	eggs
¾	onion, chopped	4	ounces tortilla chips broken into pieces
4	jalapeño peppers, chopped and seeded	½	pound mild cheddar cheese, grated
1	clove garlic, chopped	3	green onion tops, chopped
1	(4 ounce) can tomatoes broken up		

Fry bacon. Remove from grease and crumble. Brown onion, jalapeño pepper and garlic in bacon drippings. Add tomatoes and boil 5 minutes. Add eggs, stir just to break yellow. Add chips and grated cheese. Mix gently. Let simmer until cheese melts. Cover with onion tops and bacon crumbles. Serves 4-6.

GOOD MORNING MEXICAN FIESTA

12	corn tortillas, cut into bite size pieces oil	1	tablespoon oil
2	large tomatoes	12	eggs, beaten
½	onion, chopped	1	(4 ounce) carton sour cream
1-2	jalapeño peppers	10	ounces Monterey Jack cheese, grated

Fry tortillas in oil. Do not overcook. Sauté tomatoes, onions and pepper in 1 tablespoon oil. Add tortillas. Add eggs and cook until eggs set. Top with cheese and sour cream. Pass under broiler. Serves 8.

EGGS & STARCHES

℞

CORNBREAD DRESSING FOR AN ARMY AND A FEW OTHERS

Cornbread

1	cup flour, sifted	1	cup cornmeal
4	teaspoons baking powder	2	eggs
		1	cup milk
¾	teaspoon salt	¼	cup bacon grease

Sift flour, baking powder and salt. Stir in cornmeal. Add eggs, milk and bacon grease. Beat until just smooth. Pour into greased cast iron skillet. Bake at 425° for 20-25 minutes. Be sure and let brown well.

Dressing

4	cups water	3	bunches green onions, chopped
2	(8 ounce) boxes chicken giblets	1	box plain croutons
1	(8 ounce) box chicken livers		salt and pepper
	turkey neck	⅛	teaspoon garlic powder
	salt and pepper	1	pound fresh mushrooms, sliced and sautéed in margarine, divided
	garlic powder		
1	green bell pepper, finely chopped		
1	onion, chopped		
½	bunch celery, chopped, including some leaves		

Clean giblets and livers and cook with water, turkey neck, salt, pepper and garlic powder. Chop giblets and livers and store separate from liquid in refrigerator.

Crumble cornbread in a large roaster. Add green pepper, onion, celery, green onions, croutons, salt and pepper and garlic powder. Mix well. Cover with foil and let season overnight at room temperature. This allows onion flavor, etc. to permeate the corn-

EGGS & STARCHES

℞

bread. Add chicken livers and giblets, liquid broth from cooked turkey and ½ of mushrooms. Keep adding broth until mixture is wet and fluid line present on sides of container. Puddles of broth can be seen. Correct seasonings. Dressing requires a lot of salt. The flavor of the dressing comes from the flavor of the turkey. Bake at 375°-400° for about 1 hour. Stir frequently to loosen dressing from edges as it browns. Serve with turkey giblet gravy.

Gravy

Combine 4 cups of turkey broth with bits of turkey. Add salt and pepper and ⅛ teaspoon garlic powder. Dissolve 8 tablespoons flour in 1 cup water and beat vigorously to keep from clumping. Add to the 4 cups broth. Cook until it thickens and add remaining mushrooms.

When cooking for a large group, it is best to use two small turkeys rather than one large turkey since the small turkeys are more tender.

Christmas dinner is always late because my gravy will not thicken. I make enough gravy for an army and a few others. The joke at our house is that mother must have flunked gravy making at school.

ZUCCHINI DRESSING

3	medium zucchini squash with peeling	1	(2 ounce) jar chopped pimento, drained
2	cups cornbread, crumbled	2	eggs, beaten
¾	cup herb seasoned stuffing mix	¼	teaspoon basil
		1	teaspoon sugar
1	tablespoon green bell pepper, chopped	½	teaspoon salt
		¼	teaspoon black pepper
1	medium onion, chopped	1	envelope instant cream of mushroom soup
¾	cup diced cheddar cheese	¾	cup hot water

Dice zucchini ¾ inch thick. Steam until just tender. Do not overcook. Add remaining ingredients and put into greased 2 quart casserole. Bake at 350° for 45 minutes. Serves 8. Good with chicken or pork.

EGGS & STARCHES

℞

CHEESE PUDDING

- 6 eggs
- 1 cup milk
- 1 pound Monterey Jack cheese, cut into 1/2 inch cubes
- 1 (8 ounce) package cream cheese
- 1 cup cottage cheese
- ½ cup green chili peppers, chopped
- 6 tablespoons margarine
- ½ cup all purpose flour
- 1 teaspoon double acting baking powder

Beat eggs with milk. Add Monterey Jack cheese, cream cheese, cottage cheese, chili peppers and margarine. Mix well. Sift flour and baking powder together and add to pepper and cheese mixture. Transfer to greased 12 inch container and bake for 1 hour at 350°. Serves 8.

GARLIC CHEESE GRITS

- 1 cup uncooked grits
- 1½ cups grated cheddar cheese
- ¼ pound butter
- 1 teaspoon garlic powder
- ¾ cup milk
- 2 eggs, beaten stiff
- ½ cup chopped green onions

Cook grits according to box instructions. Stir in cheese, butter and garlic powder. Blend in milk. Fold in eggs and green onions. Bake 1 hour at 375°. Serves 8.

GRITS SOUFFLE

- 2 cups milk
- ½ cup instant grits
- 1 teaspoon salt
- ½ teaspoon baking powder
- 2 tablespoons butter, melted
- ½ teaspoon sugar
- 3 eggs, separated

Scald milk and stir in grits until thickened. Add salt, baking powder,

EGGS & STARCHES

℞

butter and sugar. Add beaten egg yolk to grits. Fold in beaten egg whites. Pour into greased 1½ quart souffle dish. Bake at 375° for 30 minutes. Serves 4-6.

SWEET POTATO ALEXANDER

12	tablespoons margarine	1	cup peaches
½	cup sugar	2	medium bananas, sliced
½	cup orange juice		
3	ounces Grand Marnier	2	ounces roasted almonds, slivered
1	cup apples, sliced		
2	cups sweet potatoes, cooked and sliced		

Cook margarine and sugar over low heat. Add orange juice and boil. Remove from heat. Stir in Grand Marnier. Butter baking dish. Layer apples, sweet potatoes, peaches and bananas. Pour sauce over ingredients. Spread almonds on top. Bake at 350° for 25 minutes. Serve with ham, pork or fowl. Serves 8.

JALAPEÑO POTATOES

4	medium potatoes	4	tablespoons butter
1	small bell pepper, sliced	1	tablespoon flour
		1	cup milk
1	small can pimentos	½	roll garlic cheese
	salt and pepper to taste	½	roll jalapeño cheese

Boil potatoes with jackets on. Slice and layer in buttered casserole with bell pepper and pimento. Salt and pepper each layer. Combine butter and flour in pan. Add milk and cheeses and cook until melted. Pour over potatoes. Bake at 350° for 45 minutes to 1 hour. Serves 6-8.

EGGS & STARCHES

CAVIAR POTATOES

- 6 potatoes, baked
- salt and pepper
- butter
- 1 medium onion, minced
- 4 ounces sour cream
- 2 ounces caviar

Bake potatoes, cut in half and remove pulp. Season pulp with salt, pepper, butter, onion, sour cream and caviar. Return mixture to potato shells. Just before serving return to oven and warm. Serves 12.

ITALIAN POTATOES

Cook potatoes early in the morning and allow them to marinate all day. Be sure to add enough garlic.

- 14-15 large red potatoes
- ½ cup parsley, chopped
- ½ cup green onion, chopped
- 1 teaspoon sugar
- 1 tablespoon Worcestershire sauce
- 1 (4 ounce) bottle pure olive oil
- 1 heaping teaspoon salt
- 4 ounces tarragon vinegar
- ½ teaspoon dry mustard
- 2 teaspoons garlic powder
- cracked pepper

Boil potatoes. Cut in 1 inch chunk size pieces. Sprinkle with parsley and green onion. Make sauce from sugar, Worcestershire sauce, oil, salt, vinegar, mustard, and garlic powder. Pour over hot potatoes. Stir well. *Do not refrigerate* or oil will not soak into the potatoes. Sprinkle generously with cracked pepper before serving. Serves 10-12.

EGGS & STARCHES

℞

SPRINGTIME POTATO BAKE

1¾ cups water	½ cup mayonnaise
¾ cups milk	1 (10 ounce) package frozen chopped spinach, thawed and well-drained
4 tablespoons margarine	
1 teaspoon salt	
1 (7 serving) envelope mashed potato granules	⅛ teaspoon cayenne pepper, if desired

Combine water, milk, margarine and salt in saucepan. Heat to boiling. Whip in potato granules briskly. Add mayonnaise, spinach and cayenne pepper. Spoon into buttered 1½ quart casserole. Bake at 400° for 10-15 minutes. Makes 8 servings.

SPINACH AND BROWN RICE, GREEK STYLE

1 cup brown rice	½ teaspoon salt
2 tablespoons olive oil	1 medium tomato, chopped
2 medium onions, chopped	1 tablespoon lemon juice
1 clove garlic, minced	½ teaspoon grated lemon rind
1 (10 ounce) package frozen chopped spinach, thawed and drained	1 cup shredded Swiss cheese

Cook rice according to package directions. Cook onion and garlic in oil until tender but not brown. Add spinach and salt and cook until spinach is tender. Stir in hot cooked rice, tomato, lemon juice and lemon rind. Put in casserole. Sprinkle with cheese. Heat in 350° oven until cheese melts. Makes 6 servings.

EGGS & STARCHES

℞

FRIED SWEET POTATOES REMEMBERED AS A LITTLE GIRL

- 4 long, slender sweet potatoes, baked
- ¾ cup flour
- ½ teaspoon salt
- ⅛ teaspoon pepper
- 1 egg, beaten
- vegetable oil

Let sweet potatoes cool. Peel and cut into ¼ inch slices. Mix flour, salt and pepper. Beat egg. Dip potato slices in egg and then flour. Fry in oil. Salt. Serve with ham or fowl. Serves 8.

CANDIED YAMS

- 1 (#300) can yams (1¾ cups)
- 8 ounces margarine
- ⅔ cup brown sugar
- ½ cup toasted pecans
- salt and pepper
- ¼ cup Kahlúa
- marshmallows

Cook margarine and sugar till blended. Add toasted nuts and coat with sugar mixture. Remove nuts with slotted spoon. Mix yams with margarine/sugar mixture and add salt and pepper. Beat with mixer until smooth. Add Kahlúa. Place yam mixture into buttered casserole and top with sugar coated pecans and marshmallows. Bake at 350° for 15 minutes until marshmallows are slightly browned. Serves 6-8.

HOLIDAY POTATOES

- 6 servings mashed potatoes
- salt and pepper
- 2 tablespoons margarine
- 2 (10 ounce) boxes frozen spinach in butter sauce
- ⅛ teaspoon nutmeg
- 4 ounces Mozzarella cheese, grated
- 4 green onions, chopped
- 6 small tomatoes, cut into ¼ inch slices
- ¼ teaspoon garlic powder
- 4 ounces sour cream
- 2 ounces Romano cheese

EGGS & STARCHES

℞

Season potatoes with salt, pepper and margarine. Butter 3 quart casserole. Cook spinach according to directions on box and drain. Season spinach with nutmeg. Place mashed potatoes in casserole dish and cover with ½ Mozzarella cheese. Sprinkle with green onion. Layer with spinach then sliced tomatoes. Season tomatoes with salt, pepper and garlic powder. Put dab of sour cream on center of tomatoes. Sprinkle with remaining Mozzarella and Romano cheese. Bake in 350° oven until tomatoes are barely cooked and cheese melted. Serves 12. Let some of red, green and white show through on top of the casserole.

Our apartment was small so we staggered the arrival time of the 40 invited guests. The first hour of the party went by and no one arrived. Then the door bell rang and we opened the door. All 40 people were standing in a line that appeared to be a block long.

POTATOES O'BRIEN

1 (20 ounce) package frozen Potatoes O'Brien	1 pint (2 cups) sour cream
½ cup melted margarine	10 ounces cheddar cheese, grated
¼ cup chopped onion	1 (4 ounce) can sliced mushrooms
1 (10¾ ounce) can condensed cream of chicken soup (1¼ cups)	seasoned bread crumbs

Thaw potatoes and drain. In 3 quart baking dish combine potatoes, margarine, onion, soup, sour cream, cheese, and mushrooms and stir. Top with bread crumbs. Bake 1 hour at 350°. Serves 8-10.

EGGS & STARCHES

CRABMEAT STUFFED POTATOES

4	medium Idaho potatoes	4	teaspoons minced onion
4	tablespoons margarine	1	cup sharp yellow cheese
½	cup cream		
1	teaspoon salt	6½	ounces crabmeat
⅛	teaspoon pepper	½	teaspoon paprika

Bake potatoes. Halve and scoop out pulp. Whip the pulp with margarine, cream, salt, pepper, onion, and cheese. Mix in crabmeat. Refill potato shells and sprinkle with paprika. Reheat before serving. Serves 8.

POTATOES WITH SPICED CHEESE, TOMATOES AND ONIONS

2	tablespoons margarine		dash cumin
4	green onions, chopped	½	teaspoon salt
½	cup onions, chopped		fresh ground pepper
1⅔	cups Italian plum tomatoes, chopped	1	cup grated Mozzarella or Muenster cheese
½	cup heavy cream	8	large potatoes, peeled, boiled and cut into large cubes
1	teaspoon coriander (cilantro)		
¼	teaspoon dried oregano		

Cook green onion and onion in margarine until soft. Add tomatoes and cook for 5 minutes. Add cream and seasonings. Add cheese and cook until melted. Pour over potatoes or cooked string breans. Serves 10.

EGGS & STARCHES

SPINACH STUFFED POTATOES

6	potatoes, baked and halved
6	tablespoons margarine
1½	cups Mornay sauce
1	(10 ounce) box of frozen chopped spinach, cooked according to box directions
	salt and pepper
	dash nutmeg
1	cup grated Swiss cheese

Scoop out pulp from potatoes. Mix potato pulp with margarine, Mornay sauce and spinach which has been drained well. Season with salt, pepper and nutmeg. Stuff into potato skins. Top with cheese and warm in oven just long enough to melt cheese. Can also be made with chopped broccoli. Serves 12.

POTATO BROCCOLI CHEESE BAKE

2	tablespoons margarine
2	tablespoons flour
2	cups milk
1	(3 ounce) package cream cheese, cubed
½	cup Swiss cheese, grated
1	teaspoon salt
⅛	teaspoon nutmeg
⅛	teaspoon pepper
1	(32 ounce) package frozen, shredded hash brown potatoes, thawed
1	(10 ounce) package frozen chopped broccoli, cooked and drained
¼	cup bread crumbs
1	tablespoon margarine

Melt margarine. Add flour. Cook, stirring constantly. Add milk and cook until thickened. Add cheeses, salt, nutmeg, pepper and cook until cheese melts. Add potatoes. Spoon ½ mixture into buttered 2 quart casserole dish then add layer of broccoli and top with remaining potato mixture. Sprinkle with bread crumbs and dot with margarine. Bake at 350° until top slightly browned. Serves 6-8.

EGGS & STARCHES

℞

WILD RICE AND SPINACH CASSEROLE

- 1 (6 ounce) package wild rice mix
- 1 (4 ounce) can sliced mushrooms
- 2 teaspoons prepared mustard
- ½ teaspoon salt
- 2¼ cups water
- 1 (10 ounce) package frozen chopped spinach
- ¾ cup onion, chopped
- 1 tablespoon margarine
- 1 (8 ounce) package cream cheese, cubed

Place rice and seasoning packet, mushrooms, mustard and salt in 2 quart casserole. Combine water, spinach, onion and margarine and bring to boil. Pour over rice and stir. Cover and bake at 375° for 30 minutes. Add cheese and return to oven for 15 minutes. Serves 6-8.

WILD RICE WITH GRAPES

- 1 box Uncle Ben's Wild Rice, cooked according to directions; (Substitute chicken broth for ½ amount of water)
- ½ cup margarine
- ½ cup sherry
- 1 cup green seedless grapes
- 4 tablespoons parsley
- ½ cup toasted almonds

Add margarine and sherry to wild rice at end of cooking period. Just before serving, mix in grapes, parsley and almonds. Serves 6-8.

RICE-STUFFED GREEN PEPPERS

- 6 large sweet green peppers
- ¼ cup oil
- 1 small onion, finely chopped
- 1 cup diced celery
- ½ cup sliced fresh mushrooms
- ½ cup shredded cheddar cheese
- 3 cups cooked brown rice
- salt and pepper to taste
- 3 tablespoons freshly grated Parmesan cheese

EGGS & STARCHES

℞

Cut a thin slice off top of peppers; remove seeds and core. Chop tops of green peppers and reserve. Sauté onions in oil. Add chopped pepper, celery and mushrooms and cook 5 minutes longer. Stir in the cheddar cheese, brown rice, salt and pepper. Use mixture to stuff peppers. Set in an oiled baking dish with one half inch of hot water in the bottom. Sprinkle tops of stuffed peppers with Parmesan cheese. Bake at 375° for 35-40 minutes or until tender. Makes 6 servings.

EMERALD RICE

½ cup converted rice
3 eggs, separated
1 cup shredded sharp cheddar cheese
½ cup fresh parsley, minced
2 tablespoons chopped onion
½ cup margarine, melted
salt and pepper

Cook rice according to package directions. Beat egg yolks until light and fluffy. Combine and mix rice, cheese, parsley, onion, margarine, salt, pepper and beaten egg yolks. Beat egg whites until they hold soft peaks; fold into rice mixture. Pour into 1½ quart casserole or souffle dish. Bake at 350° for 25-30 minutes. Makes 4-6 servings.

GREEN RICE

3 cups cooked rice
1 cup parsley, chopped
½ cup shredded cheddar cheese
⅓ cup chopped onion
1 (4 ounce) can chopped green chilies
1 clove garlic, minced
1 (13 ounce) can evaporated milk (1½ cups)
2 eggs, beaten
½ cup vegetable oil
1 teaspoon salt
½ teaspoon pepper
juice and grated rind of 1 small lemon
paprika

Mix rice, parsley, cheese, onions, chilies and garlic in a greased 2 quart baking dish. Blend milk, eggs, oil, salt, pepper and lemon and mix into rice. Sprinkle with paprika and bake at 350° for 45 minutes until set. Serves 8.

EGGS & STARCHES

℞

ZUCCHINI RICE BAKE

3	medium zucchini, thinly sliced		salt
1	cup regular rice, cooked according to package directions	2	cups sour cream or yogurt
		1	teaspoon oregano
		1	teaspoon garlic salt
1	(4 ounce) can chopped green chilies	¼	cup chopped green pepper
12	ounces Monterey Jack cheese, grated, divided	¼	cup chopped green onion
		2	tablespoons chopped fresh parsley
1	large tomato, thinly sliced		

Cook zucchini in salted water until tender. Drain and set aside. In 3 quart buttered casserole, place cooked rice. Cover with chopped chilies. Sprinkle with half of cheese; arrange zucchini slices over cheese. Add tomato slices. Sprinkle with salt. Combine sour cream, oregano, garlic salt, green pepper and onion. Spoon over tomato layer. Sprinkle with remaining cheese. Bake at 350° for 30-40 minutes or until bubbly. Do not boil. Sprinkle with parsley and serve immediately. Serves 8.

GARLIC BROWN RICE

2	tablespoons butter	¼	teaspoon cayenne pepper
1	tablespoon finely minced onion	2¼	cups boiling chicken stock
1	clove garlic, minced		
1	cup brown rice, uncooked		

Sauté onion and garlic in butter. Add rice and stir to coat rice. Add pepper and chicken stock. Cook covered 20-25 minutes until rice is tender.

EGGS & STARCHES

RIGATONI WITH BROCCOLI

½	pound fresh mushrooms, sliced	½	teaspoon oregano
2	tablespoons margarine	½	teaspoon basil
1½	cups cream	1	pound rigatoni, cooked
1	cup cooked broccoli, finely chopped		freshly ground black pepper
1	cup canned Italian plum tomatoes, chopped		salt to taste
		¼	cup freshly grated Parmesan cheese

Sauté mushrooms in margarine. Add cream, broccoli, tomatoes, oregano basil. Cook about 5 minutes. Place cooked rigatoni in sauce and season to taste with salt and pepper. Remove from heat and add Parmesan. Mix well and serve. Makes 8-10 servings. Fettuccini or linguine noodles may be substituted.

RIGATONI PLUS CABBAGE

8	ounces rigatoni or egg noodles, cooked	1	pound green cabbage, thinly shredded (4 firmly packed cups)
¼	pound margarine, divided in half		salt and pepper to taste
1	large onion, cut in thin strips (1 cup)		

Cook the onion in half the margarine until golden brown; add to cooked rigatoni. Gently cook the cabbage, tightly covered, in the remaining margarine until tender-crisp; toss with rigatoni and onion. Season with salt and pepper. Serves 6-8.

FETTUCCINI WITH CHICKEN AND HAM

1½	pounds fettuccini cooked	2	ounces margarine
2	ounces cooked ham, diced	2½	ounces heavy cream
		½	teaspoon pepper
4½	ounces boiled chicken, diced	2	ounces grated Parmesan or Romano cheese

Sauté ham and chicken in margarine. Add cooked fettuccini and stir. Pour in heavy cream. Sprinkle with pepper and cheese. Serves 6 to 8.

EGGS & STARCHES

℞

FETTUCCINI SOUFFLE

- ½ pound fettuccini
- ¼ pound margarine
- 1⅓ cups milk
- ¼ teaspoon garlic powder
- ½ cup plus 3 tablespoons grated Parmesan cheese
- ¼ pound Fontina cheese
- salt and pepper
- 1 teaspoon parsley
- ½ cup peas, frozen or canned
- 2 eggs, separated
- 1 tablespoon butter

Cook fettuccini in salted water until just done and drain. Add margarine to fettuccini. Bring milk to boil and add garlic powder and ½ cup Parmesan cheese and Fontina cheese. Add fettuccini. Season with salt and pepper. Add parsley. Cool mixture. Add peas and blend in egg yolks. Beat egg whites until stiff. Add pinch of salt. Fold egg whites into fettuccini mixture. Butter 2 quart souffle dish and dust with extra 3 tablespoons of Parmesan cheese. Bake at 350° for 45 minutes. Last 5 minutes of cooking, turn oven to 425°. Serve immediately. Serves 6.

VERMICELLI WITH SPINACH PESTO SAUCE

- 4 cups washed, packed, torn spinach leaves, stems removed
- 3 garlic cloves, halved
- 3 tablespoons pine nuts
- ½ teaspoon dried basil
- ¼ cup olive oil
- ⅓ cup freshly grated Parmesan cheese
- ⅛ teaspoon salt
- 8 ounces vermicelli
- 1 tablespoon salt
- 3 quarts boiling water

Blend a few spinach leaves, garlic, pine nuts, basil and a little oil in electric blender until pureed. Continue adding spinach leaves and oil to blender. Add cheese and salt. Cover and whirl until mixture is smooth. Cook vermicelli in salted boiling water until tender. Drain. Serve vermicelli on heated serving platter with pesto sauce. Makes 4-6 servings.

EGGS & STARCHES

VERMICELLI WITH BROCCOLI

1 pound fresh broccoli	3 cups well-seasoned chicken or beef broth
¼ cup olive oil	
4 large cloves garlic, chopped	
½ teaspoon hot red pepper flakes	½ cup parsley, minced
½ pound vermicelli broken into 2 inch pieces	

Cut broccoli flowerets and stems into bite-size pieces. Sauté garlic in oil. Add broccoli, pepper flakes, vermicelli and broth. Boil over high heat and cook covered for 5 minutes. When done, pasta will be cooked but broccoli will be crisp. Sprinkle with parsley and serve immediately. Serves 4-6.

MACARONI AND CHEESE

12 ounces short elbow macaroni noodles	1½ cups milk
salt and pepper	1 egg, beaten
16 ounces extra sharp cheddar cheese, shredded	½ teaspoon sugar

Cook macaroni noodles in water, but do not overcook. Place a layer of macaroni in a 3 quart casserole. Sprinkle with salt and pepper. Generously layer cheese over noodles. Place another layer of noodles and season with salt and pepper. Layer with cheese. Mix milk, egg and sugar and pour over macaroni. A fluid line should be seen on the side of the dish. Bake at 400° for 40 minutes. Serves 10. This is the most requested dish from my children when they come home from college.

The secret to this dish is to be generous with the amount of cheese used.

EGGS & STARCHES

℞

PASTA, ZUCCHINI AND MUSHROOMS

3	slender zucchini, cut in ½ inch slices	6	tablespoons margarine
2	tablespoons margarine	1½	cups whipping cream
½	pound fresh mushrooms, sliced		salt
⅛	teaspoon garlic powder		pepper
1	(8 ounce) package linguine	1	cup grated Parmesan cheese
			nutmeg

Place zucchini on rack in pot of water and steam until just tender. Sauté mushrooms in margarine and season with garlic powder. Cook linguine in salted water until just tender. Drain. Melt 6 tablespoons margarine in large pan and add ½ cream. Cook until slightly thickened. Add ½ of Parmesan cheese. Mix in sprinkle of nutmeg. Add vegetables and linguine and remaining cream and cheese. Serves 6-8.

CHEESE CANNELLONI

1	(1 pound) box cannelloni	3	cups freshly grated Parmesan cheese
6	tablespoons butter		

Cook cannelloni noodles in salted water until just tender. Drain. Stuff noodles with filling. Cover with sauce. Dot with butter and sprinkle heavily with Parmesan cheese. Bake at 350° for 15 minutes. Serves 10-12.

Filling

1½	cups Ricotta cheese	1	teaspoon salt
1	pound Mozzarella cheese, finely diced		freshly ground pepper
4	ounces Prosciutto, cut into thin strips	4	eggs

Whirl Ricotta in blender and combine Mozzarella, Prosciutto strips, salt, pepper and eggs. Mash with fork until it is a smooth paste.

EGGS & STARCHES

℞

Sauce

6	tablespoons margarine	1	teaspoon salt
8	tomatoes, peeled, seeded, drained and chopped	½	teaspoon freshly ground pepper
		2	teaspoons dried basil

Melt margarine and add tomatoes, salt, pepper and basil. Simmer 15 minutes.

VEGETABLES AND PASTA

½	pound fresh asparagus, sliced into 1 inch lengths	¼	cup slivered Prosciutto ham
½	pound mushrooms, sliced	3	green onions including tops, sliced
2	tablespoons margarine	½	cup frozen tiny peas, thawed
1	medium size carrot, cut in ¼ inch slices	1	teaspoon dry basil
		½	teaspoon salt
1	medium zucchini, cut in ¼ inch slices	1	(8 ounce) package linguine

Sauce

4	tablespoons flour		pepper
4	tablespoons butter	¼	cup grated Parmesan cheese
2	cups cream		
⅛	teaspoon nutmeg		parsley, chopped
	salt		

Place asparagus, mushrooms, carrots and zucchini on a rack in covered pot of water and steam until just tender. Salt and pepper vegetables and reserve. Do not overcook. Sauté ham, green onions, peas in margarine. Add basil and salt. Make sauce of flour, butter and cream. Add nutmeg, salt, pepper and Parmesan cheese to sauce. Cook linguine in salted water until just tender. Drain. Combine linguine, vegetables and sauce. Sprinkle with parsley. Serve with extra Parmesan cheese. Serves 6-8.

EGGS & STARCHES

LINGUINE WITH PARSLEY PESTO SAUCE

1	pound linguine or spaghetti	½	cup olive or salad oil
1	cup chopped parsley sprigs	¼	cup water
		½	cup grated Parmesan cheese
½	cup pine nuts		dash pepper
2	cloves garlic		salt
1	tablespoon dried basil		

Cook linguine in salted water until tender and drain in colander. Combine parsley, nuts, garlic, basil, oil and water in blender. Blend until smooth. Gradually add cheese until well mixed. Season to taste with salt and pepper. Toss linguine with sauce and serve immediately. Serves 6-8.

SPAGHETTI WITH PARSLEY AND WALNUT SAUCE

3	cups fresh parsley sprigs	1	cup olive oil
			salt to taste
1	cup walnut halves or pieces	1	(16 ounce) package spaghetti
3	cloves garlic		additional walnut halves
3	tablespoons grated Parmesan cheese		additional Parmesan cheese
1	teaspoon basil leaves		

Combine parsley, walnuts, garlic, Parmesan cheese, basil and olive oil in blender; process until smooth. Add salt. Cook spaghetti according to package directions; drain well. Pour parsley mixture over hot spaghetti and toss. Garnish with additional walnut halves and serve with additional Parmesan cheese. Serves 8.

EGGS & STARCHES

LAURIE'S FAVORITE CHICKEN SPAGHETTI

1 broiler chicken plus 2 chicken breasts	1 can tomatoes
water	salt and pepper
salt and pepper	garlic powder
garlic powder	Tabasco sauce
¼ pound margarine	1 (8 ounce) package thin spaghetti
1 large onion, chopped	chicken broth
3 ribs celery, sliced	Romano cheese
1 large green pepper	red cracked pepper
1 pound mushrooms, sliced and sautéed in margarine	

Cook chicken in water with salt, pepper and garlic powder. In separate pan, sauté onion, celery and green pepper in margarine until just soft. Add mushrooms. Remove chicken, debone and cut into bite size pieces. Break tomatoes up and add with juice to onion/pepper mixture. Cook until thickened. Season with salt, pepper, garlic powder and Tabasco. Add chicken. Cook spaghetti in water until just done. Drain well. Combine tomato mixture with spaghetti and add 1-2 cups of chicken broth. Serve with Romano cheese and red cracked pepper.

This is best made the day before serving so seasoning can go through the spaghetti. Re-warm before serving and correct seasoning. It is important that you use a whole chicken and not just parts so that you have a good strong chicken flavor.

One weekend when I had to work unusually long hours, my daughter Laurie, then 10 years old, said she would cook chicken spaghetti. I went over the recipe with her in detail. When I arrived home she said it was ready. When I took the lid off the roaster a cooked whole chicken was staring at me. She said I did not tell her how to take the chicken off the bone so she waited for me to come home. We started at squre one on making chicken spaghetti. Dinner was quite late that night.

EGGS & STARCHES

℞

SPAGHETTI SPINACH BAKE

- 2 cups sliced mushrooms
- ¾ cup chopped onion
- ⅓ cup corn oil
- 1 (10 ounce) package frozen chopped spinach, thawed, drained
- 1 pound cottage cheese
- ½ teaspoon salt
- ¼ teaspoon nutmeg
- ¼ teaspoon pepper
- 1 (8 ounce) package thin spaghetti, cooked, drained
- 1 cup grated Mozzarella cheese

Sauté mushrooms and onion in oil. Stir in spinach; cook 2 minutes. Stir in cottage cheese, salt, nutmeg, and pepper. Toss with spaghetti until well-coated. Place in oiled 10 x 5 x 2 inch baking dish. Top with Mozzarella. Bake at 425° for 20 minutes. Serves 8.

SPINACH CREPES

- 1 cup cold water
- 1 cup cold milk
- 4 eggs, large
- ½ teaspoon salt
- 4 tablespoons margarine, melted
- 2 cups sifted all-purpose flour (or 1½ cups instant flour)

Whirl all ingredients in electric blender at high speed for 1 minute. If all-purpose flour is used, refrigerate 2 hours. If instant flour is used, you may proceed immediately. Slightly oil 2 small Teflon skillets. Pour batter in pan to just cover bottom and cook until the crepe moves when you shake the pan. Turn out on waxpaper squares. The first crepe is always a failure - try again. Do not overcook. After awhile you can cook simultaneously with two pans. Crepes made with instant flour will not freeze. To store crepes made with all-purpose flour in freezer, place waxpaper between crepes. Place in sealed plastic bags. Makes 12.

EGGS & STARCHES

℞
Sauce

4	tablespoons margarine, melted		pepper dash nutmeg
5	tablespoons flour	¼	cup heavy cream
2¾	cups hot milk	1	cup grated Swiss cheese
½	teaspoon salt		

Add flour to melted margarine and cook for 2 minutes. Remove from heat. Add milk, salt, pepper, nutmeg and bring to boil. Add cream and cheese. Cook until thickened.

Stuffing

2	tablespoons minced shallots	1	cup Ricotta cheese garlic powder
1	cup sliced fresh mushrooms	1	egg
½	pound plus 4 tablespoons margarine	4	tablespoons shredded Swiss cheese
1½	cup cooked spinach in butter sauce		

Sauté shallots and mushrooms in margarine. Add spinach, Ricotta cheese, garlic powder and blend with 4 tablespoons sauce and egg to make paste. Place spinach paste at lateral edge of crepe and roll in cigar fashion. Place sealed edge on bottom of lightly buttered casserole dish. Pour cheese sauce over crepes and cover with cheese. Bake at 425° for 15-20 minutes or until cheese is bubbly and lightly browned. Wine-Cheese Sauce (see Index) may be used but add dash of nutmeg.

After Dr. Hill made and served 200 spinach crepes a Resident was heard to say to her, "I sure enjoyed the green burritos."

Date: *Daily*

For Those Who Enjoy Eating
Patient's name

℞: MEATS

Dispense: *Moderate Helping*

Sig: *Eat Once Daily*

Refill: yes ✔
       no _____

[signature]
Physician
DEA Number AH 0000000

MEATS

℞

DOTTY'S MARINATED FLANK STEAK

3	tablespoons scallions		dash Tabasco
3	tablespoons soy sauce		juice of ½ lemon
4	tablespoons olive oil	1-2	pounds flank steak
1	teaspoon thyme		

Combine marinade ingredients. Score steak on both sides. Marinate overnight. Broil 3-5 minutes on each side. Slice diagonally. Serves 4-6 people.

MARINATED BEEF TENDER

5-6	pounds beef tender, larded for roasting	2	pounds mushrooms, optional
	all-season salt		margarine
	pepper		garlic powder
1	(25 ounce) bottle dry sherry		

Sprinkle roast with all-season salt and pepper and marinate in sherry for 24 hours. Refrigerate. Remove from marinade, reserve. Place tender on rack in pan. Cook at 400° for 30 minutes and 350° for 20 minutes. It should be rare at this time. Cook marinade over high heat to allow alcohol to evaporate. Add pan juices from meat. Sauté fresh mushrooms in margarine and add to marinade juice. Season with salt, pepper and garlic powder to taste.

Slice tender thin and place in chafing dish and add sherry-mushroom mixture. Do not cover chafing dish or meat will continue to cook. Serve with Pepperidge Farm Parker House rolls or party rolls. This will serve 12 people if cut 1 inch thick or 20 people if cut thin.

The key to this recipe is the quality of meat you buy. It is best to buy the best tender you can find at the most reliable store.

Always go to a store that you know serves quality meat. It is better to pay a few cents more for that guarantee. Jamail's in Houston is such a

MEATS

℞

store. Jamail's is a grocery store where you can find anything called for in a recipe. The women shop in minks and diamonds. Chauffeurs wait in Mercedes and Rolls Royce for the housekeepers to grocery shop. The housekeepers know the butchers on a first name basis. It is a status symbol to have a charge account at Jamail's. There is a waiting list to get an account since their number of accounts is limited to 500.

One of the few times I have seen an employee of Jamail's Grocery Store in Houston shaken was when I asked for 15 five pound tenders. The butcher blinked and courteously said, "Ma'am, may I ask how many people you plan to serve?" I said, "250." He said, "You're just about right."

BEEF TOURNEDOS AND MUSHROOMS

4	(6 ounce) beef filets, 1 inch thick	1	shallot, finely chopped
1	tablespoon Dijon-style mustard	½	pound fresh mushrooms, sliced
1	tablespoon tomato paste		dried tarragon to taste
¾	cup olive oil	2	tablespoons margarine
			juice of 1 lemon
			fresh parsley, chopped

Mix mustard with tomato paste, oil, and shallot. Brush meat and mushrooms with sauce and sprinkle with tarragon. Refrigerate for 2 hours. Bring to room temperature. Place meat on barbecue grill and barbecue 2 minutes on each side for rare. (Mushrooms may be placed in foil to cook). Mix margarine with lemon juice, a dash of tarragon and chopped parsley. Pour over meat and mushrooms. Serves 4.

A call one night from a resident who asked "How do you make gravy?" Answer: "Let me tell you a thousand ways that fail."

MEATS

ROAST BEEF AND GRAVY

fat for larding
5 pound roast
all-season salt
1 onion, chopped
3 cups water
garlic powder
1 pound fresh mushrooms, sliced
2 tablespoons margarine
flour
water
salt and pepper

Season roast with all-season salt. Place larded roast in uncovered roaster and cook for 1 hour at 400°. Whirl onions in blender with 3 cups of water. Add to roaster. Sprinkle meat with garlic powder. Cover and cook at 350° for 2 hours. Remove from drippings. Sauté mushrooms in margarine. Combine 3-4 tablespoons flour in ½ cup of water for each 2 cups of drippings. Add to meat drippings and cook to thicken. Season with garlic powder, salt, pepper and add mushrooms.

MEAT BALLS

2 pounds hamburger
salt and pepper
⅛ teaspoon garlic powder
3-4 dashes Worcestershire sauce
1 tablespoon Parmesan cheese
3 tablespoons olive oil

Mix all ingredients and form into meat balls. Sauté in olive oil until just brown. Add to favorite homemade spaghetti sauce. Do not overcook meat balls before putting them into the sauce or they will be hard. Olive oil gives this a special flavor so do not substitute. Serves 6-8.

Have you ever asked your sister-in-law from out of town to come to your party? When she politely asks if there is anything she can do, you say, "Will you form this meat into 200 meat balls?"

MEATS

CRANBERRY ROAST

1-2	pounds beef roast	1	envelope onion soup mix
1	cup white wine		
1	cup whole cranberry sauce	2	tablespoons cornstarch

Pour wine over meat. Marinate several hours. Mix cranberries and soup mix together and let stand ½ hour. Spread mixture over top of meat. Roast at 350° uncovered until meat is tender. Add water to pan as wine evaporates. Remove roast from pan. Add 2-3 cups of water to pan to loosen drippings. Add cornstarch to 1 cup cold water and stir into drippings. Cook until thickened. Salt and pepper to taste. Pork can also be used.

SAUERBRATEN

4	pounds beef rump or sirloin tip	3	black peppers
2	cups vinegar	2	tablespoons salt
2	cups water	3	tablespoons sugar
2	onions		flour
1	bay leaf	2	tablespoons cooking oil
1	clove		

Combine all ingredients except oil and marinate beef for 3 to 4 days in the refrigerator.

Remove meat from marinade. Dry. Rub with flour. Heat oil in roaster; brown meat on all sides. Cook meat in ½ of marinade at 350° for 3 hours or until tender. Add more marinade to keep ½ inch of liquid in the roaster. Thicken marinade with 3-4 tablespoons flour in ½ cup water for each 2 cups of marinade. You may add raisins to the sauce. Serve over meat. Serves 10.

This recipe came from my husband's first secretary who was from Germany. Note no ginger snaps in recipe.

MEATS

FILET OF BEEF WITH CRABMEAT

4-6 ounces filet mignon
1   cup Madeira wine

Crabmeat au Gratin
(see Index)

Make pocket in filet. Place 1 tablespoon Crabmeat au Gratin in pocket. Secure with toothpick and saute in frying pan. Just before meat is done, add Madeira wine. Serves 4.

TACOS

Stuffing

2   pounds hamburger
1   package taco seasoning mix
1   (10 ounce) can Rotel tomatoes (tomatoes with green chilies) (1 ¼ cups)
1   can water
     salt and pepper
1   can tomatoes, chopped
⅛   teaspoon garlic powder

Topping

2   tomatoes, chopped
½   head small lettuce, thinly sliced
1   onion, chopped
6   ounces cheddar cheese, grated
     salt and pepper
12   cornmeal taco shells

Cook hamburger meat until just brown. Add next 6 ingredients and stir well. Cook covered for about 20 minutes. Warm taco shells in oven at 300°. Fill with meat, tomatoes, lettuce, onions and cheese. Makes 10-12. If shells are not available, use tortilla chips.

MEATS

℞

Each year we vacation in Ponce Inlet, Florida, at the same condominium. When I arrive the kids begin to ask "When will we have tacos?" One year I served 125 large tacos. I think every child from condos within a 5 mile radius came. One young man reported to me with a smile on his face that he was eating his 13th. I suddenly became nauseated.

CABBAGE ROLLS

1	medium sized cabbage, cored	2	small cans tomato paste
1	pound ground meat	1	(#2) can beef bouillon (2½ cups)
¼	teaspoon salt		
⅛	teaspoon pepper	2	teaspoons crushed sour salt
½	cup rice, cooked		

Steam cabbage until barely tender. Mix ground meat with salt, pepper and rice. Make sauce with tomato paste, bouillon and sour salt. Cook until slightly thickened. Take 1 tablespoon of meat mixture and place on edge of cabbage leaf and roll cigar fashion. Place in buttered casserole seam edge down. Continue until all meat mixture used. Coarsely chop remaining cabbage and sprinkle it on the cabbage rolls. Cover with sauce. Bake at 350° for 1 hour.

MEATS

℞

TACOS DESPERADO

Marinade

- 1 part soy sauce
- ½ part vinegar
- 1 part water
- steak, 1 to 1-½ inches thick
- ½ teaspoon garlic powder
- salt and pepper

6-12 hours before serving, place steak in ingredients for marinade.

flour tortillas

Topping

- lettuce, thinly sliced
- tomatoes, chopped
- sour cream
- salsa
- Guacamole Relish

Guacamole Relish

- 3 ripe avocados, chopped
- juice of ½ lemon
- ½ medium onion, chopped
- 1 medium tomato, chopped
- 1 small jalapeño, chopped
- ¼ bunch cilantro
- salt and pepper
- ¼ teaspoon garlic powder
- ⅛ teaspoon oregano
- ⅛ cup plain yogurt

Combine all ingredients and mix with yogurt several hours before serving.

MEATS

℞

Salsa

3	tomatoes, chopped	¼	teaspoon garlic powder
½	medium onion, chopped	¼	bunch cilantro
¼	teaspoon salt	1	jalapeño pepper
¼	teaspoon oregano		

Combine ingredients 2 hours before serving.

Grill steak over charcoal to desired doneness. Cut into thinly sliced bite size pieces. Roll beef in warm flour tortillas. Serve with topping, guacamole relish and salsa. To warm tortillas, wrap in cloth and put in colander which fits a pan that contains about one inch of water. Simmer water with pan covered.

EMPANADAS

⅓	cup chopped onion	¾	teaspoon salt
½	cup peeled, chopped tomatoes	⅛	teaspoon pepper
⅓	cup chopped green pepper		few drops liquid hot pepper sauce
1	tablespoon margarine	1	hard boiled egg, chopped
½	pound lean ground beef	1½	tablespoons seedless raisins
3	(8 ounce) packages refrigerated crescent rolls	¼	cup chopped green olives

Sauté onion, tomatoes and green pepper in margarine. Add meat. Stir in salt, pepper, pepper sauce, egg, raisins and olives. Do not overcook. Cool. Roll out each crescent roll to form a 4 inch round. Place 1 tablespoon filling in center of each round. Brush edges with water and fold dough to cover. Put hole in each to allow steam to escape. Bake in a 425° oven until lightly browned. Makes about 2½ dozen.

MEATS

℞

SPECIAL CHILI RELLENO

1 package flour tortillas (8-10)	cooking oil

Stuffing

1 pound hamburger	salt and pepper
8 ounces water	garlic powder
1 tablespoon chili powder	1 small box raisins
1 tablespoon sugar	½ cup toasted pecans, chopped
1 tablespoon cumin	
1 can Rotel tomatoes (tomatoes with green chilies), broken up (1¼ cups)	

Topping

lettuce	sour cream
tomatoes	onions (optional)

Sauce

2 large onions, cut in rings	8 ounces tomato juice
2 (4 ounce) cans green chilies	1 teaspoon cornstarch
oil	salt and pepper
	1 teaspoon sugar

Cook hamburger until slightly browned. Add water, chili powder, sugar, cumin, Rotel tomatoes, salt, pepper and garlic powder. Plump raisins in water, drain. Add raisins and pecans near the end of the cooking time. Do not overcook. Meat should be soft.

To make sauce, sauté onion rings and green chilies in small amount of oil. Add tomato juice and cornstarch, salt, pepper and sugar. Cook until thickened.

MEATS

℞

Place spoonful of meat in center of warmed tortilla and roll over at ends and then at sides so it is rectangular. Secure with toothpick. Fry in oil until slightly brown. Remove and drain. Top meat filled tortilla with sauce and then add topping of lettuce, tomatoes, sour cream and onions. Serves 4-6.

Stuffing may be used alone as a dip for a buffet or cocktail party served with fried tortillas.

MEAT PIES

1½	pounds ground chuck	1	tablespoon oil
1	onion, chopped	3	cans refrigerated biscuits
1	(No. 2) can tomatoes (2½ cups)		
	salt, pepper, allspice and chili powder to taste		

Sauté meat, onion, tomatoes, salt, pepper, allspice and chili powder in oil. Simmer until juice cooks out. Roll out each biscuit into 4 inch circle. Fill with 1 tablespoon meat mixture and pinch together at 3 corners. Bake close together on greased cookie sheet at 350° until brown. Makes 30-36 pies.

POOR BOYS

French rolls or bread
mayonnaise
leftover roast
gravy with mushrooms
onions
tomatoes
lettuce
sour pickles

Take leftover roast and place on rolls which have been spread with mayonnaise on one cut side and gravy with mushrooms on the opposite. Layer with onions, tomatoes, lettuce and sour pickles. Place sandwiches in 350° oven for 5 minutes to toast bread. Great for Sunday night suppers.

MEATS

℞

CALF'S LIVER

1½	pounds calf's liver, cut in ⅛ inch slices	1½	teaspoon dried sage
	salt and pepper	¼	cup olive oil
2	cloves garlic	2	tablespoons lemon juice

Salt and pepper liver. Brown in mixture of garlic, sage and olive oil for 2-3 minutes. Do not overcook. Add lemon juice. To serve, pour pan juice over liver. Serves 6.

CALF'S LIVER AND ONIONS

3	cups onion, thinly sliced	1¼	pounds calf's liver, cut in thin slices
2	tablespoons olive oil	6	tablespoons margarine
2	tablespoons margarine	2	tablespoons parsley
3	tablespoons white wine vinegar	¼	teaspoon dried thyme
	salt and pepper		dash nutmeg
			juice of 1 lemon

Cook onions in olive oil and 2 tablespoons margarine until golden. Add vinegar, salt and pepper and cook until vinegar reduced. In separate skillet, heat liver for 2 minutes with ¾ stick margarine, parsley, thyme, nutmeg. Add onion/vinegar mixture. Correct seasoning. Pour lemon juice over liver before serving. Serves 4.

LIVER MARENGO

1	pound liver	1	bay leaf
¼	cup flour	½	teaspoon garlic powder
⅛	teaspoon salt		
¼	teaspoon pepper	¼	cup white wine
1½	tablespoons oil	3	cups cooked rice (1 cup raw)
1	cup beef bouillon		
½	cup sour cream		
1	(#303) can tomatoes, chopped (2 cups)		

MEATS

℞

Cut liver in thin strips. Roll in flour, salt and pepper. Brown in oil. Combine leftover flour with bouillon and sour cream. Add tomatoes, bay leaf and garlic powder. Pour over meat and simmer covered for 30 minutes. Add wine and cook 10 minutes. Remove bay leaf. Serve over rice. Serves 6.

PORK IN CRUST

2½	pounds pork tender, cut into 3 inch portions		salt and pepper
	all-season salt	½	teaspoon rosemary
½	pound mushrooms, chopped		refrigerated crescent rolls
1	tablespoon margarine	1	egg
⅛	teaspoon garlic powder	2	tablespoons water
		1	can whole cranberry sauce
		2	teaspoons cornstarch

Season tender with all-season salt. Bake tender at 400° for 20 minutes. Remove and cool. Save drippings. Sauté mushrooms in margarine. Season with garlic powder, salt, pepper and rosemary. Form 2 triangles of crescent roll to form a rectangle. Place pork on pastry and cover with mushrooms. Fold pastry over meat. Mix egg with water and coat pastry and meat. Bake at 350° until crust is golden. Add a small amount of water to reserved pan drippings. Add whole cranberry sauce. Season with salt and pepper. Add cornstarch to sauce and stir until thickened. Serve each pork crescent with cranberry sauce. Lamb can also be used. Serves 8.

MEATS

TEXAS PORK CHOPS

6	pork chops, 1 inch thick	1	tablespoon mustard with horseradish
	salt and pepper	1	tablespoon Tabasco
½	cup margarine	1	tablespoon Worcestershire sauce
½	cup tomato juice		
½	cup ketchup	1½	ounces quick chili mix
¼	cup tomato sauce	1	(20 ounce) can pineapple slices, drained
2½	tablespoons vinegar		
1	tablespoon lemon juice		

Season pork chops with salt and pepper. Refrigerate 1-2 hours. Melt margarine. Add tomato juice, ketchup, tomato sauce, vinegar, lemon juice, mustard, Tabasco sauce, Worcestershire sauce, and chili mix. Cook until well combined. Grill chops over charcoal for 10 minutes. Coat chops with sauce and place in foil with 1-2 pineapple slices. Wrap and return to grill and cook an additional 15 minutes. Serves 6.

SWEET AND SOUR PORK WITH CRANBERRIES

1	pound lean pork, cut into 1 inch cubes	1	large onion, sliced ¼ inch thick
	salt and pepper	2	small zucchini, cut in ¼ inch cubes
¼	cup cornstarch		
6	tablespoons flour	½	cup cranberry juice cocktail
1	egg		
¼	cup chicken bouillon	½	cup whole cranberry sauce
	peanut oil		
1	green pepper, cut into ¼ inch cubes		

Season pork with salt and pepper. Make batter with cornstarch, flour, egg and bouillon. Dip pork cubes into batter and fry in peanut oil. Remove meat and drain. In 1 tablespoon oil, sauté green pepper, onion slices and the zucchini cubes. Heat whole cranberry sauce and cranberry juice and combine with zucchini mixture and pork cubes. Correct seasoning with salt and pepper. Serve with rice. Serves 4.

MEATS

PORK, PEPPERS AND MUSHROOMS

6	pork chops, ½ inch thick	1	cup tomato juice
	olive oil		juice of ½ lime
1	pound mushrooms, sliced	1	teaspoon thyme
		1	teaspoon oregano
2	bell peppers, cut in ¼ inch strips	1	teaspoon basil
		¼	teaspoon garlic powder
4	tablespoons margarine or ¼ cup olive oil	1	tablespoon flour
		¼	cup water
3	medium tomatoes, peeled and cut in large pieces	2	ounces Marsala wine

Salt and pepper pork chops and sauté until brown. In a separate pan, sauté mushrooms and peppers in margarine or oil until just limp. Add tomatoes, tomato and lime juice, thyme, oregano, basil and garlic powder. Cook for 5 minutes. Remove vegetables. Add flour and water to drippings and then Marsala and cook for about 10 minutes. Return vegetables to sauce and pour over pork chops. Serves 6.

MARINATED PORK ROAST

1	cup soy sauce	1	teaspoon ginger
½	cup dry sherry	1	teaspoon crushed thyme
2	cloves garlic		
1	tablespoon dry mustard	4-5	pounds pork loin roast

Combine first 6 ingredients to make marinade. Place roast in plastic bag. Pour marinade in bag and seal tightly. Turn frequently. Marinate overnight. Cook roast at 325° for 3 hours. Baste occasionally with marinade. Serves 8.

MEATS

℞ PORK ROAST, AVOCADO AND LEMON GARLIC SAUCE

1 (2-3 pound) boneless pork roast	1 clove garlic, sliced
seasoned salt and pepper	Lemon Garlic Sauce
	2 avocados

Rub roast with salt and pepper and sliced clove of garlic. Additional cloves may be inserted into meat. Cook at 325° (30 minutes per pound). Let stand 10 minutes. Slice fairly thin. Arrange slices in shallow serving platter. Pour ¾ of Lemon Garlic Dressing over meat and let stand at room temperature for at least 2 hours. Slice avocado and garnish meat. Pour rest of Lemon Garlic Sauce over avocado. Serves 4-6.

Lemon Garlic Sauce

- 3 tablespoons lemon juice
- 3 tablespoons water
- 1 tablespoon parsley, finely minced
- ½ teaspoon grated lemon peel
- ½ teaspoon dry mustard
- ½ teaspoon sugar
- ½ teaspoon seasoned salt
- ½ teaspoon garlic powder
- ¼ teaspoon turmeric
- dash seasoned pepper
- ⅔ cup salad oil

Combine all ingredients except oil in blender and mix well. Add oil gradually to mixture and blend. Refrigerate overnight. Makes 1 cup.

PORK POT ROAST

- 4-6 pound pork roast
- all-season salt
- salt and pepper
- garlic powder
- 1 slender eggplant, unpeeled, cut into 1 inch pieces
- 3 onions, cut in large pieces
- 1 (#300) can tomatoes, broken (1¾ cups)
- 4-6 zucchini squash, cut in 1 inch pieces
- 1 bay leaf
- 1 teaspoon oregano

MEATS

℞

Season roast with all-season salt, pepper and garlic powder. Place roast in 400° oven and brown one hour. Pour off excess grease. Add eggplant, onions, tomatoes, zucchini, bay leaf and oregano. Bake 1½ hours. Correct seasoning with salt and pepper to taste. Serves 6-8. Beef roast can also be used.

EASY GOURMET PORK CASSEROLE

6	pork chops, 1 inch thick	1	can cheddar cheese soup, undiluted
2-3	large California potatoes, cut in ½ inch slices	1	can mushroom soup, undiluted
	salt and pepper to taste	1-2	ounces sherry
	garlic powder to taste	2	teaspoons cornstarch
2-3	large onions, cut in ½ inch slices		
1	can sliced mushrooms, or equivalent fresh mushrooms, sautéed in margarine		

Put potato slices in 3 quart buttered casserole and season with salt, pepper and garlic powder. Layer with onions and mushrooms. Place pork chops on layer of onions. Salt and pepper chops and sprinkle with garlic powder to taste. Mix cheddar cheese and mushroom soups over low heat to liquify. Pour over chops. Cover with foil and bake at 350° for 40 minutes. Mix cornstarch with sherry and stir into casserole. Cook an additional 5-10 minutes to thicken sauce. Serves 6. Easy to serve to large group.

MEATS

GLAZED HAM WITH AMBROSIA SAUCE

1 (10-12 pound) ham	2 tablespoons prepared yellow mustard, divided
12 whole cloves	
1 (10 ounce) jar pineapple preserves, divided	1 cup coconut, toasted
	¼ cup orange juice

Stud ham with cloves. Bake ham on rack at 325° for 15-18 minutes per pound. Combine ¼ cup preserves with 1 tablespoon mustard. Brush ham with preserve mixture. Increase oven temperature to 400°. Bake 30 minutes longer. Combine remaining preserves, coconut, orange juice and 1 tablespoon mustard. Serve as sauce with sliced ham.

We frequently had foreign house staff to our house for Thanksgiving lunch. One resident from Lebanon who attended was to eat supper with a group of Lebanese physicians. He asked to use the phone and was overheard to say, "Forgive me, but I will not be able to attend the supper. I'm at the Hill's house and they have just had a food orgy."

BOSTON CUTLETS

6 (5 ounce) veal cutlets	4 green onions, finely chopped
flour	
3 tablespoons margarine, divided	¼ cup vermouth
½ pound mushrooms, finely chopped	

Sauce

12 tablespoons Hollandaise Sauce	1 tablespoon Gruyère cheese, grated
12 tablespoons whipped cream	

MEATS

℞

Flour cutlets and brown in 2 tablespoons margarine. Place cutlets in casserole dish. Sauté green onions and mushrooms in 1 tablespoon margarine. Add vermouth. In separate container combine Hollandaise sauce, whipped cream and cheese. Spoon mushroom mixture over cutlets and top with sauce. Brown under broiler. Serves 6. Chicken breast put through cutlet blade may be used instead of veal.

LAURIE'S VEAL POCKETS

½ pound mushrooms, sliced
3 tablespoons olive oil
salt and pepper
dash garlic powder
½ cup ripe olives, sliced
12 thin slices ham
12 slices of Mozzarella cheese

flour
salt and pepper
2 eggs, beaten
olive oil
juice of 1 lemon
¼ cup vermouth

Sauté mushrooms in olive oil. Season with salt, pepper and garlic. Add sliced olives. Layer ham, cheese, and 2 tablespoons mushroom/olive mixture over veal. Fold over to enclose all sides and secure with toothpicks. Combine flour and salt and pepper. Dip the veal roll in egg and roll in flour mixture then fry in olive oil until brown. Remove. Add lemon and vermouth to the pan. Simmer 1 minute. Pour sauce over veal. Serves 12.

MEATS

VEAL LASAGNA LIKE MAMA POLI'S

2	pounds milk fed veal, cut thin for scallopini	1	(28 ounce) can tomato sauce (3½ cups)
1	cup sauterne	1	(6 ounce) can tomato paste (¾ cup)
2	tablespoons olive oil	1	bay leaf
6	whole lasagna noodles	1	whole clove
1	can beef bouillon		salt and pepper
1	medium onion, cut in pieces	1	pound Mozzarella cheese, grated
½	teaspoon garlic powder	1	pound Romano cheese, grated
½	pound mushrooms, sliced and sautéed in margarine		

Cut veal into bite size pieces. Marinate in sauterne overnight. Sauté veal in olive oil until just done. Reserve drippings. Cook lasagna noodles in water until just done. DO NOT OVERCOOK. Blend bouillon and onion in blender. In pan add bouillon, onion, garlic powder, mushrooms, tomato sauce, tomato paste, bay leaf, clove, salt and pepper. Cook over low heat until sauce thickens and becomes brownish red. About 4 hours. Add sauterne from marinade and meat drippings to tomato mixture. Cook sauce for an additional 15-20 minutes to evaporate alcohol.

Cover bottom of casserole with small layer of sauce. Add lasagna noodles to cover bottom of casserole dish. Add veal. Cover with Romano and Mozzarella cheeses. Add ½ of sauce. Cover with lasagna noodles and top with remaining sauce and Romano and Mozzarella cheese. Bake at 350° until bubbly.

Chicken breasts that have been put through the cutlet blade may also be used. Few know the difference. Serves 6.

The secret of this dish is to have a generous hand with cheese. The idea for using veal in this recipe is Mama Poli's. The sauce is my creation.

MEATS

GRILLADES

- 4 pound veal round, cut in small pieces
- salt and pepper
- 1½ cups flour
- 3 tablespoons oil
- 1 bunch green onion, chopped (keep green tops separated)
- ¼ cup chopped bell pepper
- 2 (6 ounce) cans Italian tomato paste
- water
- 1 teaspoon thyme
- 1 bay leaf
- 1 clove garlic, minced
- 2 tablespoons parsley, chopped
- salt and pepper to taste

Season meat with salt and pepper. Dredge in flour and fry in oil until brown. Remove from pan. Cook onions and green pepper in oil until limp. Add tomato paste and 2 cans of water. Add thyme, bay leaf, garlic, parsley, salt and pepper. Add meat and simmer slowly until meat tender. Serve with grits. Serves 8.

Good for post theatre meal or after the football game. When in New Orleans, these are a must for brunch at the Royal Orleans preceded by Bloody Marys.

VEAL SCALLOPS

- 2 pounds veal, cut thin as for scallopini
- ¾ cup bread crumbs, Italian style
- ⅛ teaspoon garlic powder
- 1 tablespoon grated Parmesan cheese
- salt and pepper
- 2 eggs, beaten
- olive oil

Mix bread crumbs, garlic, Parmesan, salt and pepper. Dip veal scallops in egg and then dredge in bread crumb mixture. Refrigerate for several hours or preferably overnight. Place scallops in flat pan and drizzle with olive oil. Bake at 375° for 10 minutes or until golden. Serve immediately. Serves 8.

MEATS

GREEK LAMB WITH BASIC GREEK SALSA

- 3 pound leg of lamb
- 1 large onion, chopped
- 3 cloves garlic, chopped
- ⅓ cup olive oil
- 1 (28 ounce) can tomatoes, chopped (3½ cups)
- 3½ cups water
- salt and pepper to taste
- 2 tablespoons oregano
- 3 whole allspice
- 1 clove garlic, whole

Sauté onions and garlic in olive oil. Add remaining ingredients except lamb and simmer for 15-20 minutes. Make deep holes in lamb with sharp knife and insert halves of garlic cloves. Place lamb in roaster and pour sauce over it. Cover and bake at 350° until done.

LEG OF LAMB

- 3 pound leg of lamb
- ¼ cup olive oil
- salt and pepper
- 1 teaspoon garlic powder
- 2 teaspoons oregano
- 1 can chicken bouillon
- 1 (#300) can tomato sauce (1¾ cups)
- 3 carrots, scraped and cut into 1 inch pieces
- 4 large white potatoes, peeled and cut into 1 inch cubes
- 1 cup fresh mushrooms, sliced

Place lamb in roaster with olive oil. Season with salt, pepper, garlic powder and oregano. Add tomato sauce and chicken bouillon. Bake at 350° for 3 hours. 30 minutes before serving add carrots, mushrooms and potatoes. Any that is left over is good served over cooked rice. Serve 8-10.

LAMB KIDNEYS IN SHERRY-MUSTARD SAUCE

- 6 lamb kidneys
- salt and pepper
- 4 tablespoons margarine, divided
- ⅓ pound fresh mushrooms, sliced
- ¼ cup onions, chopped
- ¼ cup dry sherry
- 2 teaspoons Dijon-style mustard
- ½ cup sour cream
- parsley, chopped

MEATS

℞
Remove the exterior membrane from kidneys; slice in half and remove the interior suet. Season with salt and pepper. Melt half of the margarine and cook the kidneys with mushrooms and onions. Remove from skillet. Add sherry and mustard to pan, stirring until mixture is smooth. Return kidneys, mushrooms and onions to pan. Stir in sour cream and heat through. Garnish with parsley. Serves 4.

EASY GOURMET CHICKEN

2	large California potatoes, cut in ½ inch slices	1	(10¾ ounce) can cheddar cheese soup, undiluted (1¼ cups)
	salt and pepper	1	(10¾ ounce) can cream of mushroom soup, undiluted (1¼ cups)
	garlic powder		
1	large onion, cut in ½ inch slices, separated into rings	1	ounce sherry
		1	tablespoon cornstarch
2-4	whole chicken breasts, deboned to make 4-8 filets of chicken	1	(16 ounce) can pear halves, drained (2 cups)
3	slices of cooked ham, ⅛ inch thick, the size of chicken filets		
1	(4 ounce) can sliced mushrooms or fresh mushrooms sautéed in butter		

Put a layer of potatoes in the bottom of a deep baking dish. Season with salt and pepper and sprinkle with a little garlic powder. Add a layer onion rings, chicken breasts and ham. Season with pepper and garlic—no salt as ham contributes salt. Cover with mushrooms. Warm soups together and pour over mixture. Cover and bake at 350° until chicken is tender, about 30 minutes. Mix sherry with cornstarch and stir into chicken mixture. Add pear halves. Spoon some of cheddar cheese sauce over pears. Bake for an additional 10 minutes uncovered. Serves 4-8.

This makes a lovely one dish meal that is covered with a light wine cheese sauce. It is just as good without ham and pears.

MEATS

CHICKEN AND ARTICHOKES

8	chicken breast halves		salt and pepper
1	(14¾ ounce) jar marinated artichokes	½	cup grated Parmesan cheese

Place breasts of chicken in pan in single layer. Pour juice from artichokes over chicken breasts and allow to marinate several hours. Season chicken with salt, pepper and Parmesan cheese. Cook chicken in 350° oven for 15-20 minutes. Add artichoke hearts and cook an additional 10 minutes. Serve over brown rice or with linguine.

CUBAN CHICKEN

2½- 3	pound chicken, quartered	½	teaspoon ground cinnamon
	salt and pepper	1 ¼	cup chicken broth
2	tablespoons margarine	¼	cup almonds, sliced
1	onion, chopped	3	tablespoons raisins, plumped
2	cloves garlic, minced		
3	fresh tomatoes, chopped	3	tablespoons ripe olives, sliced
¼	cup dry white wine	2	tablespoons drained capers
¼	teaspoon ground cumin		parsley
2	teaspoons oregano		

Sprinkle chicken with salt and pepper and roast at 350° until brown. Remove from pan. Lower temperature to 325°. Add ¼ cup water to pan to loosen particles. Sauté onion and garlic in margarine and combine with tomatoes, wine, cumin, oregano, cinnamon, broth, almonds, raisins, olives and capers. Cook for 15-20 minutes until thickened. Spoon sauce over chicken and bake at 325° for 20-25 minutes. Serve over rice. Garnish with parsley. Serves 4-6.

MEATS

SAN ANTONIO GREEN ENCHILADAS

1	chicken	3	chicken bouillon cubes
⅛	teaspoon garlic powder	2	pints chicken broth, from chicken
1	small onion, chopped	32	corn tortillas
1	rib celery	½	cup cooking oil
	salt and pepper	1½	pounds Monterey Jack cheese, grated
5	pounds green Mexican tomatoes, chopped	1	(4 ounce) carton sour cream
2	bell peppers, chopped		
3	onions, chopped		

Boil chicken in water with garlic powder, onion, celery, salt and pepper. Debone and dice chicken. Make sure chicken is well salted. Make sauce of green Mexican tomatoes, pepper, onions, chicken bouillon and chicken broth. Dip tortillas in hot oil to soften. Place 1 tablespoon chicken and 1 tablespoon cheese at edge of tortilla and roll cigar fashion. Place in greased casserole with seams down. Pour green tomato sauce over tortilla and top with sour cream. Heat for 20 minutes in 400° oven. Serves 8-16 depending on how many enchiladas served per guest.

MEATS

℞

COUNTRY CAPTAIN

1	hen chicken	1	teaspoon salt
2	medium onions, chopped	1	teaspoon sugar
1	bell pepper, chopped	½	teaspoon garlic powder
3	tablespoons olive oil	⅛	teaspoon red pepper
2	(#303) cans tomatoes, chopped (2 cups each)	½	cup currants
		1	small can sliced almonds
2	teaspoons curry powder		peanuts, ground
			coconut, shredded
1	teaspoon powdered thyme		chutney
		2	cups wild rice, cooked

Boil hen, debone and cut into bite size pieces. Sauté onions and green pepper in olive oil. Add tomatoes and then curry powder, thyme, salt, sugar, garlic powder and red pepper. Add currants that have been soaked in ½ cup chicken stock and almonds. Sprinkle peanuts, coconut and chutney over dish. Serve over rice. Serves 6-8.

CHICKEN INTERLAKEN

2-2½	pounds chicken, cut into serving pieces	2	tablespoons Spanish saffron
½	cup olive oil	½	pound fresh mushrooms, sliced
2	onions, chopped	1	small bottle capers, drained
1	large green pepper, chopped		
1	teaspoon garlic powder	½	cup almonds, sliced
		1	cup stuffed olives, halved
1	(#2) can tomatoes (2½ cups)	¾	cup seedless raisins
1	bay leaf	¾	cup dry white wine
1	can chicken bouillon	8	medium potatoes

Brown chicken in oil. Add onions, green pepper, garlic powder, tomatoes and bay leaf and cook covered for 15 minutes. Add remaining ingredients except potatoes and cook until chicken tender. Add

MEATS

potatoes; canned potatoes are better since they do not cook apart. This tastes better if cooked early in the day and allowed to season. Serves 10.

CHICKEN SUPREME

6	whole chicken breasts, halved and skinned	1½	cups half and half, divided
¼	cup flour	¼	cup sherry
2½	teaspoons salt	1	teaspoon lemon peel
1	teaspoon paprika	1	tablespoon lemon juice
¼	cup butter	1	cup grated Swiss cheese
¼	cup water		
2	tablespoons cornstarch	½	cup parsley

Dredge chicken in flour and season with salt and paprika. Brown in butter. Add water and simmer covered for 30 minutes. Remove from pan. Mix cornstarch and ¼ of the half and half in drippings and warm. Gradually add rest of half and half, sherry, lemon peel and lemon juice. Cook until thickened. Place chicken into 3 quart casserole dish and cover with sauce and sprinkle with cheese. Bake at 350° for 35 minutes. Sprinkle with parsley. Serves 12.

ITALIAN CHICKEN

8	chicken breasts, skinned and deboned		salt and pepper
		1	teaspoon grated Parmesan cheese
½	teaspoon garlic powder	2	eggs, beaten
		¾	cup olive oil
1	cup bread crumbs, Italian style		

Halve the chicken breasts and flatten like cutlets. Combine garlic powder, bread crumbs, salt, pepper and cheese. Dip chicken into beaten eggs then into bread crumb mixture. Bread chicken breast early in the morning and refrigerate so seasoning goes through chicken. Place chicken breasts on large flat pan. Drizzle with olive oil. Bake at 350° until just golden about 20 minutes. Serves 8-10. This is an easy dish to serve to a large group. Olive oil is a must; cooking oil should not be substituted.

MEATS

CHICKEN FLORIO

8	chicken breasts, halved	1	(#300) can of potatoes (1¾ cups)
2	quarts water		
½	cup chopped onion	1	medium tangerine (fresh)
2	teaspoons salt		
¼	teaspoon pepper	1-2	teaspoon tangerine peel
2	cups Marsala wine		
4	medium carrots, scrapped, cut into ½ inch slices	6	tablespoons margarine
		3	tablespoons flour
		4	small zucchini, cut into ½ inch slices
¾	pound fresh mushrooms, small and whole		

Cook chicken in 2 quarts of water with onion, salt and pepper until tender. Remove skins from chicken. Return chicken to stock. Add wine, carrots, mushrooms, potatoes, tangerine slices, and tangerine peel to chicken stock. Cook 30 minutes. Blend flour into margarine and add to chicken stock. Add zucchini and cook 20 minutes. This dish may be cooked a day ahead to season. If so, add zucchini to cook during re-warming period to retain their color. May serve with Wild Rice with Grapes (See Index). Fresh tangerine adds special taste to this dish. Quail or dove may be substituted for chicken. Serves 8-16.

CHICKEN WITH ROCHAMBEAU SAUCE

8	chicken breasts	4	tablespoons margarine
8	slices ham	8	pieces toasted bread

Salt and pepper chicken breasts and broil in oven. Sauté ham slices in margarine and keep warm.

Sauce

8	tablespoons margarine	16	tablespoons Bèarnaise sauce made from scratch or Knorr packaged Bèarnaise
3	tablespoons flour		
10	ounces pineapple juice		
1	tablespoon brown sugar	¼	cup Vermouth

MEATS

℞
Melt margarine. Add flour and stir until brown roux forms. Add pineapple juice, brown sugar and cook until thickened. Add vermouth and stir. Make Bèarnaise sauce according to directions on package. Layer toast, ham, chicken and cover with sauce. Top with 1 tablespoon Bèarnaise sauce.

CHICKEN STUFFING FOR CREPES

6	chicken breasts	2	jalapeño peppers, seeded and finely chopped
1	celery rib		
1/8	teaspoon garlic powder		
	salt and pepper	1	teaspoon salt
		1	teaspoon pepper
1 1/4	pounds Swiss cheese, grated, reserve 1 cup	12	Crepes (See Index)
		1	pint heavy cream

Boil chicken breast in water with celery rib, garlic powder, salt and pepper. Debone chicken and cut into bite size pieces. Combine with cheese, jalapeños, salt, pepper. Place 1 tablespoon chicken mixture on outer edge of crepe. Roll like cigar; place folded edge down. Top with cheese and cover with cream. Bake at 325° for 20-30 minutes. Serves 6.

SMOTHERED DOVES

14-16	doves	1 1/2	cups water
	salt and pepper	1	cup sherry
	flour	1/4	cup parsley, chopped
1/2	cup salad oil		
1/2	cup chopped green onion		

Salt, pepper and flour doves. Brown doves in oil in roaster at 400°. Add onion and water; decrease heat to 350°. Bake until tender. Add sherry and parsley. Serves 6-8.

MEATS

SLICED CHICKEN AND MUSHROOMS IN SOUR CREAM SAUCE

4	chicken breasts, deboned, skinned, and cut in ¼ inch strips	½	cup white wine
		½	cup sour cream
		1	tablespoon tomato paste
5	tablespoons margarine, divided	2-3	drops Worcestershire sauce
1	tablespoon oil	1	tablespoon salt
½	cup diced green onions		fresh ground pepper
		1	tablespoon parsley, finely chopped
¼	pound mushrooms		
1	tablespoon flour		

Brown chicken in 3 tablespoons margarine and oil. Remove chicken from pan. Add remaining margarine to skillet; sauté green onions and mushrooms until limp. Add flour and stir. Pour in wine and gradually add sour cream. Add tomato paste, Worcestershire sauce, salt and pepper. Return chicken to pan and cook covered until tender. Sprinkle with parsley and serve over noodles. Serves 4-6.

CHICKEN, MUSHROOMS AND RED WINE

Marinade

1½	cups dry red wine	4½-5	pounds chicken, cut into serving pieces
2	large carrots, cut in ½ inch slices	⅓	ounce dried black mushrooms
	garlic		salt and pepper
2	tablespoons oil		flour for dredging
1	teaspoon peppercorns	½	pound lean bacon, cut in 1 inch pieces
4	sprigs parsley		
1	bay leaf		
¼	teaspoon thyme		

MEATS

℞

2 teaspoons cornstarch	1 tablespoon parsley leaves, minced
2 tablespoons cold water	
½ cup chicken stock	12 egg-size white onions, peeled, halved lengthwise

Combine ingredients of marinade in saucepan and boil for 5 minutes. Marinate chicken parts overnight. Soak mushrooms in hot water for 20 minutes. Mince caps. Remove chicken from marinade. Pat dry. Season chicken with salt and pepper and dredge in flour. Fry bacon until crisp. Remove from pan. Brown chicken in bacon grease and then place in casserole. Mix cornstarch with cold water and combine with marinade and chicken stock. Pour over chicken. Add parsley and onions. Bake at 350° for 20 minutes or until sauce thickens and onions are cooked.

CHICKEN, TOMATOES AND BACON

6 chicken breasts, halved	3 green onions, chopped
4 tablespoons butter, melted	½ pound bacon cut in bite size pieces
all-season salt	1 (4 ounce) can mushrooms, sliced or buttons
salt and pepper	
½ teaspoon garlic powder	
1 onion, sliced and left in rings	½ cup water, divided
	2 tablespoons flour
1 (#2) can peeled tomatoes, chopped (2½ cups)	

Arrange chicken breasts in pan. Drizzle with butter. Season with all-season salt, pepper and garlic powder. Add onions, tomatoes, green onions, bacon, mushrooms and ½ of water. Bake at 350° for 20 minutes. Add flour to remaining water and pour into sauce. Return to oven for 10 minutes. Serve over rice. Serves 6-8.

MEATS

CHICKEN TORONTO

6 chicken breasts, deboned, skinned	8 tablespoons margarine
salt and pepper	1 cup Bèarnaise sauce (Knorr packaged sauce)
2 tablespoons cornstarch	
½ cup water	

Have butcher put chicken breasts through cutlet machine. Cut into 1 inch slices. Season with salt and pepper. Make batter of cornstarch and water. Dip chicken into cornstarch batter. Fry in margarine until light golden brown. Mix Bèarnaise sauce according to directions on package. Serve chicken topped with Bèarnaise sauce. Duck can also be used. Serves 8.

SAN FRANCISCO CHICKEN

2½-3 pounds chicken, cut into serving pieces	¼ cup white wine
3 tablespoons margarine	½ cup cream
8-10 small mushrooms, sliced	3 sprigs parsley
	1 bay leaf
1 teaspoon green onion, chopped	dash thyme
	salt
1 tablespoon flour	2 egg yolks
	½ cup warm cream

Brown chicken in margarine. Add mushrooms and cook 5 minutes. Stir in onions and flour. Add wine and cream, parsley, bay leaf, thyme and salt. Cook 30 minutes partly covered. Discard bay leaf. Remove chicken. Stir egg yolks and cream into sauce. Pour over chicken. Serve with rice. Serves 4.

MEATS

CHICKEN FINGERS

- 8 chicken breasts, skinned and deboned
- 1 quart buttermilk
- ¾ cup flour
- salt and pepper
- cooking oil

Cut chicken breast into strips. Marinate in buttermilk overnight. Dredge in flour seasoned with salt and pepper. Deep fry in oil until brown. Excellent finger food for cocktail party.

MOTHER'S RITZ CRACKER CHICKEN

- 8 chicken breasts, deboned and halved
- salt and pepper
- ½ pound melted margarine
- 1 small box Ritz crackers, crumbled
- ½ teaspoon garlic powder

Salt and pepper chicken and dip into margarine; roll in Ritz cracker crumbs. Sprinkle heavily with garlic powder. Bake at 350° for 20-25 minutes. Chicken needs no grease for cooking since Ritz crackers contain grease. This is a great dish to serve to a large group. Serves 12-16.

MEATS

BONNIE'S ALMOND CHICKEN

6	chicken breasts, halved	¼	teaspoon nutmeg
	salt and pepper	4	tablespoons butter
	marjoram	½	cup toasted almonds, sliced
1	(10 ounce) can mushroom soup (1¼ cups)	2	cups coarse breadcrumbs
1	soup can of milk (1¼ cups)	½	cup sherry

Season chicken with salt and pepper. Place in greased pan and sprinkle heavily with majoram. Combine soup, milk, and nutmeg and pour over chicken. Cover. Bake at 350° for 1 hour. Melt butter and add toasted almonds and breadcrumbs. Sprinkle over chicken. Add sherry and cook 30 minutes more. Serves 12.

CHICKEN JAMBALAYA

1	fryer, cut up	½	pound hot smoked sausage, crumbled
	salt, pepper, cayenne	3	cups regular long grain rice, uncooked
1	cup cooking oil	2	tablespoons tomato paste
2	medium sized onions, chopped	4	cups water
1	teaspoon chopped bell pepper	½	teaspoon garlic powder
1	teaspoon finely chopped celery		

Season chicken with salt, pepper and cayenne and fry until golden brown. Lower heat and add chopped onion, bell pepper, celery and sausage. Add rice and stir to coat. Add tomato paste, water and garlic powder. Cover. Simmer over low heat about 1 hour. Serves 8.

MEATS

CHICKEN TACOS

Chicken Mixture

- 8 chicken breasts
- 1 rib celery
- 1 small onion, chopped
- 2 teaspoons garlic powder
- 1 (4 ounce) can mild green chilies
- 1 (#303) can tomatoes, chopped (2 cups)
- 2 tablespoons chili powder
- 1 tablespoon cumin
- salt and pepper
- 1 cup water

Topping

- 2 tomatoes, chopped
- ½ head lettuce, thinly sliced
- 1 large onion, chopped
- 2 avocados, chopped
- ½ pound Monterey Jack cheese, grated
- 8 ounces sour cream
- cooking oil
- 12 flour tortillas

Combine ingredients for chicken mixture and simmer covered for 30 minutes. Remove chicken and cut into bite size pieces. Return to sauce. Fry flour tortillas in oil. Do not burn. Remove and drain. Place on plate. Add chicken mixture and top with tomatoes, lettuce, onion, avocado, sour cream and cheese. Makes 12 tacos.

MEATS

CHICKEN ENCHILADAS

½	recipe chicken mixture for Chicken Tacos	½	teaspoon sugar salt and pepper
2	tablespoons oil	1	cup chicken broth
1	large onion, sliced in rings	12	corn tortillas
1	bell pepper, sliced	1½	cups grated Monterey Jack cheese
1	(#303) can tomato sauce (2 cups)		

Sauté onion and green pepper in oil until just soft. Add tomato sauce, sugar, salt, pepper and chicken broth. Cook for 20-30 minutes. Warm tortillas in oil. Place 1 tablespoon chicken mixture and 1 tablespoon Monterey Jack cheese at edge of tortilla and roll like cigar. Place seam down in baking dish. Sprinkle with remaining cheese and cover with sauce. Bake in oven at 350° for 25 minutes. Makes 12 enchiladas.

CHICKEN AND GREEN CHILI CASSEROLE

2	cups coarsely chopped onion	2-2½	pounds chicken, cooked, deboned
4	tablespoons margarine	10-12	cornmeal tortillas, torn into small pieces
3	tablespoons flour		
2	cups milk		
1	cup chicken broth	1¾	pounds sharp cheddar cheese, grated (4 cups)
1	(4 ounce) can green chilies, seeded and cut in strips		
		1½	teaspoon salt
1	(10 ounce) can Rotel (tomatoes with green chilies), chopped (1¼ cups)		

MEATS

℞

Sauté onion in margarine and add flour; cook until bubbly. Add milk and broth. When thickened add green chilies and Rotel tomatoes. Cook 20 minutes. In 3 quart casserole layer chicken, tortillas, sauce and cheese. Salt each layer. Repeat with cheese on top. Bake at 375° until bubbly. May be prepared ahead and frozen. To make this hotter, 2 tablespoons sliced jalapeño peppers can be added. Serves 8-10.

CHICKEN LETTUCE POCKETS

1 cup Stir Fry Sauce (See Index)	1 cup chopped celery
1 teaspoon Worcestershire sauce	1 cup fresh beansprouts
2 chicken breasts, diced	1 (8 ounce) can water chestnuts, drained and chopped
1 tablespoon cornstarch	iceberg lettuce, separated
1 tablespoon soy sauce	
2 tablespoons salad oil	

Combine Stir Fry Sauce and Worcestershire sauce. Mix chicken with cornstarch and soy sauce. Stir fry in oil about 1 minute. Add celery, bean sprouts and water chestnuts. Add Stir Fry/Worcestershire sauce mixture. Cook until sauce thickens. Place 2 tablespoons on lettuce leaf and roll up cigar fashion. Serves 4.

MEATS

CHICKEN BREASTS AND TOMATO SAUCE

8	chicken breasts, split and put through cutlet machine (may pound with mallet if frustrated)	2	tablespoons olive oil
1	(28 ounce) can of peeled tomatoes, whirled in blender (3½ cups)	½	cup bread crumbs with Italian seasoning
		⅛	teaspoon garlic powder
		2	teaspoon grated Parmesan cheese
			salt and pepper
1	(28 ounce) can of tomato puree (3½ cups)	2	eggs, beaten
		¼	cup olive oil
¾	cup water	½	pound Mozzarella cheese, grated
1	teaspoon basil		
3-4	whole cloves	½	pound Romano cheese, grated

Combine tomatoes and tomato puree with water, basil, cloves and 2 tablespoons olive oil. Cook over low heat for 3-4 hours. Sauce should be brownish red. Do not cook fast or it will burn and taste bitter.

Mix bread crumbs, garlic powder, Parmesan cheese, salt and pepper. Dip chicken breast into beaten eggs and then dredge in seasoned bread crumbs. Fry in olive oil until slightly brown.

Put chicken breasts in casserole and top with grated Mozzarella and Romano cheese. Cover with tomato sauce and top with more cheese. Bake at 350° for 15-20 minutes. Serves 16. Veal can be used in this recipe, although it is expensive.

MEATS

SUPREMES WITH CHEESE LEMON SAUCE

4 chicken breasts, deboned and skinned	¼ teaspoon salt pepper
½ teaspoon lemon juice	4 tablespoons margarine

Rub chicken breast with lemon then salt and pepper. Bake in margarine in hot oven 6-8 minutes. Chicken is done when springy to touch. Remove to hot dish. Reserve drippings.

Cheese Lemon Sauce

¼ cup beef bouillon	salt and pepper
¼ cup vermouth	2 tablespoons fresh parsley
1 cup heavy cream	

Put bouillon and vermouth into casserole with chicken drippings. Cook down until syrupy. Pour in cream and add salt and pepper. Cook until thickened. Cover chicken with sauce. Sprinkle with parsley. Serve with rice. Serves 6-8.

Rice

⅓ cup onion, minced	bouquet of 2 sprigs parsley, ½ bay leaf and ⅛ teaspoon thyme
2 tablespoons butter	
1 cup rice, uncooked	
2 cups chicken stock salt and pepper	

Sauté onion in butter until translucent. Add rice and cook 3-4 minutes. Stir in chicken stock. Season with salt and pepper. Add herbs. Cover and bake in 350° oven for 18 min. Do not stir. Remove bay leaf before serving.

MEATS

MARINATED CHICKEN

1-2½ pounds chicken	1 tablespoon dry or prepared mustard
1 cup sherry	½ teaspoon black pepper
½ cup salad oil	1 teaspoon garlic salt
1 large onion	1 teaspoon soy sauce
1 tablespoon Worcestershire sauce	

Cut chicken into serving parts. Combine remaining ingredients to make marinade. Marinate chicken overnight. Remove from marinade. Bake at 350° for 25 minutes. Warm marinade and serve with chicken. Serves 4.

CHICKEN BREASTS WELLINGTON

6 chicken breasts, deboned, halved and flattened	2 egg yolks
seasoned salt	4 tablespoons water
seasoned pepper	2 (10 ounce) jars red currant jelly
1 (16 ounce) package long grain and wild rice	1 tablespoon prepared mustard
¼ cup grated orange peel	1 tablespoon water
2 egg whites	3 tablespoons port wine
3 (8 ounce) cans refrigerated crescent dinner rolls	¼ cup lemon juice

Sprinkle chicken with seasoned salt and pepper. Cook rice according to package directions for drier rice; add orange peel and cool. Beat egg whites; fold into rice mixture. Roll 2 triangular pieces of crescent dough into a circle. Repeat until you have 12 circles. Place chicken breast in center of each circle. Spoon about ¼ cup rice mixture over chicken. Fold dough over chicken. Place seam side down on baking sheet. Mix egg yolks with water, brush over dough. Bake, uncovered at 375° for 45-50 minutes. Heat currant jelly in saucepan; gradually stir in mustard, water, wine and lemon juice. Serve warm with chicken. Serves 12.

MEATS

BREAST OF CHICKEN PAPPAGALLO

5-6	boneless chicken breasts, halved and flattened as cutlet	¼	cup margarine
		2	tablespoons olive oil
		¼	cup sliced green onions
⅓	cup flour		
1	teaspoon salt	1½	cups champagne
⅛	teaspoon white pepper	1	cup whipping cream

Dredge chicken in flour, salt and pepper. Brown chicken in melted margarine and olive oil. Add green onions and cook until limp. Add champagne and cook for 12 or 15 minutes, until chicken tender and champagne reduced by one-half. Add cream. Cook until sauce thickens. Serves 10-12.

CHICKEN WITH RASPBERRY SAUCE

1	broiler-fryer chicken, cut in parts	1	teaspoon pepper
			Raspberry Sauce
1	teaspoon garlic salt		

Season chicken with garlic salt and pepper. Bake uncovered at 450° for 25 minutes. Drain. Pour Raspberry Sauce over chicken. Bake chicken at 350° for 30 minutes. Baste frequently. Makes 4 servings.

Raspberry Sauce

1	box frozen raspberries, thawed	⅛	teaspoon garlic powder
½	cup water	1	teaspoon sugar
2	teaspoons cornstarch		

Whirl defrosted raspberries in blender with water and strain. Place in pot and add cornstarch. Mix well. Cook until mixture begins to thicken. Add garlic powder and sugar. Serve over chicken.

Date: *Daily*

For Those Who Enjoy Eating
Patient's name

℞: **SALADS**

Dispense: *Large Servings*

Sig: *Enjoy Daily*

Refill: yes ✓
      no _____

Reba Michele Hill MD.
Physician
DEA Number AH 0000000

SALADS

℞

TO MAKE A GREEN SALAD

Use basic greens:
   romaine
   leafy lettuce
   spinach
   or other favorites

These remain crisp when dressing is added.

Always add:
   green onions and chopped parsley

Types of ingredients you add to salad for variation (slices, cubes, or wedges):
   tomatoes
   plum tomatoes
   yellow squash
   zucchini squash
   carrots
   celery
   radishes
   avocado
   green peppers
   purple onion rings
   marinated artichokes
   marinated eggplant
   plain artichokes
   sour pickles
   apples
   oranges
   Greek olives
   ripe olives
   Italian peppers
   Greek peppers
   pickled onions
   miniature pickled corn-on-the-cob

SALADS

℞

Additional ingredients to consider:

Cheese (shavings or cubes):

    Mozzarella cheese
    Romano cheese
    Parmesan cheese
    Feta cheese
    Brie cheese
    Monterey Jack cheese

Nuts (pieces or whole):

    pecans
    walnuts
    peanuts

Meats (chopped):

    bacon
    ham
    turkey
    chicken
    shrimp (whole, small)
    crab

SALADS

℞

Examples:

For chicken dishes make salad of basic greens plus slices of apple, avocado, ripe olives and cubes of Monterey Jack cheese with Fresh Lemon Dressing.

For Italian foods, make salad of basic greens, plum tomatoes, artichokes, purple onion, Italian peppers, Feta cheese and ripe olives with Simple Salad Dressing.

For seafood dishes, make salad of basic greens, plum tomatoes, zucchini, yellow squash, radishes, green peppers and Romano cheese with Tangy French Dressing.

For Mexican food, make salad of basic greens, avocado, tomato slices, sour pickles, purple onion and cubes of Monterey Jack cheese with Simple Salad Dressing.

There are endless combinations.

My greatest salvation from entertaining failure came when I was a bride of 3 months and entertaining our first couple who had been married 10 years. I was tossing the salad and the bowl fell to the floor—spilling all of the contents. With horror I looked at my female guest who looked critically at the floor, scooped up the salad and placed it back into the bowl. She responded, "The floor looks clean and you did say it was a tossed salad."

SALADS

℞

LAYERED SALAD

- 3 large tomatoes, peeled and thinly sliced
- 2 medium cucumbers, peeled and thinly sliced
- 2 red or green peppers, julienned
- ½ pound mushrooms, sliced
- 1 large red onion, thinly sliced
- salt and ground pepper to taste
- 12 pitted black olives, sliced round
- 2 green onions, chopped

Dressing

- ½ cup olive oil
- 2 tablespoons tarragon white wine vinegar
- 1 clove garlic, minced
- ¼ teaspoon salt
- ¼ teaspoon ground pepper
- 1 tablespoon parsley, chopped
- ¾ teaspoon dried basil

Combine ingredients for dressing and let refrigerate overnight. Layer vegetables for salad. Sprinkle each layer with salt and pepper. Top with olives and green onions. Sprinkle with dressing. Cover and refrigerate overnight. Serves 6.

SPINACH SALAD WITH MANGO CHUTNEY DRESSING

- 2 heads spinach torn in bite size pieces
- 4 green onions, sliced
- ½ can ripe olives, halved cracked pepper and salt
- 1 (4 ounce) can Mandarin orange slices, drained

Combine ingredients and serve with Mango Chutney Salad Dressing (see Index).

SALADS

TUNA AND POTATO SALAD

1	(10 ounce) package frozen hash brown potatoes, defrosted and drained	¼	cup chopped parsley
		1½	teaspoons salt
		¼	teaspoon pepper
		2	(6½ or 7 ounce) cans tuna, drained
¾	cup mayonnaise		
¼	cup lemon juice	2	cups tomatoes, peeled, chopped
1	cup chopped celery		
¼	cup finely chopped onion	8	slices bacon, cooked and crumbled

Combine potatoes with mayonnaise, lemon juice, celery, onion, parsley, salt and pepper. Cover and refrigerate for several hours. At serving time, stir in tuna, tomatoes and bacon. Serves 6.

GERMAN POTATO SALAD

3	pounds potatoes, peeled, cut in ½ inch cubes	¼	cup vinegar
			salt and pepper
		⅛	teaspoon sugar
½	pound bacon, fried and cut in ¼ inch pieces (reserve bacon grease)	½	cup green onions, chopped

Boil potatoes in salted water. Drain. Fry bacon and crumble into potatoes. Mix vinegar with bacon grease, salt, pepper and sugar. Pour over potatoes. Add onions. Serves 8-10.

GRANDMOTHER'S MASHED POTATO SALAD

2	cups *hot* mashed potatoes (do not add butter)	4	green onions, chopped
		1	small green pepper, chopped fine
	salt and pepper	8	small sweet gherkin pickles, chopped fine
2	teaspoons vinegar		
2	tablespoons mustard	2	boiled eggs, sliced
½	cup mayonnaise		

SALADS

℞

Mashed potatoes must be hot to add ingredients. Salt and pepper while hot. Mix vinegar, mustard and mayonnaise. Add onions, green peppers, pickles, egg and mayonnaise mixture to potatoes. Stir and refrigerate. Best made the day before it is to be used. Serves 6.

EGGPLANT SALAD

2	medium sized eggplants (1 pound apiece)	2	tablespoons olive oil
		¼	cup chopped parsley
		½	teaspoon dried oregano
2	cloves garlic		
½	teaspoon salt	1	large tomato, chopped
⅛	teaspoon pepper	½	cup Greek olives
1	tablespoon white wine vinegar		

Peel and cube eggplants. Cook in boiling water 10 min. Do not overcook. Drain. Combine all ingredients except olives and refrigerate overnight. Add olives before serving. Serves 10-12.

HEARTS OF PALM SALAD

1	can hearts of palm	1	(2 ounce) jar chopped pimento
1	small onion, minced		
¼	cup sliced ripe olives		

Marinate hearts of palm and onion in Simple Salad dressing (See Index). Serve on lettuce leaf and top with pimento, onion and olives. Spoon some of marinade over salad. Serves 8-10.

One time at a very formal dinner we gave, I noted a resident diligently digging in the bottom of a large salad bowl meant to feed 50 people. I asked, "Joe, what are you doing?" He said, "No one knows it yet but there are marinated artichokes in here and I'm going to get my share."

SALADS

GREEN SALAD WITH APPLES AND CHEESE

1 head leafy lettuce	Roquefort or Bleu cheese, crumbled, or small pieces of Brie cheese
1 head romaine lettuce	
½ cup parsley	
4 green onions, sliced	
2 Granny Smith apples	20 black olives
juice of ½ lemon	sour pickle slices
2 boiled eggs	

Tear lettuce and romaine into bite size pieces. Add parsley and green onions. Slice green apples and place in plastic bag with juice of ½ lemon. Secure plastic bag and refrigerate. At serving time toss greens with Simple Salad Dressing (See Index). Crumble cheese on top. Dress each salad with slice of egg, 2 black olives, 2 slices of apple and 2 slices of sour pickle. Serves 10.

AMBROSIA

6 oranges, sliced, fiber removed	¾ cup pecans, toasted
	¾ cup coconut
1 (8 ounce) jar maraschino cherries, halved	1 cup sugar
	8 bananas, sliced thick

Cut oranges and save juice. Add cherries, pecans, coconut and orange juice. Add sugar and stir. Refrigerate overnight. Add bananas just before serving. Serves 8. May be used as a salad or a dessert.

FRUIT HEAVEN

1 box fresh strawberries, halved	3 bananas, sliced
	2 avocados, cubed

Combine bananas, strawberries and avocados and toss with Le Martinique Poppyseed dressing. Serve in glass bowl or on individual lettuce leaves. Serves 6.

SALADS

TWENTY-FOUR HOUR SALAD

3	cups bite size pieces of lettuce	1	cup shredded Swiss cheese
	coarsely ground black pepper	1	(10 ounce) package frozen green peas, thawed but uncooked
	salt		
3	hard boiled eggs, sliced	2	green onions, chopped
½	pound bacon, fried crisp and crumbled	½	cup mayonnaise
		¼	teaspoon sugar

Salt and pepper lettuce. Layer eggs, bacon, cheese, green peas and green onions over lettuce. Combine mayonnaise and sugar. Spread mayonnaise over top to cover ingredients. Seal bowl with plastic wrap and refrigerate overnight. Must prepare 24 hours before using. Serves 8.

KOLBS SALAD

1	head leafy lettuce, bite size pieces	10	cherry tomatoes, halved
1	head romaine, bite size pieces	3	green onions, cut
		2	boiled eggs, sliced
1	(8½ ounce) can English peas, drained	1	cup small boiled shrimp
		½	pound crabmeat

Combine lettuce, romaine, peas, tomatoes and onions. Toss with dressing. Dress salad with eggs, shrimp and crabmeat. Serves 10.

Dressing

½	cup white wine vinegar	1	tablespoon Creole mustard
½	cup blended oil		salt and cracked pepper

Combine all ingredients and mix until well blended.

SALADS

GREEK SALAD

- 3 California potatoes boiled in skins
- ½ cup white wine vinegar
- 2 tablespoons mayonnaise
- salt and pepper
- 1 tablespoon oregano
- ½ head lettuce, cut into strips
- 2 tomatoes, chopped
- 1 cucumber, sliced with skin on
- 2 avocados, sliced
- 8-10 radishes, sliced
- 1 cup sliced ripe olives
- ½ cup green olives, sliced
- 2 small green peppers, cut in rings
- anchovies (optional)
- 2 pounds Feta cheese, crumbled

Dressing

- ½ cup olive oil
- ½ cup white wine
- Good Seasons Italian dressing mix

Peel and slice potatoes. Marinate in wine vinegar and mayonnaise overnight. Place potatoes on platter. Sprinkle generously with salt, pepper and oregano. Cover with strips of lettuce and layer with rest of ingredients. For dressing, combine olive oil and white wine with Italian dressing mix. Pour dressing over salad. Do not substitute salad oil. Do not mix salad. Serves 8.

GREEN BEAN SALAD

- 1 pound fresh string beans
- 12 cherry tomatoes
- 1 red onion, cut in rings
- 3 tablespoons red wine vinegar
- ½ teaspoon salt
- ½ teaspoon dry mustard
- ground pepper
- ½ cup olive oil

SALADS

℞

Cook beans in salted boiling water until they are just tender. Combine beans, tomatoes and onions. For dressing, combine vinegar, salt, mustard, pepper and oil. Pour over beans, tomatoes and onions. Marinate overnight. Serves 6.

MARINATED CHERRY TOMATOES

10-12	cherry tomatoes	5	tablespoons olive oil
3	tablespoons lemon juice		salt and cracked pepper
2	tablespoons minced, fresh basil		

Prick cherry tomatoes with fork or tooth pick. Make marinade of lemon juice, basil, olive oil, salt and pepper. Mix well. Pour over tomatoes and marinate overnight. Serve over lettuce or spinach leaves.

CHICKEN SALAD

2½	cups chicken	1	cup celery, chopped
1	celery rib	2	tablespoons minced parsley
	salt and pepper		
	garlic powder	1	cup of fresh fruit (seedless grapes, strawberries and/or bananas)
1	cup mayonnaise		
½	cup whipping cream		
⅛	teaspoon garlic powder	½	cup toasted almonds, shredded
1	teaspoon salt		

Cook chicken with celery rib, salt, pepper and dash of garlic powder so chicken is seasoned. Cool and dice chicken. Mix mayonnaise, whipping cream, garlic powder, salt, celery, parsley and combine with chicken. A good combination of fruits to add to the salad are grapes and strawberries, or grapes and bananas. If you choose bananas, they should be coated with lemon juice to keep them from turning brown. Add almonds just before serving so they remain crunchy. Serves 8.

SALADS

CHICKEN-CRANBERRY SALAD

Layer 1

- 1 envelope unflavored gelatin
- ¼ cup cold water
- 1 can whole cranberry sauce
- 1 (8 ounce) can crushed pineapple (1 cup)
- ½ cup toasted pecans
- 1 tablespoon lemon juice

Mix gelatin in cold water and dissolve over low heat. Cook until it starts to bubble. Add remaining ingredients. Pour into 10 x 6 x 1½ dish. Chill until firm.

Layer 2

- 1 envelope unflavored gelatin
- ¼ cup cold water
- 1 cup mayonnaise
- ½ cup water
- 3 tablespoons lemon juice
- ¾ teaspoon salt
- 2 cups cooked, diced chicken
- ½ cup diced celery
- 2 tablespoons parsley

Soften gelatin in cold water and heat to dissolve. Combine with mayonnaise, water, lemon juice and salt. Add remaining ingredients and pour over first layer. Chill until firm. Serves 8.

HOT CHICKEN SALAD

- 3 cups cooked, diced chicken
- 3 boiled eggs, chopped
- 1½ cups chopped celery
- ½ cup chopped onion
- 2 tablespoons lemon juice
- ⅛ teaspoon pepper
- 1½ cups mayonnaise
- ½ cup toasted almonds
- salt
- cayenne pepper
- ½ cup pimento, chopped
- 4 tablespoons chicken stock
- sour cream and chive potato chips, crushed
- 1½ cups cheddar cheese, grated

SALADS

℞

Mix all together except potato chips and cheese and place in greased casserole. Top with cheese and potato chips. Bake at 375° for 35 minutes. Serves 8-10.

FRIED CHICKEN SALAD

2	chicken breasts, deboned and skinned, cut in ¼ inch strips	1	cup Mandarin oranges
		½	cup chopped celery
		⅓	cup walnuts, coarsely chopped
¾	cup prepared biscuit mix, divided	½	teaspoon seasoned salt
		4	cups fresh spinach, shredded
¼	teaspoon garlic powder		
		½	cup white wine vinegar
½	teaspoon salt		
⅓	cup milk	½	cup blended oil
½	cup cooking oil		

Combine ¼ cup of biscuit mix, garlic powder, and salt. Make batter out of remaining ½ cup biscuit mix and milk. Dredge chicken in dry mix and then into batter. Fry chicken in oil. Do not overcook. Combine fried chicken with oranges, celery, walnuts, seasoned salt and spinach. Toss with vinegar and oil. Makes 4 servings.

ANN'S WILD RICE AND CHICKEN SALAD

1	(6 ounce) box wild rice and long grain rice mix	⅓	cup dry white wine
		¼	cup vegetable oil
		2	teaspoons sugar
2⅓	cups water	¾	teaspoon salt
2	cups cut up chicken	¼	teaspoon pepper
¼	pound fresh mushrooms, sliced	1	carton cherry tomatoes, halved
1	cup fresh spinach, cut into strips	½	cup water chestnuts, sliced
2	green onions, sliced		

Cook rice with seasoning packet in water until just tender. Chill. Add chicken, mushrooms, spinach, and green onions to rice. Make dressing from wine, oil, sugar, salt and pepper. Add to rice mixture and chill. Add tomatoes and water chestnuts just before serving. Serves 6.

SALADS

SHRIMP SALAD

Salad

1½	pounds shrimp, cooked	1	cup mayonnaise
¾	cup celery		juice of ½ lemon
			salt and pepper

Rémoulade Sauce

1	egg, boiled	1	tablespoon Worcestershire sauce
¼	teaspoon garlic powder	1	tablespoon Creole mustard
¼	cup fresh spinach, finely chopped	1	tablespoon lemon juice
2	green onions, minced	1⅓	ounces anchovy paste
2	cups mayonnaise		dash Tabasco

Mix shrimp, celery, mayonnaise, lemon juice, salt and pepper. Make Rémoulade sauce by combining egg, garlic powder, spinach, onions, mayonnaise, Worcestershire sauce, mustard, lemon juice, anchovy paste and Tabasco sauce. Mix in blender. Pour over shrimp/celery mixture. Serves 6.

GUACAMOLE AND SHRIMP SALAD

½	cup small shrimp, cooked	2	cups boiling water
4	ounces French dressing	4	cups mashed avocado
		¼	cup lemon juice
2	packages of unflavored gelatin	⅛	teaspoon garlic powder
1	cup cold water	1	teaspoon salt
			Tabasco

Marinate shrimp in French dressing. Drain. Soften gelatin in cold water and dissolve in boiling water. Pour small amount of gelatin in bottom of mold. Arrange shrimp in gelatin and chill. Mash avocado with lemon juice, garlic, salt and Tabasco. Add remaining gelatin and pour on top of firm shrimp layer. Chill until firm. Unmold on lettuce. Serve with mayonnaise. Serves 10-12.

SALADS

MARGARET'S SHRIMP SALAD

- 1 pound shrimp cooked, shelled and deveined
- 1 (12 ounce) package small elbow macaroni, cooked
- 1 (0.56 ounce) package Lowry's green onion dip mix
- 1/3 cup sweet pickle relish
- 3 boiled eggs, chopped
- salt and pepper to taste
- dash of paprika
- 3 tablespoons mayonnaise
- 1/2 cup celery, diced (optional)
- 1 small bell pepper, diced (optional)

If shrimp are large, they may be cut into bite-size pieces. If shrimp and macaroni are warm, 3 tablespoons of mayonnaise will be adequate. But if ingredients are cold, it will take more. Mix all ingredients together and refrigerate overnight before serving. Serves 8-10.

YELLOW SQUASH SALAD

- 1½ pounds yellow squash
- 1 red onion, grated
- 1 green pepper chopped
- salted water
- 1 (2 ounce) jar sliced pimento

Dressing

- 1 cup sugar
- 1 teaspoon mustard seed
- 1 cup vinegar
- cracked pepper

Slice squash thinly. Soak onion and green pepper in salt water for 2 hours. Pour off water and mix with squash. Add pimento. For dressing, bring sugar, vinegar and mustard seed to boil. Cool. Pour over squash and refrigerate 8 hours. Drain. Add cracked pepper. Serves 6.

SALADS

℞ MARINATED ANTIPASTO

1½ cups wine vinegar	1 clove garlic
¼ cup sugar	2 cups cauliflower sprigs
1 cup olive oil	1½ cups carrot sticks
½ teaspoon tarragon	1 cup green pepper strips
½ teaspoon oregano	¾ cup red onion slices
½ teaspoon salt	1 cup black olives
½ teaspoon lemon pepper	

Heat vinegar and sugar. Add oil and spices. Place vegetables in marinade at room temperature for 2 hours and then in refrigerator overnight. Drain. Dress with black olives. Serves 8-10.

HOLIDAY CRANBERRY SALAD

2 (3 ounce) packages cream cheese	1 cup crushed pineapple
2 tablespoons mayonnaise	½ cup chopped nuts
2 tablespoons sugar	1 cup whipping cream, whipped
1 cup whole canned cranberry sauce	½ cup confectioner's sugar
	1 teaspoon vanilla

Soften cream cheese. Blend with mayonnaise and sugar. Add cranberry, pineapple and nuts. Fold in cream which has been whipped with confectioner's sugar. Add vanilla. Pour in 9 x 13 container and freeze 6 hours. Cut into squares. Serves 6-8 people. Triple recipe for 3 quart container. Keeps in freezer. Seal well. This dish does not stay around long.

Beautiful. May be served as a salad or a dessert.

SALADS

℞ MARINATED CARROTS (COPPER PENNIES)

2 pounds carrots, sliced into rounds
1 small green pepper, chopped
1 small onion, chopped
1 (10½ ounce) can tomato soup (1¼ cups)
½ cup salad oil
1 cup sugar
¾ cup vinegar
1 teaspoon prepared dry mustard
1 teaspoon Worcestershire sauce

Cook carrots in salt water until *just* tender. Do not overcook. Make marinade of remaining ingredients. Place carrots in the marinade for 3-4 days before serving. Carrots may be served as a cold vegetable or salad. Excellent with all meats. Serves 10-12. Keeps 2-3 weeks in refrigerator. The marinade makes an excellent French salad dressing.

Intern said, "Dr. Hill, I really liked the salad. What was it?" Reply, "Carrots." Intern, "I hate carrots. You're just like my mother. You are always finding ways to make me eat carrots. May I have the recipe?"

COLORFUL RICE SALAD

1 (10 ounce) package frozen English peas
3 cups cooked rice
1 (4 ounce) jar diced pimento
1 cup diced cooked ham
6 green onions, chopped
4 hard boiled eggs, chopped
¾ cup sliced pimento-stuffed green olives
½ cup chopped celery
⅓ cup sweet pickle relish
2 cups shredded cheddar cheese
½ teaspoon pepper
¼ cup salad dressing or mayonnaise
lettuce leaves
cherry tomatoes

Cook peas according to package directions; drain and cool. Combine peas with next 10 ingredients; stir well. Add salad dressing, tossing until well mixed. Chill thoroughly. Correct seasoning with salt and pepper. Serve on lettuce leaves and garnish with cherry tomatoes. 6 to 8 servings.

SALADS

℞

ITALIAN VEGETABLE SALAD

- 2 (10 ounce) packages frozen broccoli spears
- 1 (8 ounce) can sliced water chestnuts, drained
- 1 (6 ounce) can ripe olives, drained and sliced
- ½ pound fresh mushrooms, sliced
- 1 pint cherry tomatoes, halved
- 1 medium green pepper, thinly sliced
- 1 medium onion, coarsely chopped
- 2 cups sliced celery
- 1 (8 ounce) bottle commercial Italian salad dressing

Cook broccoli according to package directions, omitting salt; drain well. Cut spears in half crosswise. Combine with remaining ingredients, tossing gently. Cover and chill at least 4 hours before serving. Makes 12 servings.

BROCCOLI AND WHITE BEAN SALAD

- 1 cup dried Great Northern or white beans
- 2 cups chicken broth
- ½ cup Fresh Lemon Dressing (See Index)
- ½ cup thinly sliced red onion
- 1 pound broccoli
- salt and pepper
- juice of ½ lemon

Soak beans overnight. Add chicken broth and bring to boil. Simmer for 1¼ hours. Drain beans. Toss with Lemon Dressing, and red onion. Place broccoli flowerets into salted, boiling water for 3-4 minutes. Drain and place under cold water. Dry well. Add broccoli to the beans and toss. Season with pepper, salt and lemon juice. Serves 8.

SALADS

TOMATOES CAMILLE

- 4 tomatoes, cut
- ½ cup white wine vinegar
- ½ cup sesame oil
- ½ teaspoon cracked pepper
- ¼ teaspoon salt
- ⅛ teaspoon garlic powder
- 1 teaspoon Creole mustard
- 1 medium onion, chopped fine

Cut tomatoes to even thickness. Mix vinegar, oil, pepper, salt, garlic powder, and mustard and pour over tomatoes. Add chopped onion. Refrigerate at least 2 hours before serving. Sprinkle with cracked pepper. Serve very cold. Serves 8.

Date: *Today*

For Those Who Enjoy Eating
Patient's name

℞: SAUCES AND DRESSINGS

Dispense: *Small Measures*

Sig: *Use Small Serving Spoons*

Refill: yes _____
      no ✓

Reba Michele Hill M.D.

Physician
DEA Number AH 0000000

SAUCES & DRESSINGS

SPINACH PESTO

4 cups washed, torn spinach leaves, stems removed	½ teaspoon diced basil
	¼ cup olive oil
	⅓ cup grated Parmesan cheese
3 garlic cloves, halved	
3 tablespoons pine nuts	⅛ teaspoon salt

Place spinach, garlic, pine nuts, basil, oil in blender and mix well. Add cheese and salt. Whirl until smooth.

PISTOU SAUCE

1 cup olive oil	1 teaspoon chives
1½ tablespoons chopped basil	½ teaspoon garlic powder
2 tablespoons chopped parsley	juice of 1 lemon
	1½ teaspoons salt
1 teaspoon tarragon	1 teaspoon pepper
1 teaspoon chervil	

Blend all ingredients together in food processor and pour over fish or pasta. Yields 1 cup.

STIR FRY SAUCE

3 tablespoons brown sugar	½ cup soy sauce
	½ cup sherry
⅓ cup cornstarch	¼ teaspoon Tabasco
2 teaspoons ground ginger	3 tablespoons wine vinegar
4 garlic cloves, crushed	2½ cups chicken broth

Combine all ingredients in blender and mix well. Place in jar in refrigerator. May store 10 days to 2 weeks.

SAUCES & DRESSINGS

BÈARNAISE SAUCE

1 cup tarragon vinegar	6 egg yolks
1 tablespoon dried tarragon	1 cup butter
1 slice onion	dash cayenne

Boil vinegar, tarragon and onion until liquid is reduced to ⅓ cup. Strain liquid into top of double boiler over hot water. Add egg yolks and whip. Melt butter and add dash cayenne. Pour slowly into egg mixture, beating constantly. Cook until thickened. Place pan in cold water. Keep at room temperature until served. Makes ½ cup.

HORSERADISH SAUCE

1 cup mayonnaise	4 tablespoons undrained horseradish
½ cup sour cream	
¼ teaspoon dry mustard	½ teaspoon garlic powder

Combine and refrigerate. Good on cold meats, fish, or beef. Makes 1½ cups.

SWEET MUSTARD SAUCE

½ cup prepared mustard (Grey Poupon)	¼ cup Madeira or cream sherry
2 tablespoons vinegar	1 cup yogurt or mayonnaise
3 tablespoons sugar	
¼ teaspoon salt	

Combine all ingredients and fold into mayonnaise. Keeps in refrigerator for 2 weeks. Makes 1¾ cups. Good over salad greens or with poached fish or beef.

SAUCES & DRESSINGS

ASPARAGUS SAUCE

1 can undiluted cream of asparagus soup	1-2 teaspoon lemon juice
½ cup milk	$1/16$ teaspoon ground marjoram
1 tablespoon minced onion	salt and pepper to taste
1 tablespoon pimento	⅓ cup toasted walnuts, chopped

Blend all ingredients except walnuts and cook at low temperature for 10-15 minutes. Add toasted walnuts. Makes 2⅓ cups. Good over fresh asparagus, green beans or cauliflower.

AVOCADO SAUCE

1 ripe avocado	¼ teaspoon salt
¼ cup sour cream	¼ teaspoon dried cilantro
¼ cup milk	⅛ teaspoon Tabasco sauce
1 teaspoon minced onion	2-3 tablespoons lemon juice
⅛ teaspoon garlic powder	

Mash avocado and add rest of ingredients. May serve as dip with tortilla chips or sauce over chicken, tostados or tacos. Makes ⅔ cup.

CHEESE WINE SAUCE

1 cup milk	4 ounces Swiss cheese, grated
2 teaspoons flour	1 ounce vermouth
2 teaspoons margarine salt and pepper	

Make white sauce with milk, flour and margarine. Add cheese, salt and pepper. Cook until cheese melts and sauce is thickened. Add vermouth. Makes 1½ cups. Good on stuffed seafood, mushrooms or over vegetables.

SAUCES & DRESSINGS

SHERRY MUSTARD SAUCE

⅓ pound fresh mushrooms, sliced	¼ cup dry sherry
¼ cup chopped onions	2 teaspoons Dijon style mustard
4 tablespoons margarine	½ cup sour cream
	salt and pepper

Sauté mushrooms and onions in margarine. Add sherry and mustard. Stir in sour cream. Season with salt and pepper. This may be served over lamb chops, kidneys or pork chops. Serves 4.

ITALIAN SPAGHETTI SAUCE

2 (15 ounce) cans tomato sauce	1 bay leaf
1 (10½ ounce) can chicken bouillon (1¼ cups)	1 (6 ounce) can tomato paste
1 small onion, minced	1 (4 ounce) can sliced mushrooms or fresh mushrooms
3 whole cloves	fresh Parmesan cheese, grated
garlic powder	

Simmer tomato sauce, chicken bouillon, onion, cloves, garlic and bay leaf until sauce begins to thicken (about 1 hour). Then add tomato paste. Simmer until sauce thickens (about 3 hours). Do not cook too fast or sauce will burn and taste bitter. Add mushrooms and pour sauce over spaghetti. Sprinkle with fresh grated Parmesan cheese. Recipe for sauce may be doubled, tripled, etc. for amount needed.

SAUCES & DRESSINGS

REVEREND NOTAR'S QUICK TOMATO SAUCE

1 (#2) can peeled tomatoes, chopped (2½ cups)	1 tablespoon olive oil salt and pepper 1 garlic clove, minced

Combine ingredients and cook over moderate heat for 20 minutes. Serve over pasta with fresh Parmesan cheese. This is supposed to taste like fresh tomato sauce and not heavy full flavored spaghetti sauce. Serve with Italian Chicken (see Index).

WHITE SAUCE

	Thin	Medium	Thick
Butter	3 tablespoons	4 tablespoons	6 tablespoons
Flour	2 tablespoons	4 tablespoons	8 tablespoons
Salt	1 teaspoon	1 teaspoon	1 teaspoon
Pepper	¼ teaspoon	¼ teaspoon	¼ teaspoon
Milk	2 cups	2 cups	2 cups

Melt butter and stir in flour, salt and pepper. Remove from heat and pour in milk. Cook until sauce is the right consistency. Makes 2 cups.

PAT'S GREEK TOMATO SALSA

1 large onion, chopped	1 large can water
⅓ cup olive oil	salt and pepper
3 cloves garlic, chopped	3 tablespoons oregano
1 large can tomatoes, mashed	3 whole allspice
	1 whole clove

Sauté onions in oil. Add remaining ingredients and simmer for 20 minutes. Good with lamb or roast beef. Makes 1½ cups.

SAUCES & DRESSINGS

℞

GOLDEN YOGURT SAUCE

2	small onions, thinly sliced crosswise, in rings	2	tablespoons prepared mustard
¼	cup butter	1	teaspoon prepared horseradish
3	tablespoons flour	1	cup plain yogurt
½	teaspoon salt	⅔	cup pitted ripe olives, sliced
1¼	cups apple juice		
2	tablespoons honey		

Sauté onions in butter. Sprinkle flour and salt over onions. Gradually add apple juice and cook, stirring constantly until mixture is smooth and thickened. Stir in honey, mustard and horseradish and cook 5 minutes. Fold in yogurt and olives. Yield 3 cups. Good over green vegetables.

CUCUMBER SAUCE FOR FISH

½	cup mayonnaise or salad dressing	2	teaspoon lemon juice
½	cup cucumber, peeled and coarsely chopped	¼	teaspoon dried dill weed
1	teaspoon lemon peel, grated		salt and pepper

Combine mayonnaise, cucumber, lemon peel, juice and dill weed. Salt and pepper to taste. Serve over fried, broiled or poached fish. Makes about 1 cup.

SAUCES & DRESSINGS

DOUBLE CHEESE SAUCE

- 2 tablespoons margarine, melted
- 2 tablespoons flour
- ¼ teaspoon salt
- dash pepper
- 1¼ cups milk
- 2 ounces sharp natural cheddar cheese, shredded
- 2 ounces Swiss cheese, shredded

To melted margarine, add flour, salt and pepper and cook until bubbly. Add milk and cook until thickened. Add cheeses and stir until melted. Makes 1½ cups. Serve over green vegetables.

FRESH SALSA

- 4 small tomatoes, peeled and chopped
- ½ cup finely chopped onion
- 3-4 fresh jalapeño peppers
- 2 teaspoon olive oil
- 1 teaspoon vinegar
- 1 teaspoon lime juice
- ½ teaspoon dried oregano
- ½ teaspoon salt
- ¼ teaspoon dried cilantro

Combine all ingredients and let stand at room temperature at least 2 hours. Makes 2 cups. Good with Mexican food.

CHICKEN MARINADE

- 1 cup sherry
- ½ cup oil
- 1 large onion, chopped
- 1 tablespoon Worcestershire sauce
- 1 tablespoon dry mustard or prepared mustard
- 1 teaspoon rosemary
- 1 teaspoon marjoram
- 1 teaspoon oregano
- ½ teaspoon black pepper
- 1 teaspoon garlic powder

Mix all ingredients together. Place chicken in marinade and refrigerate overnight. Excellent for grilled chicken.

SAUCES & DRESSINGS

℞

BASTING SAUCE FOR FISH OR GAME

¾ cup butter	1 tablespoon Durkee's sauce
juice of 1 lemon	3 tablespoons dry white wine or sherry
6 dashes Tabasco	
3 dashes celery salt	½ teaspoon Liquid Smoke (optional)
1 tablespoon Worcestershire sauce	

Mix all ingredients and simmer over low heat until well blended. Use for basting fish, game or chicken while broiling. Makes 1 cup.

TUJAQUE'S BOILED BEEF SAUCE

1 cup ketchup	½ cup horseradish
½ cup Creole mustard	

Mix all ingredients together and warm before serving with beef or pork. This is very spicy. Makes 2 cups.

RED SAUCE
(MILDER VERSION)

1 (4 ounce) can tomato sauce	1 teaspoon Worcestershire sauce
3 teaspoons horseradish	juice from ½ lemon

Mix ingredients and cook just long enough to warm.

MY RENDITION OF TIGER HORSERADISH SAUCE

8 ounces sour cream	1 (6 ounce) jar Tulkoff's Hot Horseradish
8 ounces yogurt mayonnaise	
⅛-¼ teaspoon garlic powder	

Mix all ingredients together.

SAUCES & DRESSINGS

ARNAUD LIKE RÈMOULADE SAUCE

- ½ cup vinegar
- 1 (6 ounce) jar Zatarian prepared mustard
- ⅓ (1 ounce) can paprika
- salt and pepper
- 1 ounce Worcestershire sauce
- ⅓ bottle horseradish
- 10 ounces olive oil
- 1 bunch green onions, chopped
- ⅓ bunch parsley, chopped

Combine vinegar, mustard, paprika, salt, pepper, Worcestershire, and horseradish. Add olive oil and beat vigorously. Do not add green onions and parsley until ready to use. Makes 1 quart.

BARBEQUE SAUCE

- ¼ cup vinegar
- ½ cup water
- 2 tablespoons sugar
- 1 tablespoon prepared mustard
- ½ teaspoon pepper
- 1½ teaspoons salt
- ¼ teaspoon cayenne pepper
- 1 thick slice lemon
- 1 slice onion
- ½ cup ketchup
- 2 tablespoons Worcestershire sauce
- 1½ teaspoons Liquid Smoke

Mix all ingredients except last 3. Simmer 20 minutes. Add remaining ingredients and bring to boil. Makes 1¾ cups.

MORNAY SAUCE

- 2 tablespoons margarine
- 2 tablespoons flour
- 1 cup milk
- salt
- 1 cup grated cheese (½ Gruyère and ½ Parmesan)

Melt margarine and add flour. Add milk and mix well. Add cheese and salt. Cook until thickened. Makes 1½ cups.

SAUCES & DRESSINGS

ANGEL SALAD DRESSING

1 cup mayonnaise
½ cup whipping cream
¼ cup raspberry preserves

Combine all ingredients and serve over fruit salad. Yields 1½ cups.

HOT FRENCH DRESSING

1 cup French dressing
2 hard boiled eggs, chopped
1 tablespoon minced parsley
1 tablespoon minced celery leaves
1 tablespoon minced green onion
1 teaspoon Dijon-style mustard
½ teaspoon Worcestershire sauce

Combine all ingredients and bring to a boil. Pour over asparagus, hot potato salad or boiled beef. Makes 1½ cups.

MANGO CHUTNEY SALAD DRESSING

17 ounces mango chutney
2 teaspoons minced garlic
1½ tablespoons stone ground mustard
1 cup red wine vinegar
1 cup vegetable oil
raisins (optional)

Chop chutney in blender or food processor. Blend in garlic, mustard and vinegar. Add oil. Let stand overnight. Serve dressing over spinach. Makes 3 cups.

SAUCES & DRESSINGS

SIMPLE SALAD DRESSING

- ½ cup Hunza sesame or blended oil
- ½ cup Spice Islands white wine vinegar
- ½ teaspoon champagne, Creole, or Grey Poupon mustard
- ¼ teaspoon salt cracked pepper
- ¼ teaspoon garlic powder

Combine all ingredients and mix well. Let stand at room temperature 1 hour to blend flavors. Makes 1 cup.

POPPYSEED COLESLAW DRESSING

- 1 small onion, finely chopped
- ⅓ cup white vinegar
- ¼ cup sugar
- ¼ cup honey
- 1 teaspoon dry mustard
- 1 teaspoon salt
- 3 teaspoons poppyseeds
- 1 cup vegetable oil

Blend onion, vinegar, sugar, honey, seasonings and poppyseeds. Slowly pour in oil. Pour over shredded cabbage and toss lightly. Makes 2 cups. Good also on fruit.

FRESH LEMON DRESSING

- 3 tablespoons fresh lemon juice
- 6 tablespoons salad oil
- ½ teaspoon salt
- ⅛ teaspoon pepper
- ⅛ teaspoon dry mustard
- 2 tablespoons chopped parsley
- ½ clove garlic, bruised

Mix all ingredients in blender. Let stand at room temperature about 1 hour. Remove garlic before serving. Makes about ⅔ cups. Good on salads or to marinate meat.

SAUCES & DRESSINGS

℞

TANGY FRENCH DRESSING

½ cup salad oil
2 tablespoons fresh lemon or lime juice
2 tablespoons vinegar
1 teaspoon sugar
1 teaspoon grated fresh lemon or lime rind
½ teaspoon salt
½ teaspoon mustard

Combine all ingredients in blender and mix well. Makes ¾ cup. Serve over greens or fresh vegetables.

CHILI SALAD DRESSING

1 clove garlic, quartered
½ teaspoon salt
¼ teaspoon pepper
1 teaspoon chili powder
½ cup olive or salad oil
3 tablespoons cider vinegar
3 tablespoons fresh lemon juice

Combine all ingredients. Let stand 1 hour. Remove garlic, cover and refrigerate. Makes ¾ cup. Serve over mixed greens and tomatoes.

HOT BACON DRESSING

4 slices bacon, diced
½ cup finely chopped onion
2 tablespoons brown sugar
1 tablespoon flour
¼ teaspoon dry mustard
1 tablespoon lemon juice
¾ cup water
¼ cup mayonnaise

Fry bacon until crisp. Remove and drain. Sauté onion in bacon grease. Stir in brown sugar, flour, dry mustard, lemon juice and water. Cook until thickened. Blend in mayonnaise until mixture is smooth. Add reserved bacon; stir. Makes 1¼ cups. Serve over spinach leaves.

Date: *Today*

For Those Who Enjoy Eating
Patient's name

℞: **SEAFOODS**

Dispense: *Moderate Helpings*

Sig: *Eat Weekly*

Refill: yes ✔
       no ____

[signature]
Physician
DEA Number AH 0000000

SEAFOODS

SHRIMP, TOMATOES, WINE AND FETA CHEESE

¼	cup finely chopped onion	½	teaspoon crushed oregano
6	tablespoons olive oil	1	teaspoon salt
1½	pounds canned tomatoes, drained, finely chopped		pepper
		1½	pounds shrimp, peeled but with tails on
½	cup dry white wine	2	ounces Feta cheese, cut in cubes
2	tablespoons mint, finely chopped		

Sauté onions in oil. Stir in tomatoes, wine, mint, oregano, salt and pepper. Bring to boil and cook until it thickens. Add shrimp. Cook until shrimp are pink. Stir in Feta cheese and heat until cheese melts. Serve over Garlic Brown Rice (See Index). Serves 6.

SHRIMP CREOLE WITH EGGPLANT AND BROWN GARLIC RICE

2	cups coarsely chopped onion	1	tablespoon grated lemon rind
1	cup chopped green pepper	3	whole cloves
		1	bay leaf
1	cup coarsely chopped celery	½	teaspoon thyme
		¼	teaspoon honey
½	cup margarine, divided	½	cup water
		1	small eggplant with skin left on, diced
2	cloves garlic, minced		
4	large tomatoes, peeled and chopped	¼	cup olive oil
		½	teaspoon salt
½	cup tomato sauce	2	pounds raw shrimp
½	teaspoon pepper	3	tablespoons parsley

Cook onion, green pepper and celery in 3 tablespoons margarine. Add garlic and tomatoes and bring to a boil. Add tomato sauce, pepper, lemon rind, cloves, bay leaf, thyme, honey and water. Simmer 15-20 minutes. Sauté eggplant in separate skillet in olive oil until brown.

SEAFOODS

℞

Season with salt. Combine with tomato sauce mixture and add shrimp. Cook until shrimp are pink. Serve over Garlic Brown Rice (See Index). Sprinkle with parsley. Serves 6.

SHRIMP FIORENTINA

2	pounds shrimp, uncooked, shelled	4	tablespoons olive oil
3	cups dry white wine	¼	cup white wine vinegar
4	bay leaves	¼	cup olive oil
1	teaspoon thyme	1	medium onion, chopped
¼	cup chopped green onions	1	clove garlic, chopped
1	teaspoon chopped parsley	4	medium tomatoes, peeled and chopped
1	teaspoon salt	½	cup fresh basil leaves, chopped, or ⅛ cup dried basil
½	teaspoon black pepper corns		

Make stock of wine, bay leaves, thyme, green onion, parsley, salt and pepper corns. Boil for 10 minutes. Add shrimp and take off heat. Leave in broth until shrimp become pink. Remove shrimp. Sprinkle shrimp with vinegar and oil. Sauté onion, garlic and tomatoes in ¼ cup olive oil until just soft. Add basil and remove from heat. Serve shrimp covered with sauce. This dish may be served warm or cold. Sauce good over warm pasta. Serves 6.

SEAFOODS

SHRIMP BROCHETTES

- ⅔ cup bread crumbs
- ¼ teaspoon garlic powder
- 2 teaspoons chopped parsley
- ¾ teaspoon salt
- ground pepper
- 1½ pounds medium shrimp
- 3½ tablespoons olive oil
- 3½ tablespoons vegetable oil
- lemon wedges

Mix bread crumbs, garlic powder, parsley, salt and pepper. Put shrimp in just enough oil to coat and then cover with bread crumb mixture. Mix so that shrimp are well coated. Marinate overnight. Put shrimp on skewers and cook 2 minutes on one side and 3 minutes on the other under hot broiler. Garnish with lemon. Serves 6.

BARBECUED SHRIMP IN WINE

- 2 pounds uncooked shrimp, peeled and deveined
- 1 cup olive oil
- 1 teaspoon salt
- 3 tablespoons parsley, chopped
- 1 tablespoon basil
- 2 cloves garlic
- 1 tablespoon tomato sauce or chili sauce
- 1 teaspoon ground pepper
- 1 tablespoon vinegar
- ½ cup white wine

Peel and devein shrimp but leave tail on. Combine remaining ingredients to make marinade. Put shrimp in marinade and leave for several hours or overnight. Bake at 400° for 5-8 minutes. Serve with French bread and extra sauce. Serves 6-8.

SEAFOODS

BARBECUED SHRIMP

- 8 pounds large unpeeled shrimp
- ½ pound butter
- 1 cup olive oil
- 1 (8 ounce) bottle chili sauce
- 3 tablespoons Worcestershire sauce
- 2 lemons, sliced
- 4 cloves garlic
- 3 tablespoons lemon juice
- 1 tablespoon parsley, chopped
- 2 teaspoons paprika
- 2 teaspoons oregano
- 2 teaspoons red pepper
- 1 teaspoon liquid pepper sauce
- 3 tablespoons Liquid Smoke

Combine all ingredients except shrimp to make marinade. Marinate shrimp in sauce for several hours in the refrigerator. Bake at 350° for 30 minutes. Serve in bowl with sauce and French bread to dip. Unused sauce keeps well and can be used on other dishes. Serves 25.

SHRIMP ETOUFFEE

- 2 pounds raw shrimp, peeled and deveined
- 1 teaspoon Tony Chachere's Creole Seasoning
- 1 onion, chopped
- 3 cups water
- 1 bay leaf
- 1 tablespoon flour
- 2 tablespoons margarine
- 1 teaspoon Pickapeppa Sauce
- ¼ teaspoon garlic powder

Season shrimp with creole seasoning. Mince onion in blender with 3 cups of water. Pour onion and water into pot and add shrimp shells and bay leaf to make stock. Strain. Combine flour and margarine. Sauté shrimp in margarine/flour mixture until pink. Combine shrimp, stock, Pickapeppa Sauce, garlic and cook until thickened. Serve over rice. Serves 6. If Tony Chachere's Creole Seasoning not available, use Creole Seasoning.

SEAFOODS

CREOLE SEASONING

- ⅓ cup plus 1 tablespoon salt
- ⅓ cup plus 1 tablespoon paprika
- ¹⁄₁₆ cup cayenne pepper
- ¼ cup black pepper
- ⅛ cup lemon pepper
- ¼ cup granulated garlic
- 3 tablespoons granulated onion
- 2 tablespoons thyme
- 1 tablespoon chili powder

Combine all ingredients and store in tightly sealed glass jar. Makes 1½ cups. Good to use on meats, fish, poultry. Stores indefinitely.

GUTSEY SHRIMP

Marinade

- 1 pound large raw shrimp, shelled and deveined
- juice of ½ lemon
- 1 bay leaf
- salt and pepper

Stock

- 1½-2 cups water
- 1 bay leaf
- 1 slice onion
- ⅛ teaspoon oregano
- ⅛ teaspoon thyme
- salt and pepper

- 1 onion, sliced and separated into rings
- 1 teaspoon garlic powder
- 1 teaspoon parsley, chopped fine
- 2 tablespoons olive oil
- 1 tablespoon margarine
- ⅓ cup dry white wine
- 1 large tomato, peeled, seeded and chopped
- ¼ cup flour
- 3 tablespoons olive oil

Marinate shrimp in lemon juice, bay leaf, salt and pepper for 1 hour. Make stock of shrimp shells, using water, bay leaf, onion slice, oregano, thyme, salt and pepper. Cook onion rings, garlic powder and parsley in oil and margarine. Add wine and simmer until almost evaporated. Add tomatoes and ½ cup stock. Dredge shrimp in flour

SEAFOODS

and brown in oil. Add to sauce and simmer 15-20 minutes. Serve over cooked vermicelli. Serves 4.

SPANISH SHRIMP CASSEROLE

¾ cup uncooked rice	½ cup chopped green onion
½ cup onion, separated into rings	1 (6 ounce) can tomato paste (¾ cup)
1½ pounds raw shrimp, shelled and deveined	⅛ teaspoon garlic powder to taste
12 tablespoons margarine, divided	juice of large lemon
½ cup sherry, divided	½ pound cheddar cheese, grated
½ cup Rotel tomatoes (tomatoes with chilies) (1¼ cups)	

Cook rice according to directions on box. Add raw onion to rice. In pan, lay shrimp in single layer on rice. Combine 8 tablespoons melted margarine with ¼ cup sherry and pour over rice/shrimp mixture. Place under broiler and barely cook until shrimp are pink. Puree tomatoes in blender. Sauté green onions in remaining butter. Combine tomatoes, green onion, tomato paste, garlic powder, rest of sherry and lemon juice and cook 5 minutes. Pour over shrimp and rice. Top with cheese and bake covered at 350° until cheese melts. Serves 6.

SEAFOODS

SHRIMP VERACRUZ

1	pound medium size shrimp	2	medium tomatoes, chopped
3	tablespoons oil, divided	12	pimento stuffed olives
1	large green pepper, cut in 1½ inch strips	1½	teaspoons capers
		¼	teaspoon cumin
		1	bay leaf
1	small onion, chopped	1	teaspoon salt
1	(4 ounce) can green chilies	½	teaspoon sugar
			lime juice
1	(16 ounce) jar taco sauce		

In 2 tablespoons oil, sauté green pepper and onion. Add green chilies, taco sauce, tomatoes, olives, capers, cumin, bay leaf, salt and sugar. Simmer 10 minutes. Cook shrimp in remaining oil until they turn pink. Sprinkle with lime juice. Add to sauce. Serve over rice. Serves 4.

CRANBERRY BUTTERFLY SHRIMP

2	pounds raw shrimp, shelled and deveined	⅓	cup all purpose flour
½	cup margarine	1	cup cranberry juice cocktail
1	pound small mushroom caps	1	(10¾ ounce) can chicken broth (1¼ cups)
1	clove garlic		salt and pepper
1	small onion, minced		
½	cup cranberry orange relish		

Melt margarine and cook mushrooms, garlic and onion for 5 minutes. Stir in relish, flour, cranberry juice and chicken broth. Cook until sauce thickens. Add shrimp and cook until they turn pink. Season with salt and pepper. Serve over rice. Serves 8.

SEAFOODS

BAKED OYSTERS

2	tablespoons butter	2	dozen fresh oysters
1	cup fresh bread crumbs	3	tablespoons grated Parmesan cheese
1	clove garlic, finely chopped	2	tablespoons margarine or butter
2	tablespoons finely chopped fresh parsley		

Sauté ½ of the bread crumbs and garlic in butter for 2-3 minutes. Stir in chopped parsley. Spread bread mixture in buttered 2 quart baking dish. Place oysters in one layer on crumbs. Mix the rest of the crumbs with cheese and spread on top of oysters. Dot with butter. Bake for 12-15 minutes at 450° or until crumbs are golden. Serve immediately. Serves 4-6.

OYSTER LOAF

	whole loaf French or Italian bread	salt and pepper
36	oysters, drained	butter
	flour	lemon juice

Cut a horizontal slice off top of loaf and reserve. Hollow out center of bread to make a large well. Dredge oysters in flour seasoned with salt and pepper. Fry in butter and place fried oysters in hollow of bread. Season with lemon juice. Cover immediately with horizontal slice of bread. Put in oven and warm bread. The juice from the oysters permeates the bread. Serve with red sauce or tartar sauce.

SEAFOODS

OYSTERS IN A PASTRY CUP

2	dozen shucked oysters, reserve liquid		water
		2	tablespoons cornstarch
½	cup chopped green onions	1	tablespoon oil
			salt and pepper
¼	cup parsley		garlic powder
2	tablespoons margarine	1	cup sherry

Sauté onions and parsley in margarine. Combine liquid from oysters and water to make 1½ cups. Put onion, parsley and juice in blender or food processor and puree. Stir cornstarch into mixture. In saucepan, cook oysters in oil until edges curl. Add onion/parsley mixture, salt, pepper and garlic powder to oysters. Cook until mixture thickens. Stir in sherry and cook 5 minutes longer. Serve over pastry shells. Serves 6.

OYSTERS DUNBAR

¼	pound margarine	1	tablespoon poultry seasoning
1	large onion, finely chopped	1	teaspoon salt
1	bunch green onions, chopped	½	teaspoon black pepper
		½	cup sherry
1	clove of garlic	1	(4 ounce) can sliced mushrooms, finely chopped
1	(14 ounce) can artichoke hearts, sliced (1¾ cups)		
		1	small jar pimentos, chopped
3	pints oysters		
2	(10½ ounce) cans mushroom soup (1¼ cups)	1	cup seasoned Italian bread crumbs
¾	cups parsley		
3	tablespoons Worcestershire sauce		

SEAFOODS

℞

Melt margarine and sauté onion, green onions and garlic. Add artichoke hearts and cook for 10 minutes. Strain oysters, reserve the liquid. Cut oysters into quarters if large and combine with oyster liquid and all ingredients except pimentos and bread crumbs and simmer for 15 minutes. Add bread crumbs and pimento. May be used as a dip or served in a pastry shell. Serves 8-10.

COQUILLE CRAB ARTICHOKE

¼	cup chopped green pepper	¼	teaspoon salt
¼	cup chopped green onions		cayenne
		1	teaspoon English mustard
4	artichoke hearts, drained and sliced	¾	pound crabmeat
		1	slice pimento, chopped
4	tablespoons margarine		chopped parsley
¼	cup dry white wine		herb seasoned bread crumbs
1	cup sliced mushrooms sautéed in margarine		butter, melted

Sauté green pepper, green onions and artichokes in margarine. Add wine and mushrooms. Stir in salt, cayenne, mustard and crabmeat. Fold in pimento and parsley. Put in ramekins and sprinkle with bread crumbs and butter. Bake at 375° for 15 minutes. Serves 6.

SEAFOODS

DON'S CRABMEAT CASSEROLE
LAFAYETTE, LOUISIANA

2	cups finely chopped onions	2	teaspoons cornstarch
⅓	cup finely chopped celery	2	cups cornflakes
		2	tablespoons mayonnaise
¼	pound margarine	1	pound crabmeat
⅛	teaspoon sage	1	cup Ritz crackers, crumbled
⅛	teaspoon thyme		
⅛	teaspoon nutmeg		margarine
½	cup evaporated milk		

Sauté onions and celery in margarine. Add sage, thyme, nutmeg, evaporated milk and cornstarch. Toast cornflakes, crumble and combine with onions/celery mixture. Add mayonnaise and crabmeat and mix. Put in casserole and crumble Ritz crackers on top. Dot with margarine and bake for 20-25 minutes at 375°. Serves 6. Serve with tartar sauce.

NEW ORLEANS STUFFED BELL PEPPER

8	medium sized bell peppers	1	cup cooked rice
		1	(5 ounce) can crabmeat or lobster meat
½	cup chopped celery		salt and pepper
½	cup chopped onions		cayenne pepper
¼	pound margarine		
1	teaspoon tomato paste	½	cup bread crumbs
½	pound raw shrimp, peeled and deveined		margarine

Cut off tops and remove centers from bell peppers. Put peppers into cold water and bring to boil for 10 minutes. Drain and set aside. Mince tops of green peppers. Sauté celery, onions and minced peppers in margarine until just tender. Add tomato paste and shrimp. Cook about 6 minutes. Add rice, crabmeat and seasoning. Mix well. Fill peppers with stuffing. Top with bread crumbs and dot with margarine. Bake at 350° for 15 minutes. Serve with Brown Gravy. Serves 8.

SEAFOODS

℞

Brown Gravy

- 1½ tablespoons margarine
- 1 tablespoon flour
- 1 cup chicken broth
- 2 tablespoons white wine
- ⅛ teaspoon garlic powder
- salt and pepper

Cook margarine and flour until brown roux forms. Add chicken broth and white wine. Cook until thickened. Season with garlic powder, salt and pepper.

CRABMEAT MORNAY

- ¼ pound margarine
- 1 small bunch green onions, chopped
- ½ cup finely chopped parsley
- ½ pound fresh mushrooms, sliced
- 2 tablespoons flour
- 1 pint breakfast cream
- ½ pound Swiss cheese, grated
- 1 tablespoon sherry
- cayenne to taste
- 1 pound crabmeat

In margarine, sauté onion, parsley and mushrooms. Blend in flour, cream, cheese and cook until cheese is melted. Add wine, cayenne and crabmeat. Serve in chafing dish with melba toast or in a pastry cup. Serves 12 or more as dip or 6 as a main course.

Everyone loves Crabmeat Mornay. It is always a winner.

SEAFOODS

CRABMEAT AU GRATIN

- 1 rib celery, finely chopped
- 1 onion, finely chopped
- ¼ pound margarine
- ½ cup flour
- 1 cup evaporated milk (13 ounces)
- 2 egg yolks
- ½ teaspoon salt
- ⅛ teaspoon cayenne
- dash black pepper
- dash nutmeg
- 1 pound crabmeat
- ¾ pound cheddar cheese grated and divided

Sauté celery and onion in margarine. Blend in flour. Pour in milk, stirring constantly. Cool. Add egg yolk, salt, cayenne, black pepper and nutmeg. Cook 5 minutes. Mix with crabmeat and ½ pound grated cheese and place in greased casserole. Sprinkle top with ¼ pound of cheese. Bake at 375° for 10-15 minutes. Serves 6 as a main course.

This can be put into small scallop seashells and served as an appetizer. Serves 8-12.

MUSHROOMS STUFFED WITH CRABMEAT

- 2 teaspoons margarine
- 2 teaspoons flour
- 1 cup milk
- salt and pepper
- garlic powder
- 1 tablespoon grated Parmesan cheese
- 1 triangle Gruyère cheese, grated
- 2 tablespoons sherry
- ½ pound crabmeat
- 2 shallots, sautéed in margarine
- 8 large mushrooms, sauteed in margarine
- 12 small shrimp, peeled and deveined
- paprika
- parsley, minced
- 1 (8½ ounce) can English peas, drained (1 cup)
- small onions, cooked

SEAFOODS

℞

Make sauce with margarine, flour and milk. Add salt, pepper and garlic powder. Add Parmesan and Gruyère cheese and sherry to sauce. Combine crabmeat, shallots and 2 tablespoons of sauce. Stuff mushrooms with mixture and place in buttered individual casseroles. Cover with remaining sauce. Top each with 3-4 small raw shrimp. Sprinkle with paprika and minced parsley. Bake at 350° for 20 minutes. Garnish side of dish with English peas and small onions. Serves 4.

CRAWFISH ETOUFFEE

1	pound crawfish and fat	½	teaspoon dried thyme
	Tony Chachere's Creole Seasoning	1	tablespoon flour
		2	cups water
			salt and pepper
¼	pound margarine	1	tablespoon paprika
2	cloves garlic	1	tablespoon chopped parsley
1	medium onion		
½	green pepper, chopped	1	tablespoon green onion tops, chopped
1	teaspoon dried basil		

Season crawfish with Tony Chachere's Creole Seasoning. If seasoning is not available, use Creole Seasoning (See Index). Cook garlic, onion, green pepper, basil and thyme in margarine. Add crawfish and flour and cook 2-3 minutes. Add water and cook until thickened. Season with salt, pepper and paprika. Cook 40 minutes. Serve over rice. Sprinkle with chopped parsley and green onions. Serves 4. If crawfish is not available, use shrimp or lobster.

SEAFOODS

℞ SHELLFISH CREPES IN WINE-CHEESE SAUCE

Crepes (see Index)

Stuffing

- 2 tablespoons margarine
- 3 tablespoons minced shallots
- 1 pound fresh crabmeat
- salt and pepper
- dash garlic powder
- ¼ cup vermouth
- ½ pound mushrooms, sliced, sautéed in margarine
- 4 tablespoons grated Swiss cheese

Sauté shallots in margarine. Add crabmeat, salt, pepper and garlic powder. Stir in vermouth and boil to evaporate liquid. Add mushrooms. Makes enough stuffing for 12 crepes.

Place shellfish stuffing at lateral third of crepe. Roll in cigar fashion. Place seam on bottom of lightly buttered casserole. Twelve crepes fit into 3 quart casserole. Cover with Wine-Cheese Sauce. Sprinkle with Swiss cheese. Cook at 425° for 15-20 minutes until bubbly and lightly browned.

Wine-Cheese Sauce

- ⅓ cup dry vermouth
- 2 tablespoons cornstarch
- 1½ cups heavy cream
- ¼ teaspoon salt
- pepper
- ½ cup grated Swiss cheese

Add vermouth to skillet and heat to reduce volume to 1 tablespoon. Remove from heat. Stir in cornstarch, cream, salt and pepper. Cook 2 minutes. Stir in cheese.

SEAFOODS

BAKED SNAPPER SOUTH PACIFIC

4	pounds red snapper	¾	cup milk
¼	cup lemon juice	4	dashes Tabasco
1	teaspoon celery salt	¼	cup white wine
1¼	cups grated cheddar cheese	1	teaspoon nutmeg
1½	cups cashews, chopped	1¼	cups bread crumbs, toasted
1	clove garlic, crushed	5	tablespoons butter
1	tablespoon minced onion		

Sprinkle fish inside and out with lemon juice and celery salt. Chill. Place fish in buttered baking dish. Combine cheese, nuts, garlic and onion. Add just enough milk to make paste and stuff snapper. Combine Tabasco, wine, nutmeg and crumbs. Spread over fish and dot with butter. Bake at 350° for 1½ hours. Serves 8.

RED SNAPPER EXCELSOR
MAXIM'S
HOUSTON, TEXAS

4	red snapper filets	¼	cup parsley, chopped
¼	pound butter	¼	cup red wine
1½	cups sliced mushrooms	2	eggs, beaten
3	artichoke bottoms, canned or bottled, sliced		flour
			salt and pepper to taste
		¼	cup cooking oil
		1	tablespoon lemon juice

In browned butter, cook mushrooms and artichoke bottoms. Add parsley and wine, mix and cook briefly. Dip filets in egg and dredge in flour. Season with salt and pepper. Cook in oil over *high* heat so that coating is crusty. Fish should remain moist. Drain. Place on serving dish. Sprinkle filets with lemon juice and then cover with mushroom and artichoke mixture. Serve at once. Serves 4.

SEAFOODS

RED SNAPPER WITH TOMATO SAUCE, OLIVES AND POTATOES

6	red snapper filets (about 2½-3 pounds)	1	tablespoon fresh lime juice
½	cup flour	½	teaspoon sugar
¼	cup olive oil	⅛	teaspoon ground cinnamon
12	medium tomatoes, peeled, seeded and chopped	⅛	teaspoon ground cloves
1	cup coarsely chopped onion	1	teaspoon salt
		⅛	teaspoon pepper
2	tablespoons margarine	6	medium new potatoes, cooked and peeled (about 2 pounds)
¼	teaspoon minced garlic		
4	canned jalapeño chilies, split, seeded and cut into strips	1	tablespoon finely chopped parsley
¼	cup pimento-stuffed olives		

Salt fish filets and dredge in flour. Fry filets in olive oil until golden brown. Puree tomatoes in blender. Sauté onions in 2 tablespoons margarine. Add pureed tomatoes, garlic, chilies, olives, lime juice, sugar, cinnamon, cloves, salt and pepper and cook for 5 minutes. Place filets in casserole and cover with sauce. Add new potatoes. Sprinkle with parsley. Bake at 350° until warm and bubbly. Serves 6.

DADDY'S LOBSTER NEWBURG

2	cups cooked lobster		salt
½	cup butter, melted		cayenne
⅔	cup cream		nutmeg
4	egg yolks, slightly beaten	2	tablespoons sherry
		2	tablespoons brandy

Sauté lobster in butter about 3 minutes. Add cream. Cool mixture. Stir in egg yolks. Season with salt, cayenne, nutmeg, sherry and brandy. Stir until thickened. Serve with rice or in chafing dish as dip. Serves 6.

SEAFOODS

℞

My dad was paralyzed in an automobile accident when I was 11 years old. One of his favorite pastimes was to think of foods he would like to eat and have me try to create them. This dish was one of his favorites.

YE OLDE COLLEGE INN STUFFING FOR FLOUNDER
HOUSTON, TEXAS

2	large or 4 small flounder	2	tablespoons Worcestershire sauce
½	cup margarine		
4	tablespoons minced celery	2	teaspoons prepared yellow mustard
4	tablespoons minced onion	¼	teaspoon Tabasco salt and pepper
1	tablespoon minced green onion	1	egg
		1	cup bread crumbs
1	clove garlic, minced	1	tablespoon parsley
3	tablespoons flour		
1	cup milk		
1	pound claw crabmeat or shrimp or ½ of each		

In margarine, sauté vegetables and garlic until limp. Blend in flour. Add milk and cook until thickened. Add seafood and seasoning. Blend a little of sauce into egg. Add egg to the rest of sauce while stirring. Add crumbs and parsley. Stuff into fish. Bake at 375° for 25 minutes or until fish flakes. This will stuff 2 large flounder or 4-6 small ones. May be used to stuff shrimp. Serves 6-8.

SEAFOODS

℞

FISH, MUSHROOMS AND ARTICHOKES

- 1 pound fresh mushroom caps, sautéed in butter
- 4 (6 ounce) jars marinated artichokes, sliced
- Fish Stuffing From the Doggie Bag
- Swiss Cheese and Wine Sauce (see Index)
- Pepperidge Farm seasoned croutons with cheese, whirled in food processor

Place mushrooms in buttered casserole. Divide sliced artichokes between mushroom caps and cover with Fish Stuffing From the Doggie Bag. Cover with Swiss Cheese and Wine Sauce. Top with crouton crumbs. Serves 6-8 as a main course. Good as an appetizer; serves 10-12. If serving a large group, the mushrooms may be sliced instead of served whole.

FISH STUFFING — FROM THE DOGGIE BAG

- 4-6 small fish filets, fried
- 2 shallots, sautéed in margarine
- juice of ½ lemon
- ⅛ teaspoon garlic powder
- salt and pepper
- 2-3 dashes Tabasco
- ½ cup mayonnaise
- 1 teaspoon horseradish

Whirl fish, shallots, lemon juice, garlic powder, salt, pepper, Tabasco, mayonnaise and horseradish in blender. Use to stuff mushrooms.

This recipe originated after a visit to a seafood restaurant where one is served all the fresh seafood catch of the day. Being born during the depression, I could not leave all that untouched fish on my plate. Fish stuffing from the doggie bag was born that day.

SEAFOODS

CUBAN FISH

4 cups Italian plum tomatoes drained (break up in blender)	⅛ teaspoon ground cinnamon
1 cup chopped onion	⅛ teaspoon cloves
2 tablespoons margarine	⅛ teaspoon pepper
¼ teaspoon finely chopped garlic	1 teaspoon salt
	½ cup flour
4 (4 ounce) cans mild jalapeño chilies, rinsed, seeded and cut in ⅛ inch strips	6 red snapper filets (about 2½-3 pounds)
	¼ cup olive oil
¼ cup pimento-stuffed olives	6 new potatoes, peeled and cooked in salted water
1 tablespoon lime juice	1 tablespoon chopped fresh parsley
½ teaspoon sugar	

Puree tomatoes in blender. Sauté onion in margarine. Stir in tomatoes, garlic, chilies, olives, lime juice, sugar, cinnamon, cloves, pepper and salt. Cook 5 minutes. Flour filets and fry in olive oil 2 minutes on each side. Place fish on serving platter. Pour sauce over fish and garnish with potatoes and parsley. Serves 6.

SEAFOODS

FISH FILETS LAS BRISAS

8 fresh fish filets
2 tablespoons margarine

Stuffing

4 slices bread, trimmed and diced to make bread cubes
4 tablespoons margarine
3 tablespoons green onions, minced
¼ teaspoon thyme
½ teaspoon tarragon
½ teaspoon salt
¼ teaspoon pepper

Sauce

½ cup sour cream
1 tablespoon flour
1 teaspoon lemon juice
½ teaspoon salt
1 tablespoon tomato puree

Sauté fish in 2 tablespoons margarine and cook until white. Brown bread cubes in 4 tablespoons margarine. Add green onions, thyme, tarragon, salt and pepper. Place 2 tablespoons stuffing on small end of fish filet and roll jelly roll fashion. With edge surface down, place in buttered container and bake 12-15 minutes at 350°. Combine sour cream and flour. Heat. Gradually add lemon juice and salt. Stir in tomato puree. Spoon over fish. Serves 8.

STUFFED EGGPLANT

3 medium eggplants
½ cup margarine
1 cup chopped green onion
½ cup chopped onion
½ cup parsley
1 bell pepper, chopped
1 teaspoon garlic powder
1 tablespoon thyme
2 bay leaves
1 cup wet bread, squeezed dry
1 pound shrimp, chopped
1 pound crabmeat
3 eggs
salt and pepper
margarine
bread crumbs

SEAFOODS

℞

Parboil eggplants in skins. Split in half. Let cool. Scoop out pulp and save skins. Sauté onions, green onions, parsley, bell peppers in margarine with garlic, thyme and bay leaves. Add wet bread, shrimp, crabmeat and eggplant pulp. Mix together and add eggs. Season with salt and pepper. Cook for 5 minutes. Put stuffing into eggplant skins, top with bread crumbs and dot with margarine. Bake at 350° for 10-15 minutes. Serves 6 as main course. You can also buy the tiny young eggplants and stuff them this way to serve as a vegetable.

SEAFOOD CHEESECAKE

1 cup crushed Ritz crackers	1 cup drained and flaked salmon or 1 cup fresh crabmeat
3 tablespoons margarine, melted	1 teaspoon lemon juice
2 (8 ounce) packages cream cheese, softened	2 tablespoons grated onion
3 eggs	⅛ teaspoon ground black pepper
¾ cup sour cream, divided	

Combine crackers and margarine and press into bottom of 9 inch springform pan. Bake at 350° for 10 minutes. Combine cheese, eggs, ¼ cup sour cream, fish, lemon juice, onion and pepper. Pour over crust. Bake at 325° for 45-50 minutes. Cool. Spread top with remaining sour cream. Serves 12 as appetizer and 6 as main course. Serve with crackers or melba toast.

SEAFOODS

℞

SEAFOOD MOUSSE

Fish Stock

	fish bones	1	teaspoon salt
1	quart water	6	whole black peppers
1	onion, chopped	½	pound raw shrimp
1	medium bay leaf		

Mousse

1	pound fish filet	1	tablespoon lemon juice
1	cup light cream, divided	¼	teaspoon nutmeg
		¼	teaspoon pepper
8	ounces crabmeat	4	egg whites
4	egg yolks	1	tablespoon oil
1	tablespoon grated onion		

Sauce

1	cup fish stock	2	egg yolks
2	teaspoons cornstarch mixed with 2 teaspoons water	½	cup light cream
		2	tablespoons sherry

Make stock by combining fish bones, water, onion, bay leaf, salt and pepper. Cook shrimp in stock 5 minutes. Remove shrimp, peel and chop. Reserve for sauce. Return shells and tails to stock and cook to reduce stock to 1 cup. Strain. To make mousse, combine fish filet and ¼ cup light cream and puree in blender. Combine crabmeat with remaining cream and puree together. Add to fish mixture. Combine egg yolk, grated onion, lemon juice, nutmeg and pepper. Add to fish/crabmeat mixture. Beat egg whites and fold into fish mixture until well blended. Put into oiled mold and bake in pan of water for 35-40 minutes at 350°.

SEAFOODS

℞

To make sauce, warm fish stock and add cornstarch. Cook until mixture clears and thickens. Remove from heat. Beat egg yolks and add to cream slowly. Pour into fish stock and cook over low heat for 2-3 minutes. Stir in sherry and chopped shrimp. Serve mousse with shrimp sauce. Serves 8.

Date: *Daily*

For Those Who Enjoy Eating
Patient's name

℞: SOUPS

Dispense: *Large Servings*

Sig: *Use a Large Spoon*

Refill: yes ✔
      no _____

Physician
DEA Number AH 0000000

SOUPS

℞

MUSHROOM SOUP

4	tablespoons margarine	¼	cup flour
1	cup finely chopped onion		salt and pepper
		3	cups chicken broth
1	pound fresh mushrooms, sliced	1	cup whipping cream

In margarine sauté onions. Add mushrooms and cook until soft. Add flour, salt and pepper. Stir to coat mushrooms and then add broth. When mushrooms are thoroughly cooked, puree mixture. Return to heat and add cream. Serves 8-12.

LOBSTER BISQUE

1	cup lobster meat	1	teaspoon salt
1	tablespoon finely chopped onions		paprika (to give pink color)
3	tablespoons margarine	1	cup heavy cream
3	cups milk		dry sherry to taste

Sauté lobster and onion in margarine until soft. Add milk, salt, paprika and cream. Cook over low heat. Add sherry. Serves 6.

ZUCCHINI BISQUE

1	medium onion, finely chopped	½	teaspoon nutmeg
		1	teaspoon basil
½	cup butter	1	teaspoon salt
2½	cups chicken stock		ground pepper
1½	pounds zucchini, shredded	1	cup heavy cream

Sauté onion in butter. Add chicken stock. Shred zucchini in food processor and add to chicken stock and onions. Simmer for 15 minutes. Add seasoning and cream and mix well. Serve hot or cold. Makes 1½ quarts.

SOUPS

COLD CREAM OF AVOCADO

- 2 ripe avocados
- juice of 1 lemon
- salt
- ¼ cup dry white wine
- 2 cups degreased chicken stock
- 6 dashes Tabasco
- ½ cup heavy cream
- ½ cup sour cream
- 1 small green onion, chopped

Put avocado pulp, lemon juice, and salt into blender and puree. Add wine, chicken stock. Tabasco and cream. Chill. Beat sour cream until smooth and place spoonful on each bowl of soup. Sprinkle green onion on top. Serves 6.

BOOLA-BOOLA SOUP

- 3½ cups green pea soup
- 3½ cups clear green turtle soup
- 2 tablespoons dry sherry
- ½ cup heavy cream, whipped

Add ½ the amount of water called for on directions to make soup. Heat soups together. Flavor with sherry. Transfer to individual dishes or a baking dish. Top with whipped cream and pass under the broiler quickly. Makes 7 cups.

SOUPS

CREAM OF SPINACH SOUP

- 2 quarts chicken stock
- 2 pounds spinach chopped
- 4 tablespoons butter
- ½ teaspoon chopped garlic
- 1 cup chopped onion
- ⅛ teaspoon ground nutmeg
- 1 teaspoon salt
- ⅓ teaspoon white pepper
- 1 cup heavy cream
- 2 hard boiled eggs, chopped (optional)

Heat chicken stock and add spinach. Cook 10 minutes. Sauté garlic and onion in butter and add to spinach mixture. Add seasonings. Cook. Blend thoroughly in blender. Return to pan, add cream and beat. Garnish with chopped egg. Serves 8-10.

MOCK TURTLE SOUP

- 1 small onion
- 2 tablespoons margarine
- 1 quart water
- ½ pound red kidney beans (do not use more)
- 2 cloves garlic
- 2 ribs celery, chopped
- 2 bay leaves
- 1 teaspoon dried thyme
- 1 teaspoon Worcestershire sauce
- ½ pound ham, finely ground
- salt and pepper
- ½ cup claret wine
- 2 hard boiled eggs, riced
- lemon slices

Brown onion in margarine. Add water, beans, garlic, celery, bay leaves, thyme and Worcestershire sauce. Simmer for about 2 hours then strain. Add ham, salt and pepper. Place 1 tablespoon of claret in bottom of each serving bowl. Pour soup into bowl and top with riced egg and lemon slice. Serves 6.

SOUPS

LETTUCE SOUP

- 4 heads iceberg lettuce, cored and shredded
- 3 tablespoons butter
- 2 cups chopped onion
- 2 quarts chicken broth
- 3 cups frozen peas
- 2 teaspoons sugar
- ½ teaspoon salt
- ¼ cup mint leaves

Cut cores out and shred lettuce. Sauté onions in butter. In broth, combine onions, lettuce, peas, sugar and salt. Boil. Reduce heat; cook covered for 1½ hours. Puree contents in blender and remove any pulp. Refrigerate for four hours before serving. Garnish with mint leaves. May serve cold or warm. Serves 8-10.

GAZPACHO

- 1 (10 ounce) can Rotel tomatoes (tomatoes with green chilies) (1¼ cups)
- 6 tablespoons vinegar
- 4 tablespoons olive oil
- 1 onion, quartered
- 1 bell pepper, seeded and quartered
- 3 ripe tomatoes
- 1 cup tomato juice
- salt and pepper
- ½ cup ice water

Garnish

- onions, chopped
- tomatoes, chopped
- bell peppers, chopped
- seasoned Pepperidge Farm croutons

Put Rotel juice, vinegar and olive oil in large container and mix. Put onion, bell pepper, tomatoes into blender or food processor with 1 cup tomato juice and water and chop. Add to Rotel mixture. Salt and pepper to taste. Garnish with onions, tomatoes, croutons and/or bell peppers. Serves 6. The olive oil adds a special flavor. Do not substitute salad oil.

This is great to serve in cups on Thanksgiving Day while dinner is being placed on the buffet.

SOUPS

℞

SENEGLASE

1	hen chicken	2-4	tablespoons curry powder
1	quart chicken broth		
1-2	onions, chopped	2	tablespoons flour
2	ribs celery, chopped	1	pint cream
2	tablespoons butter		salt
1-2	Granny Smith apples, peeled and chopped		

Cook chicken in water and chop. Reserve 1 quart of chicken broth. Chill broth overnight and remove chicken fat. Sauté onions and celery in butter and add apples. Combine curry powder and flour with onion mixture. Add chicken broth and simmer over low heat 40 minutes. Mash through sieve. Cool and add cream. Add salt if needed. Chill. Place 1 tablespoon chopped white meat of chicken in each serving bowl and cover with soup. Serves 12.

This is a very rich soup so servings should be small.

SPANISH FISH SOUP

1	(10½ ounce) can chicken bouillon (1¼ cups)		salt and pepper
		1	jar mild to hot banana pepper rings with juice
7	cups water		
1	(14½ ounce) can tomato juice (1¾ cups)	1	large onion, cut into rings, sautéed in olive oil
2	bay leaves	1-2	pounds trout, redfish or snapper
1	teaspoon thyme		
1	pound crabmeat	1	pound raw shrimp, peeled and deveined
2-3	tomatoes, skinned and cubed		
		1	cup vermouth
1	teaspoon garlic powder		

Combine bouillon, water, tomato juice, bay leaves and thyme in roaster and cook. Add crabmeat, fresh tomatoes, garlic powder, pepper, salt and banana pepper rings with juice. Add onions. Cook for 15

SOUPS

minutes at medium heat. Add trout and shrimp. If you add this seafood too early it will cook apart or get tough. The soup does not smell like much until you add the wine. Let it cook only about 5 minutes after wine is added. Serve with Italian or French bread for dunking. Serves 12. Seafood may be varied as to cost of fish and preference.

After eating this soup, a prominent biochemist asked me if I would mind giving him my formula. I thought at first he was teasing and then agreed to give him my recipe. Formula—recipe—who cares, it all means how do you make it.

CRAB BISQUE

4	tablespoons margarine	⅛	teaspoon white pepper
½	cup chopped onion	2	cups milk
½	cup chopped celery	2	cups heavy cream
2	tablespoons flour	1	cup cooked crabmeat
½	teaspoon paprika	¼	cup pale, dry sherry
1	teaspoon salt		

Sauté onions and celery in margarine. Add flour, paprika, salt and pepper. Add milk and cream and bring to a boil stirring constantly. Reduce heat and cook for 3 more minutes. Stir in crabmeat and sherry. Serves 6.

CHICKEN SOUP

1	broiler plus 1 whole breast of chicken	¼	teaspoon pepper
2	quarts water	1	rib celery and a few leaves, chopped
⅛	teaspoon garlic powder	1	small onion, chopped
½	teaspoon salt		thin spaghetti, broken into bite-size pieces

Cook chicken in water with garlic powder, salt, pepper, celery and onion. Remove chicken, debone and cut into bite-size pieces. Return to liquid. Add spaghetti and cook until tender. This soup makes everyone well without the need of a doctor. Maybe it's the garlic.

Date: *Daily*

For Those Who Enjoy Eating
Patient's name

℞: VEGETABLES

Dispense: *Large Servings*

Sig: *Use a Large Spoon*

Refill: yes ✔
      no _____

Physician
DEA Number AH 0000000

VEGETABLES

SPINACH AND NAVY BEANS

2	(10 ounce) boxes frozen, chopped spinach, thawed	2	cups white Navy beans, cooked
4	tablespoons margarine or olive oil	2	tablespoons whipping cream
½	cup diced cooked ham		salt and pepper dash nutmeg

Melt margarine or heat oil and add spinach, ham and beans. Stir in cream and cook until consistency of mashed potatoes. Add salt and pepper and a dash of nutmeg. Serves 8-10.

SPINACH DUMPLINGS

1	(10 ounce) box frozen chopped spinach, defrosted and squeezed dry	¼	cup green onion, chopped
		½	teaspoon salt
		1	teaspoon basil
1½	cups Ricotta cheese	¼	teaspoon nutmeg
1	cup fine dry crumbs	¼	teaspoon garlic powder
2	eggs, beaten		
¼	cup grated Parmesan cheese		flour

Combine spinach, Ricotta cheese, bread crumbs, eggs, Parmesan cheese, onion, salt, basil, nutmeg and garlic powder. Form into walnut size balls. Roll in flour. Dumplings may be frozen at this point. Put wax paper between layers of dumplings.

To cook, drop dumplings into salted simmering water. They are cooked when the dumplings rise to the top. Remove with slotted spoon and drain. Serve with favorite Italian sauce. Serves 8.

"Dr. Hill, what was that green stuff in the crepes? That was so good. I'm on my 4th helping." Reply, "Spinach." Intern, "But I don't like spinach."

VEGETABLES

LENTEN SPINACH

4 (10 ounce) boxes frozen spinach in butter sauce, thawed

6 eggs, made into deviled eggs
white sauce

Cook spinach according to directions on box. Place into a buttered 9 x 13 casserole. Make your favorite deviled eggs. Arrange them on top of spinach. Cover each egg with white sauce to keep them from getting tough. Place in oven just long enough to warm. Serves 12.

SPINACH NUT PIE

1 (9 inch) pastry shell, unbaked
2 tablespoons margarine
1 cup chopped onion
½ cup chopped red bell pepper
4 cups coarsely chopped fresh spinach
¾ cup toasted pecans, chopped
1¼ cups grated Swiss cheese
1¼ cups half and half
3 eggs
¾ teaspoon salt
⅛ teaspoon pepper

Bake pastry shell for 10 minutes at 425°. Cook onion and pepper in margarine until tender. Add spinach and cook until wilted. Sprinkle pecans and cheese on pastry shell. Spread spinach over cheese. Blend half and half, eggs, salt and pepper and pour into shell. Bake at 350° for 35 minutes. Serves 8.

VEGETABLES

SPINACH AND PINE NUTS

2	tablespoons butter	½	teaspoon garlic powder
2	tablespoons olive oil		
1	tablespoon minced green onion	⅛	teaspoon Tabasco
		3	tablespoons pine nuts
2	pounds fresh spinach	3	tablespoons seedless raisins, plumped
½	teaspoon salt		

In olive oil and butter sauté onion in skillet until just beginning to be soft. Add spinach, salt, garlic powder and Tabasco. Cook until spinach just begins to wilt. Add pine nuts and raisins. Cook 1 minute more. Serves 6.

ITALIAN SPINACH

2	pounds spinach	3	tablespoons bacon grease
2	green onions, chopped		

Sauté spinach and onion in bacon grease until just wilted. Serve immediately. Serves 6-8.

GREEK SPINACH PIE

½	cup finely chopped onion	2	tablespoons chopped parsley
¼	cup margarine	⅛	teaspoon dillweed
2	(10 ounce) packages frozen chopped spinach, defrosted and drained	½	teaspoon salt
		¾	cup margarine, melted
		16	(12 x 15) phyllo or strudel leaves at room temperature
2	eggs, slightly beaten		
1	cup crumbled Feta cheese		

Sauté onions in margarine until tender. Stir in spinach, remove from heat. Combine eggs, Feta cheese, parsley, dillweed and salt. Add to spinach mixture.

VEGETABLES

℞

Lightly brush a 13 x 9 x 2 inch baking pan with melted margarine. Layer 8 phyllo leaves in buttered pan brushing top of each with melted margarine. Spread spinach mixture evenly on top of 8th layer. Repeat layering and brushing with remaining phyllo leaves, pouring any remaining margarine over top. Bake at 375° for 25 minutes. Serves 8.

FANCY PEAS

4	tablespoons margarine	1	cup chicken broth
½	pound fresh mushrooms, sliced	¼	teaspoon pepper
		¼	teaspoon marjoram
8	green onions, chopped	3-4	sprigs parsley
4	cups frozen peas	1-1½	teaspoons salt
2	large lettuce leaves, torn in bite-size pieces	½	teaspoon nutmeg
		1	teaspoon sugar

In margarine sauté onions and mushrooms. Add peas and mix. Line a separate pan with lettuce leaves. Heat chicken broth, and add seasonings. Pour broth over lettuce and add onion, mushrooms and pea mixture. Cover and refrigerate several hours. Bake at 350° for 15-20 minutes. Sherry may be substituted for ¼ ounce broth. Serves 8-10.

VEGETABLES

SUNDAY PEAS

1	medium onion, chopped	¼	pound mushrooms, sliced and sautéed in butter
2	tablespoons margarine		
½	teaspoon salt	1	tablespoon soy sauce
¼	teaspoon pepper	¼	cup red wine
2	tablespoons chopped pimento	2	(10 ounce) package frozen green peas
1	(10½ ounce) can cream of mushroom soup (1¼ cups)	¼	cup toasted almonds, slivered

Sauté onions in margarine. Add salt, pepper, pimento, soup, mushrooms with liquid, soy sauce and wine. In separate pan cook peas as directed on package; drain. Add soup mixture and bring to boil. Simmer 1 minute. Add almonds. Serves 8.

CHILI BLACK EYED PEAS

1	cup dried black eyed peas	1	tablespoon Worcestershire sauce
4	cups water	1	teaspoon chili powder
1	medium onion, chopped	1	bay leaf
1	green pepper, chopped	½	teaspoon salt
1	(#2) can stewed tomatoes (2½ cups)	1	cup grated cheddar cheese
¼	teaspoon garlic powder		

Put peas in water in covered sauce pan and boil for 2 minutes. Turn off heat and let peas stand 1 hour. Then cook until tender. Drain. Mix with rest of ingredients except cheese and put into 2 quart casserole dish. Sprinkle with cheese and bake in 350° oven until warm.

VEGETABLES

MARINATED PEAS OR BEANS

1	quart cooked black eyed peas, lima beans or Great Northern beans	¼	teaspoon garlic powder
¾	cup salad oil	1	small purple onion, chopped
¼	cup wine vinegar		salt and pepper
			dash Tabasco

Place cooked peas or beans in container with rest of ingredients and marinate at least 24-48 hours. Keeps for 10 days. Serve on lettuce leaves as salad or as a vegetable. Serves 10-12.

JEANNINE'S ITALIAN VEGETABLE CASSEROLE

1	(13 ounce) package Pepperidge Farm seasoned croutons	⅓	cup cooked rice
		1	can mushrooms
			cheddar cheese
1	(10 ounce) package Birdseye Italian Vegetables *with Seasoned Sauce*	1	ounce white wine or vermouth
		3-4	tablespoons butter, melted
1	package hollandaise sauce mix (make as directed on package)		

Place croutons in food processor and whirl to make bread crumbs. Cook Italian vegetables until little seasoning cubes just melt. Do not overcook. Place in buttered casserole dish. Add hollandaise sauce, cooked rice, Italian vegetables and mushrooms. Mix well. Cover with cheese and bread crumbs. Sprinkle with white wine and melted butter. Bake until bubbly in 350° oven. Serves 4-6. Triple recipe for 3 quart casserole. Be sure you get Italian Vegetables *with Seasoned Sauce.*

VEGETABLES

ITALIAN WHITE BEANS

1½ cups white beans (Great Northern)	2 large tomatoes, peeled, seeded, chopped
1½ quarts water	¼ teaspoon sage
¼ cup olive oil	fresh ground pepper
1 tablespoon wine vinegar	salt
1 teaspoon garlic powder	

Soak beans overnight. Drain. Add water and next 5 ingredients. Cover and simmer beans for 2 to 2½ hours. Correct seasoning with salt, pepper, olive oil and vinegar. These beans are better cooked the day before they are served. Serves 10-12.

Cheap dish to serve with expensive meat like veal.

Among one of the cheapest parties I have had was one where I served milk-fed veal (cost $15.00 a pound), but the rest of the meal was inexpensive, i.e., Italian White Beans, Red and Green Bell Peppers sautéed in Spaghetti Sauce, Green Salad, Garlic Bread and Rum Cream Pie.

RED BEANS AND RICE PARADISE

1 (8 ounce) bag small kidney beans	½ medium onion, chopped
enough water to cover	salt and pepper
ham hock or ham with fat, cut into ¼ inch pieces	⅛ teaspoon sugar
	white rice, cooked
⅛ teaspoon soda	green onions, chopped

Put beans in cold water and bring to boil. Cover and turn heat down to simmer. Add ham hock, soda and onion. Cook covered for 30 minutes. Then add salt, pepper and sugar. Continue cooking covered for 30 minutes more. Additional water may be added to maintain a watery consistency. Beans should be cooked until just soft, but not

VEGETABLES

℞

mushy. Serve over cooked white rice and garnish with chopped green onions. Serve with Tabasco sauce and cornbread.

Dishes remembered as a child become as much a part of our heritage as the genes which make up our physical body. I never knew what red beans and rice were before I married a boy from Louisiana.

TOMATOES STUFFED WITH SQUASH

4	medium tomatoes salt	1	cup grated Swiss or Gruyère cheese
2	cups grated fresh zucchini	¾	teaspoon salt
		¼	teaspoon pepper
⅓	cup onion	¼	teaspoon dried basil

Slice tops off tomatoes. Scoop tomato pulp out. Sprinkle shells with salt and turn upside down for 30 minutes. Combine zucchini, tomato pulp, onion, cheese, salt, pepper, basil. Let stand 30 minutes. Fill tomatoes with mixture and bake at 350° for 10 minutes. Do not over bake. Serves 4 but tomatoes can be halved and prepared the same way to serve 8.

TOMATOES BOMBAY

6	tomatoes, skinned		juice of 1 lemon
½	cup raisins	½	teaspoon salt
1	tablespoon margarine	½	teaspoon curry powder
2	cups rice cooked		pepper
½	green pepper, diced	1	tablespoon chutney
½	pimento, diced	½	cup toasted almonds
3	tablespoons olive oil		

Halve tomatoes and scoop out pulp. Sauté raisins in margarine. Combine cooked rice, raisins, green peppers, pimento. Mix with dressing made with olive oil, lemon juice, salt, curry powder, pepper and chutney. Fill tomatoes with rice mixture. Top with almonds. Serves 12.

VEGETABLES

℞

BLEU CHEESE TOMATOES

4 tomatoes, peeled salt and pepper garlic powder	½ cup croutons ¼ cup crumbled Bleu 　　cheese

Remove center core of tomatoes. Cut partially through tomatoes to form 6 wedges. Sprinkle with salt, pepper and garlic powder. Mix croutons and cheese. Use to stuff tomatoes. Bake at 400° for 25 minutes or until cheese melts. Serves 4. Do not add salt since cheese is very salty.

EASY TOMATOES

2 boxes cherry tomatoes, 　　halved ⅛ teaspoon garlic 　　powder	¼ cup olive oil 　　fresh Parmesan cheese, 　　　grated 　　salt and pepper

In lightly greased casserole place halved tomatoes. Sprinkle with garlic powder, olive oil, salt, pepper and Parmesan cheese. Bake at 350° until just warm. Do not overcook. Good to serve at buffet dinners. Not as messy as whole tomatoes. Serves 8-10.

PINEAPPLE SQUASH SUPREME

3 medium acorn squash, 　　halved, seeds and 　　fibers removed ¼ cup margarine 1 (8¼ ounce) can 　　crushed pineapple, 　　drained (1 cup) ¼ cup raisins, plumped	1 cup canned apple 　　slices 3 tablespoons brown 　　sugar 3 tablespoons Amaretto 　　dash nutmeg 　　salt and pepper to taste

Cut thin slice from bottom of halved squash. Bake squash in oven in ½ inch of boiling water for 40 minutes with halved side in water.

VEGETABLES

℞

Combine margarine, pineapple, raisins, apple, brown sugar, Amaretto, nutmeg, salt and pepper. Fill squash cavity with mixture. Bake at 400° for 25 minutes. Serves 6.

BROCCOLI WITH TOMATO SAUCE

1	large onion, thinly sliced	1	cup all purpose flour, seasoned with salt and pepper
1	tablespoon olive oil		
1	(#2½) can plum tomatoes (3½ cups)	3	eggs, beaten
			hot oil
½	teaspoon basil	½	cup grated Gruyère cheese
½	teaspoon oregano		
½	teaspoon thyme	2	tablespoons grated Parmesan cheese
	salt and pepper		
1	bay leaf	2	tablespoons margarine
2	pounds fresh broccoli		

Sauté onion in olive oil. Add tomatoes, basil, oregano, thyme, salt, pepper and bay leaf. Cook for 25 minutes. Discard bay leaf. Cook flowerets of broccoli in boiling, salted water for 1 minute. Drain and dry. Dredge flowerets in seasoned flour and dip in egg. Fry in hot oil until just golden. Put broccoli into buttered, 3 quart casserole dish. Cover with tomato sauce and sprinkle with Gruyère and Parmesan cheese. Dot with margarine. Bake at 375° for 25 minutes. Serves 8.

PUFFED BROCCOLI

2	bunches broccoli, cooked or 2 (10 ounce) packages broccoli cooked according to directions	2	egg whites
		¼	teaspoon salt
		½	cup shredded Swiss cheese
		½	cup mayonnaise

Place cooked broccoli in 1½ quart casserole. Beat egg whites until stiff. Add salt, fold in cheese and mayonnaise. Pour over broccoli. Place under broiler until golden brown. Serves 6-8.

VEGETABLES

MARIPOSA VEGETABLE CASSEROLE

1	(20 ounce) package frozen broccoli, corn, peppers combination, thawed, or 1 (20 ounce) package broccoli, cauliflower or carrots, thawed	2	teaspoons margarine
		1	medium onion, chopped
		4	ounce egg noodles, cooked
			salt and pepper
			garlic powder
		½	teaspoon all season salt
1	(10 ounce) box of frozen string beans, thawed	½	cup grated Parmesan cheese
	Mornay sauce		

Mix vegetables with Mornay sauce. Sauté onion in margarine. Combine noodles, Mornay sauce/vegetable mixture and seasoning and place in buttered casserole. Top with Parmesan cheese. Heat at 350° for 15-20 minutes. Pretty to serve in individual ramekins. Serves 6-8. Any preferred combination of vegetables may be substituted for vegetables in this dish.

CREOLE ONIONS

2	medium spanish onions, sliced	¼	teaspoon salt
		½	teaspoon garlic powder
2	medium red onions, sliced	1	(8 ounce) can tomato sauce
2	medium tomatoes, sliced	2	cups grated sharp cheddar cheese
2	slices bacon, diced		
1	green pepper, sliced		

Cook onion rings in salted boiling water for 10 minutes. Drain. Alternate onions and tomatoes in buttered 1½ quart casserole dish. Fry bacon until crisp. Cook green pepper in bacon grease and add salt and garlic powder. Stir in tomato sauce and pour over onions. Cover and bake 20-25 minutes. Sprinkle with cheese and return to oven to melt cheese. Serves 8.

VEGETABLES

℞

ONIONS
THAT DON'T TAKE YOUR BREATH AWAY

1-2 onions, sliced
1 tablespoon sugar
ice cold water (a must), with ice cubes

Slice onions, sprinkle with sugar and add water with ice cubes. Refrigerate for several hours. Drain. Makes onion crisp and removes odor from your breath.

My grandfather was the proprietor of a barbeque stand. He fixed onions this way for those who did not want the after effects.

STUFFED ONIONS

6 onions
1 (10 ounce) package frozen, chopped spinach
3 tablespoons mayonnaise
1 tablespoon lemon juice
½ cup grated Parmesan cheese
½ teaspoon seasoned salt
    dash nutmeg
⅛ teaspoon pepper
    pimento strips

Peel onions and cut in half. Parboil in salted water until just tender. Remove centers to leave ¾ inch thick shells. Chop removed center of onion to make ¾ cup. Cook spinach according to directions. Mix onion, spinach, mayonnaise, lemon juice, cheese and seasoning. Put into onion shells. Bake at 350° for 20 minutes. Garnish with pimento. Serves 6.

VEGETABLES

MUSHROOMS NEWBURG

1½ pounds small fresh mushrooms	2 tablespoons flour
¼ cup chopped onion	2 cups half and half
6 tablespoons margarine, divided	¾ teaspoon nutmeg
	dash cayenne pepper
1¼ teaspoon salt, divided	2 egg yolks
3 tablespoons sherry	2 tablespoons water

Sauté mushrooms and onions in 4 tablespoons margarine. Add ½ teaspoon salt and sherry. In separate pan, melt 2 tablespoons margarine and mix in flour. Remove from heat. Add half and half, nutmeg, cayenne and ¾ teaspoon salt. Cook until thickened. Cool. Beat egg yolks with water and add to mixture. Pour sauce over mushrooms/onion mixture. This may be served as an appetizer over toast or as a vegetable with steak. If mushrooms are sliced it makes a delicious dip. Serves 6.

MUSHROOMS IN PATTY SHELLS

6 frozen patty shells, cooked per directions on box	1½ cups sour cream
	¾ cup grated Parmesan or Swiss cheese
2 tablespoons margarine, melted	3 tablespoons sherry
	garlic powder
2 pounds fresh mushrooms, sliced	fresh parsley

In margarine, sauté mushrooms. Stir in sour cream, cheese, sherry, garlic powder, and parsley. Cook until thickened. Serve in patty shell. This may be served with steak as a starch or without shells as a vegetable. Serves 6.

VEGETABLES

GREEN BEAN AND RICE PROVENCALE

- 1 cup brown rice
- 2 cups beef bouillon
- 1 pound green beans, cooked
- 1 (28 ounce) can tomatoes, drained (3½ cups)
- 1½ cups sliced onion
- 1 teaspoon garlic
- 1½ teaspoons salt
- ⅛ teaspoon pepper
- ½ teaspoon dried basil
- 1 (3½ ounce) can sliced ripe olives
- 2 green onions, chopped
- 2 tablespoons grated Parmesan cheese

Cook rice in beef bouillon. Combine all ingredients and top with cheese. Allow to stand 2 hours. Bake in 350° oven for 20 minutes. Serves 8.

RATATOUILLE STUFFED MUSHROOMS

- 1 pound medium sized mushrooms, stems chopped
- 3 tablespoons olive oil, divided
- ¼ pound eggplant, diced
- ¼ pound zucchini, diced
- ½ cup diced onion
- ½ teaspoon garlic powder
- ½ cup diced green peppers
- 1 (8¼ ounce) can tomatoes, chopped, reserve liquid (1 cup)
- 2 teaspoons cornstarch
- 1 teaspoon capers
- ½ teaspoon Italian seasoning
- ½ teaspoon salt
- ⅛ teaspoon ground black pepper

Sauté mushroom caps in 1 tablespoon oil. Sauté eggplant and zucchini with onion, garlic, ½ of mushroom stems and green pepper in remaining oil. Mix tomato liquid with cornstarch and add to zucchini/eggplant mixture along with tomatoes and capers. Season with Italian seasoning, salt, pepper. Cook until thickened (10 minutes). Chill to let flavor permeate eggplant and zucchini. Spoon into mushroom caps. May serve cold or warm. Makes 18-24 servings depending on size of mushrooms. The stuffing is best made a day ahead. Good with poultry, steak or Italian food.

VEGETABLES

RATATOUILLE SAVANNAH

- ⅓ cup olive oil
- 2 large cloves
- 1 teaspoon garlic
- ½ teaspoon marjoram
- ½ teaspoon oregano
- ¼ teaspoon dillweed
- 2 teaspoons salt
- ⅛ teaspoon pepper
  Tabasco
- 2 (10 ounce) package frozen sliced summer squash, thawed
- 1 medium eggplant, peeled and cubed
- 1 cup thinly sliced onion
- 2 green peppers, cut in slices
- 4 medium firm ripe tomatoes, peeled and sliced
  cracked pepper

Mix olive oil with all seasonings and let stand to blend flavors. Butter a 3 quart casserole. Layer vegetables starting and ending with squash. Sprinkle each layer with seasoned oil. Cover. Bake in 350° oven for 1 hour. Bake an additional 15 minutes uncovered. Sprinkle with cracked pepper. Serve hot or cold. Serves 8-10.

MUSHROOMS SUPREME

- 1 (10 ounce) package frozen chopped spinach, drained
  salt and pepper
  dash garlic
- 1 can cream of mushroom soup (1¼ cups
- 1 (8 ounce) package Ricotta cheese
- 18 large fresh mushrooms
- ¼ pound margarine
- 1 (3 ounce) can french fried onions (broken into pieces)
- 1 (13 ounce) package Pepperidge Farm herbed bread croutons whirled in blender to make bread crumbs

Cook spinach according to directions and drain well. Season with salt, pepper and garlic. Heat soup and cheese together. Combine

246

VEGETABLES

℞

soups and cheese with spinach. Stuff mushrooms with spinach/cheese mixture. Dot with margarine. Top with French fried onion rings and bread crumbs. Place in greased baking dish and bake at 350° for 25 minutes. Allow 2 mushrooms per person. Spinach can also be served as a casserole with mushroom slices at the bottom. Can be made ahead and refrigerated. If refrigerated, do not add onion until ready to cook. Serves 8.

MARINATED EGGPLANT

4½ pounds eggplant, halved, score cut sides	4 cloves garlic minced
	¼ cup lemon juice
2 cups French dressing, divided	1 tablespoon ground coriander
1 cup fresh, chopped basil	1 tablespoon ground cumin
1 cup chopped, fresh parsley	1 teaspoon salt
	pepper
1 onion, minced	

Pour 1⅓ cups French dressing over eggplant. Bake eggplant scored side up in 400° oven 30 minutes. Cool. Scoop out pulp to leave ¼ inch thick shell and reserve. In food processor with steel blade, blend eggplant pulp, basil, parsley, ⅔ cup French dressing, onion, garlic, lemon juice, coriander, cumin, salt and pepper. Divide mixture between eggplant shells. Drizzle with 2 tablespoons dressing then bake at 400° for 25 minutes. Let cool and chill. Good for 4 days when refrigerated. Serves 8. This may be used also as a salad.

VEGETABLES

℞

EGGPLANT PIZZA

1	tablespoon olive oil		salt and pepper
1	large eggplant, sliced ¼ inch thick		Mozzarella cheese, sliced
3	large tomatoes, sliced ¼ inch thick	½	cup olive oil

Coat a baking pan with olive oil. Layer part of eggplant and tomatoes in casserole and sprinkle with salt and pepper. Top with part of Mozzarella cheese. Repeat layering and drizzle with olive oil. Bake at 325° for 1½ hours.

ITALIAN VEGETABLES WITH PASTA

2	cups thinly sliced onions	1	(10 ounce) can chicken broth (1¼ cups)
3	tablespoons olive oil	2	teaspoons garlic powder
1	(28 ounce) can Italian plum tomatoes, chopped (3½ cups)	1	tablespoon dried basil
		1	teaspoon thyme
3	tablespoons red wine vinegar		salt and pepper
		1	bay leaf
1	(6 ounce) can tomato paste	½	cup sliced, pitted black olives
½	pound zucchini, cut into 1 inch slices	3	tablespoons fresh parsley
1	pound eggplant, cut into 1 inch cubes (leave skin on each cube)	½	pound mushrooms, sliced and sautéed in butter
		¼	box (8 ounce) fettuccini or linguine, cooked
1	large green pepper, cut into ¼ inch strips		

Sauté onions in olive oil and cook 3 minutes. Add tomatoes, red wine vinegar, tomato paste, zucchini; then add eggplant, green pepper and chicken broth. Sprinkle with garlic, basil, thyme, salt and pepper. Add bay leaf. Cook until vegetables just begin to soften, but do not

VEGETABLES

℞

overcook. Remove bay leaf. Add black olives, parsley, and sautéed mushrooms. Combine with cooked fettuccini or linguine.

This is basically a vegetable dish and should only have a small amount of pasta in it. It is best made the day before so that the seasoning can blend. Serves 12. Good served with Italian Chicken (see Index).

SPICY LIMA BEAN CASSEROLE

2 (10 ounce) boxes frozen baby lima beans, thawed	1 teaspoon salt
	1 tablespoon cornstarch
	1 tablespoon chili powder
1 cup chopped onion	
1 cup chopped green pepper	1 cup whole ripe olives, sliced
3 tablespoons oil	1 cup shredded cheddar cheese, divided
½ teaspoon garlic powder	

Cook lima beans according to directions. After cooking add enough water to beans to make 1¼ cup. Sauté onion and green peppers in oil. Combine garlic powder, salt, cornstarch and chili powder. Stir in ¼ cup bean liquid and mix well. Add rest of liquid, beans, olives, sautéed vegetables and ½ cup cheese. Spoon into greased 1½ quart casserole and sprinkle with remaining cheese. Bake at 375° for 30 minutes. Yields 6-8 servings.

VEGETABLES

℞

BARBECUED RICE AND LIMA BEANS

½	cup chopped green pepper	½	cup barbecue sauce
½	cup chopped onion	1	(10 ounce) package frozen baby lima beans, thawed and drained
2	tablespoons margarine		
1	cup water		
½	cup rice	2	tablespoons chopped pimento
1	teaspoon salt		

Sauté green pepper and onion in margarine until tender. Add water and bring to a boil. Add rice and salt. Reduce heat to low and cook covered 20 minutes. Remove from heat. Stir in barbecue sauce, lima beans and pimento. Let stand until all liquid is absorbed (5 minutes). Serves 6. The quality of the barbecue sauce determines the success of this dish.

Barbecue Sauce

¼	cup vinegar	1	thick slice lemon
½	cup water	1	slice onion
2	tablespoons sugar	½	cup ketchup
1	tablespoon prepared mustard	2	tablespoons Worcestershire sauce
½	teaspoon pepper		
1½	teaspoon salt	1½	teaspoons Liquid Smoke
¼	teaspoon cayenne pepper		

Mix all ingredients. Simmer 20 minutes. Makes 1¾ cups.

ARTICHOKE RING

1	can cheddar cheese soup, undiluted (1¼ cups)		salt and pepper
		2	(#300) cans artichoke hearts (1¾ cups)
4	eggs	⅔	cup small fresh mushrooms, sautéed in butter
	dash Tabasco		
¼	cup mayonnaise		
1	small onion, chopped		

VEGETABLES

℞

Blend cheese soup, eggs, Tabasco, mayonnaise, onion, salt and pepper. Pour over artichokes and mushrooms in buttered ring mold. Bake at 350° for 30-40 minutes.

DANISH ASPARAGUS

2 (10 ounce) boxes of frozen 5 minute asparagus	cayenne salt
2 cups half and half	1 egg yolk
2 cups Danish Havarti or Fontina cheese	1 cup tiny shrimp, cooked
2 tablespoons flour	

Cook asparagus according to directions. Bring half and half to soft boil. Toss cheese in flour and add to half and half. Stir sauce until smooth. Add cayenne and salt. Blend small amount of sauce into egg yolk then add back to sauce. Do not boil. Fold in shrimp. Serve sauce over asparagus. Feeds 8-10.

RICE AND ASPARAGUS

1   (10 ounce) package frozen asparagus
1   small onion, sliced
¼   pound margarine
1   cup rice
½   cup dry white wine or vermouth
2   cups chicken broth
2   tablespoons heavy cream
½   cup fresh grated Parmesan cheese
    salt and freshly ground pepper

Cut tips off asparagus and reserve. Cut rest of stalks into 1 inch lengths. Cook onion in margarine until soft. Add asparagus stalks and then rice. Stir rapidly to coat rice with margarine. Add wine and cook to evaporate. Add broth and cook covered until rice almost done. Add cream, cheese and asparagus tips. Season with salt and pepper. Serves 6.

VEGETABLES

℞

EASY ASPARAGUS

2 (10 ounce) boxes frozen 5 minute asparagus	salt and pepper
	½ teaspoon garlic powder
½ cup Spice Islands wine vinegar	1 hard boiled egg
½ cup Hunza blended oil	

Cook asparagus until just defrosted. Drain. Mix vinegar, oil, salt, pepper and garlic and marinate asparagus 2 hours. Drain. Sieve hard boiled egg over asparagus. Serve with Easy Tomatoes (see Index). If served at buffet, cut asparagus into bite size pieces. Serves 8-10.

HERMENA'S ASPARAGUS CASSEROLE

2 teaspoons margarine	salt
2 teaspoons flour	white pepper
¾ cup milk	½ cup toasted pecans
1 can all green asparagus, reserve liquid (1½ cups)	1 cup grated sharp cheddar cheese
	canned apricot sections
⅛ teaspoon garlic powder	

Melt margarine, add flour and cook. Add milk, ¼ liquid from asparagus and garlic powder, stirring constantly. Season with salt and pepper. Put asparagus in casserole dish. Cover with sauce, pecans and cheese. Dress with apricot sections. Bake in 350° oven just long enough for cheese to melt. Serves 4-6.

VEGETABLES

℞

CARROT PUDDING

4	tablespoons margarine	½	teaspoon baking soda
¼	cup shortening	½	teaspoon double acting baking powder
1½	cups light brown sugar		
3	eggs	½	teaspoon salt
3	tablespoons lemon juice	½	teaspoon ground allspice
1½	teaspoons grated lemon rind	1½	cups grated carrots (½ pound)
1	cup all purpose flour		

Sauce

1	cup whipping cream	¼	teaspoon ground ginger
2	tablespoons dark rum		

Combine margarine, shortening and sugar. Beat in eggs; add lemon juice and rind. Sift together flour, baking soda, baking powder, salt and allspice. Mix into butter/sugar mixture. Stir in carrots. Pour into buttered 6 cup mold. Cover with foil buttered on side next to pudding.

Sit mold in pan of water to reach ⅔ sides of mold. Bake 30 minutes in 325° oven. Uncover mold and cook for 30 minutes more. Cool for 10 minutes before inverting mold on platter. Serve with pork or fowl.

Beat whipping cream, ginger and rum until it forms soft peaks. Serve over carrot pudding. Serves 8. With topping can serve as a dessert.

VEGETABLES

CREOLE CABBAGE

1	(2 pound) cabbage, shredded	2½	teaspoons salt
1	(#300) can tomatoes, chopped (1¾ cups)	1½	teaspoons sugar
		¾	teaspoon oregano
¼	cup sweet pepper flakes	2	teaspoons lemon juice
2	tablespoons minced onion		

Cook cabbage in boiling water 10 minutes. Drain. In saucepan combine tomatoes, pepper flakes, onion, salt, sugar and oregano. Simmer 15 minutes. Add lemon juice and combine with cabbage. Serves 8.

CABBAGE CASSEROLE

1	head cabbage, coarsely sliced	1	(10 ounce) can Rotel tomatoes (tomatoes with green chilies), broken up (1¼ cups)
½	pound highly seasoned smoked sausage		
1	large onion, sliced		salt and pepper

Blanch cabbage. Fry sausage. Remove from pan and cook onion in drippings until limp. Add tomatoes. Cook until pan is deglazed. Combine all ingredients in casserole and bake covered in 325° oven for 30 minutes. Serves 4.

GREEN BEANS LIKE MAMA MADE

1	small onion	salt and pepper
2	cups water	water chestnuts or toasted almonds, sliced
2	tablespoons bacon grease	
3	(10 ounce) boxes frozen green beans	

Place onion in blender with 2 cups of water. Whirl it to mince onion. Place onion/water mixture into pot and combine with bacon grease. Bring to a boil. Add frozen beans. Season with salt and pepper. Boil

VEGETABLES

℞

rapidly for about 40 minutes or until beans are soft and water reduced. Add sliced water chestnuts or almonds just before serving. The beans taste like fresh string beans my mother used to make instead of like frozen beans. Serves 10-12.

CONFETTI VEGETABLE CASSEROLE

½	pound fresh green beans, cut into 1½ inch pieces	⅛	teaspoon pepper
		½	cup water
		2	cups sliced yellow squash
½	cup chopped onion		
2	tablespoons parsley, chopped	¼	cup water
		3	large tomatoes, cut into wedges
1	teaspoon salt		
¼	teaspoon dried thyme	2	tablespoons margarine
¼	teaspoon dried sage		

Combine beans, onion, parsley, salt, thyme, sage, pepper and water. Bring to boil. Cover and simmer 10 minutes. Add squash and ¼ cup water and bring to boil. Cover and simmer for 10 minutes. Add tomatoes and margarine and cook until margarine just melts. Serves 6.

SUMMER SQUASH

6	cups sliced yellow squash	1	cup sour cream
		1	cup shredded carrots
¼	cup chopped onion	1	(8 ounce) package herbed seasoned stuffing
¼	teaspoon salt		
⅛	teaspoon pepper		
1	can condensed cream of chicken soup (1¼ cups)	¼	pound margarine, melted

Cook squash and onion in water seasoned with salt and pepper, for 5 minutes. Drain. Mix soup and sour cream and combine with squash, onion and carrots. Combine herbed stuffing with margarine and pour ½ in a buttered 12 x 7½ x 2 dish. Add squash mixture and cover with rest of herbed stuffing. Bake at 350° for 25-30 minutes. Serves 6.

TABLES

℞

Beef	Uncooked	Cooked	Ounces of Cooked Meat
BEEF			
Roast			
Chuck pot roast	1 pound =	0.67 pound or	10¾ ounces
Rolled rib roast	1 pound =	0.73 pound or	11¾ ounces
Rump roast boneless	1 pound =	0.73 pound or	11¾ ounces
Steaks			
Round boneless	1 pound =	0.73 pound or	11¾ ounces
Flank	1 pound =	0.67 pound or	10¾ ounces
Short ribs	1 pound =	0.25 pound or	4 ounces
Stew meat	1 pound =	0.66 pound or	10½ ounces
VEAL			
Cutlets	1 pound =	0.75 pound or	13 ounces
Ground	1 pound =	0.64 pound or	10¼ ounces
PORK			
Roast loin	1 pound =	0.68 pound or	11 ounces
Roast ham boneless	1 pound =	0.68 pound or	11 ounces
Roast ham w/bone	1 pound =	0.54 pound or	8¾ ounces
Pork chops	1 pound =	0.75 pound or	12 ounces
Sausage bulk	1 pound =	0.48 pound or	7¾ ounces
Spare ribs	1 pound =	0.26 pound or	4¼ ounces
Smoked ham w/bone	1 pound =	0.56 pound or	9 ounces
Smoked ham boneless	1 pound =	0.64 pound or	10¼ ounces
LAMB			
Chop w/rib	1 pound =	0.54 pound or	8¾ ounces
Leg w/bone	1 pound =	0.54 pound or	8¾ ounces
Leg boneless	1 pound =	0.70 pound or	11¼ ounces
LIVER	1 pound =	0.69 pound or	11 ounces
TONGUE	1 pound =	0.51 pound or	8½ ounces
FISH			
Filet	1 pound =	0.64 pound or	10¼ ounces
Whole	1 pound =	0.27 pound or	4¼ ounces

TABLES

℞

SHRIMP
In shell	1 pound =	0.50 pound or 8 ounces
Raw, peeled	1 pound =	9 ounces
Cooked, peeled	1 pound =	16 ounces

POULTRY
To stew	1 pound =	0.34 pound or 5½ ounces

TURKEY 1 pound = 0.44 pound or 7 ounces

There is a 10% waste in carving meat.

The volumes of food in canned goods vary considerably from one type of food to another and from one distributor to the next. The following table may be helpful in telling you the volume of food in a specific can size.

Industry Term	Weight Fluid Measurement	Cups	Example of Product	Number of Servings
6 ounces	6 ounces	¾	Frozen Concentrated Juices	5
8 ounces	8 ounces	1	Fruits, Vegetables	2
Picnic 12	10½ to 12 ounces	1¼	Condensed soups	2-3
12 ounces	12 ounces	1½	Fruit juices	10
			Vacuum packed corn	3-4
#300	14-16 (14 ounces - 1 pound)	1¾	Pork and Beans	3-4
#303	16-17 (1 pound - 1 pound, 1 ounce)	2	Fruits, Vegetables	4
#2	18-20 (1 pint 2 fluid ounces - 1 pound 4 ounces)	2½	Ready to serve soups Spaghetti	5
#2½	27-29 (1 pound 11 ounces - 1 pound 13 ounces)	3½	Fruits, Vegetables	5-7
32 ounces	32 ounces	4	Frozen fruit juice	25
#3 cyl or 46 fluid ounces	46-51 (3 pounds 3 ounces - 1 quart 14 fluid ounces)	5¾	Institutional size fruits and juices	10-12
#10	(6½-7 pounds 5 ounces)	12-13	Institutional size fruits and vegetables	25

INDEX

APPETIZERS

Artichokes and Shrimp 7
Balls of Fire 14
Banana Treats 21
Beef Brisket Appetizer Like Tujaque's in New Orleans 2
California Avocado Escabeche 7
Caviar Dip 19
Cheese-Onion Marinade 23
Cheddar Cheese Pennies 17
Cheese with Mustard Sauce 24
Cheese Puff 16
Clams in Mariner Sauce 10
Confetti Dip 24
Coquilles Saint-Jacques 25
Escargots in Butter 10
Feta Cheese Greek Puffs 19
Grab - Bag Dip (Warm or Cold) 20
India Cheese Ball 23
Italian Oysters 5
Liverwurst Dip 21
Marinated Sausage 2
Marinated Eggplant-Mama Poli 4
Mexican Cerviche 8
Miniature Chalupas 3
Mexican Cheese Dip Like Ninfa's 21
Mrs. Davidson's Cheese Sausage Balls 4
Mushroom and Cheese Puff 22
Oysters Daytona 9
Oysters Rockefeller Like Antoines, New Orleans 6
Oysters in Sherry Sauce 9
Pan Fried Brie Cheese 3
Phyllo Appetizers 17
Pickled Shrimp Hermena Kelly 11
Piñata Double Dip 24
Redfish Appetizer 16
Salmon Appetizer 11
Seafood Saint-Jacques 5

Scallops in Green Sauce 12
Shrimp De Jong 12
Shrimp Dill Pâté (Dip) 25
Shrimp in Mustard Sauce #1 13
Shrimp in Mustard Sauce #2 13
Shrimp and Scallop Delight 14
Spiced Sugar Pecans 3
Special BleuCheese Dressing or Dip 18
Spinach-Cheese Appetizer 15
Stuffed Jalapeños 4
Stuffed Mushrooms 22
Stuffed Oysters 8

BEEF

Beef Tournedos and Mushrooms 123
Cabbage Rolls 127
Cranberry Roast 125
Dotty's Marinated Flank Steak 122
Empanadas 129
Filet of Beef with Crabmeat 126
Marinated Beef Tender 122
Meat Balls 124
Meat Pies 131
Poor Boys 131
Roast Beef and Gravy 124
Sauerbraten 125
Special Chili Relleno 130
Tacos 126
Tacos Desperado 128

BEVERAGES

Bloody Mary 29
Chocolate Smoothie 31
Cranberry Mist 28
Cranberry Rum Delight 34
Daddy's Eggnog 29
Fish House Punch 34

Holiday Punch 28
Lime and Strawberry Champagne Punch 33
Linda's Smoothie 35
Mango Daiquiri 30
McCulley's Punch 28
Milk Punch 34
Milk Punch Freeze 29
New Orleans Gin Fizz 30
Orange Spiced Tea Mix 32
Pineapple Brandy Frost 31
Powdered Cafe Au Lait Mix 32
Rice Field Punch 28
Spiced Coffee Punch 31
Strawberry Daiquiris 30
Tequila Allmendrada 33
Wedding Reception Punch 32

BREADS
Banana Sweet Potato Muffins 46
Breakfast Monkey Bread 42
Caramel Fruit Breakfast Rolls 38
Cheese Biscuits 38
Cranberry Orange Muffins 43
Easy Praline Biscuits 39
Gabbio's Orange Bread 44
Garlic Bread - Vintage 1960 46
Gingerbread 42
Holiday Nut Bread 42
Hot Water Cornbread 41
Hush Puppies 46
Jalapeño Cornbread #1 40
Jalapeño Cornbread #2 40
Jean's Garlic Bread 47
Louise's Blueberry Muffins, the Grand Hotel at Mackinac Island . 43
Mexican Spoon Bread with Chilies 40
Monkey Bread 41
Ricotta Muffins 39

Six Week Muffins 44
Spoon Bread Souffle 45
Sweet Potato Muffins. 45
Zucchini Fruit Loaf 47

CAKES

Apricot Brandy Pound Cake 51
Cherry Spice Cake 54
Chocolate Delights. 52
Cream Cherry Cake 54
Mrs. Davidson's German Fruit Cake 56
Dotty's Chocolate Torte 55
Dundee Cake 60
Frozen Cake. 58
Fruited Rum Cake 53
Hummingbird Cake with Brandy Sauce 52
Ice Cream Cake 51
John's Pudding Cake 57
Melanie's Angel Cake Surprise 60
Melanie's Rum Cake 59
Mincemeat Upside Down Cake with Rum Sauce 50
Mississippi Fudge Cake 56
Quick Coffee Cake 61
Quick Italian Cake 58
Trifle 67
Whiskey Cake 53

CHICKEN

Bonnie's Almond Chicken 154
Breast of Chicken Pappagallo 161
Chicken and Artichokes 144
Chicken and Green Chili Casserole 156
Chicken Breast and Tomato Sauce 158
Chicken Breast Wellington 160
Chicken Enchiladas 156
Chicken Fingers. 153
Chicken Florio 148
Chicken Interlaken 146

Chicken Jambalaya 154
Chicken Lettuce Pockets 157
Chicken, Mushrooms and Red Wine 150
Chicken Tacos 155
Chicken, Tomatoes and Bacon 151
Chicken Toronto 152
Chicken Stuffing for Crepes 149
Chicken Supreme 147
Chicken with Raspberry Sauce 161
Chicken with Rochambeau Sauce 148
Country Captain 146
Cuban Chicken 144
Easy Gourmet Chicken 143
Italian Chicken 147
Marinated Chicken 100
Mother's Ritz Cracker Chicken 153
San Antonio Green Enchiladas 145
San Francisco Chicken 152
Sliced Chicken and Mushrooms in Sour Cream Sauce 150
Supremes with Cheese Lemon Sauce 159

COOKIES AND CANDIES

Bird's Nests 65
Bunuelos 62
Chocolate Indulgence 61
Coconut Macaroons 63
French Canadian Fudge 61
Golden Tassies 62
Hello Dollies 64
Louisiana Pecan Lassies 62
Praline Crescent Cookies 63

CRAB

Coquille Crab Artichoke 207
Crabmeat Au Gratin 210
Crabmeat Mornay 209
Don's Crabmeat Casserole Lafayette, Louisiana 208

Mushrooms Stuffed with Crabmeat 210
New Orleans Stuffed Bell Pepper 208

CREPES
Mincemeat Crepes with Bourbon Sauce 72
Shellfish Crepes in Wine-Cheese Sauce 212
Spinach Crepes 118

DESSERT SAUCES
Apricot Sauce 88
Brandied Peach Sauce 90
Brandy Custard Sauce 90
Brandy Sauce 88
Fudge Sauce for Ice Cream the Grand Hotel at Mackinac Island . . 91
Lemon Sauce 90
Praline Sauce 90
Rum Sauce 89
Sauce Anglaise 89
Whiskey Sauce 89

DOVES
Smothered Doves 149

DRESSINGS
Cornbread Dressing for an Army and a Few Others 98
Zucchini Dressing 99

DRESSINGS FOR SALAD OR APPETIZER
Angel Salad Dressing 193
Chili Salad Dressing 195
Fresh Lemon Dressing 194
Hot Bacon Dressing 195
Hot French Dressing 193
Mango Chutney Salad Dressing 193
My Rendition of Tiger Horseradish Sauce 191

Poppyseed Coleslaw Dressing 194
Simple Salad Dressing 194
Tangy French Dressing 195

EGGS AND BREAKFAST CASSEROLES

Breakfast Potato Casserole 95
Breakfast Souffle 96
Breakfast Sunnyside Special 96
Chilaquiles 97
Gambler's Eggs 94
Good Morning Mexican Fiesta 97
Mushroom and Cheese Puff 95
Italian Brunch Eggs 94
Sausage Squares 96

FRUITS

Ambrosia 170
Bourbon Peaches 65
Cherry Surprise 68
Custard and Fruits 68
Hot Fruit Casserole 67
Mincemeat Peaches 65
Peaches and Cream 64
Pineapple Au Gratin 66
Raspberry Bavaria 69
Spicy Stuffed Peaches 66
Strawberries and Cream 68

GRITS

Garlic Cheese Grits 100
Grits Souffle 100

ICE CREAM

South of the Border Surprise 69
Tortoni 70

ICINGS

Confectioner's Sugar Icing 58
Orange Glaze 55
Venetian Cream Icing 55

LAMB

Greek Lamb with Basic Greek Salsa 142
Lamb Kidneys in Sherry-Mustard Sauce 142
Leg of Lamb 142

LIVER

Calf's Liver 132
Calf's Liver and Onions 132
Livor Marongo 132

MOUSSE

Chocolate Chestnut Dessert 71
Eggnog Mousse 70
Mincemeat Mousse 71
Seafood Mousse 220

OYSTERS (Also See Appetizers)

Baked Oysters 205
Oysters Dunbar 206
Oyster Loaf 205
Oysters in a Pastry Cup 206

PASTA

Cheese Cannelloni 114
Fettuccini, Chicken and Ham 111
Fettuccini Souffle 112
Laurie's Favorite Chicken Spaghetti 117
Linguine with Parsley-Pesto Sauce 116
Macaroni and Cheese 113
Pasta, Zucchini and Mushrooms 114
Rigatoni with Broccoli 111

Rigatoni Plus Cabbage 111
Spaghetti with Parsley Walnut Sauce 116
Spaghetti Spinach Bake 118
Vegetables and Pasta 115
Vermicelli with Broccoli 113
Vermicelli with Spinach Pesto Sauce 112

PIE CRUST

Chocolate Nut Crust 74
Graham Cracker Crust 73
June's Pie Crust 73
Vinegar Crust 73

PIES

Amaretto Coconut Cream Pie 75
Apple Custard Pie 81
Balkan Yogurt Pie 84
Bourbon Pie 84
Bourbon Street Cheesecake 84
Brandy Alexander Pie 74
Candy Bar Pie 77
Cheese Pie 79
Chocolate Pecan Pie 74
Chocolate Meringue 85
Coconut Kahlúa Cream Pie 82
College Inn's Pumpkin Bourbon Pie 78
Cottage Cheese Apple Pie 82
Edelweiss Fudge No Crust Pie 80
German Chocolate Pie 76
Jeannine's Fruit Pizza 78
Marilyn's Crème de Cassis Pie 83
Mincemeat Cream Pie 78
Nesselrode Chiffon Pie 83
Nut Delight - A Football Recipe 76
Rum Cream Pie 77
Whiskey Apple Pie 80

PORK

Easy Gourmet Pork Casserole	137
Glazed Ham with Ambrosia Sauce	138
Marinated Pork Roast	135
Pork in Crust	133
Pork, Peppers and Mushrooms	135
Pork Pot Roast	136
Pork Roast, Avocado and Lemon Garlic Sauce	136
Sweet and Sour Pork with Cranberries	134
Texas Pork Chops	134

POTATOES

Candied Yams	104
Caviar Potatoes	102
Crabmeat Stuffed Potatoes	106
Fried Sweet Potatoes Remembered as a Little Girl	104
Holiday Potatoes	104
Italian Potatoes	102
Jalapeño Potatoes	101
Potato Broccoli Cheese Bake	107
Potatoes O'Brien	105
Potatoes with Spiced Cheese, Tomatoes and Onions	106
Spinach Stuffed Potatoes	107
Springtime Potato Bake	103
Sweet Potato Alexander	101

PUDDINGS AND CREAMS

Bread Pudding	86
Bread Pudding Bon Ton Restaurant	87
Carrot Pudding	253
Cheese Pudding	100
Zabaglione Cream	86

RICE

Barbecued Rice and Lima Beans	250
Emerald Rice	109

Green Rice 109
Garlic Brown Rice 110
Green Beans and Rice Provencale 245
Rice Stuffed Green Peppers 108
Rice and Asparagus 251
Spinach and Brown Rice Greek Style 103
Wild Rice with Grapes 108
Wild Rice and Spinach Casserole 108
Zucchini Rice Bake 110

SALADS

Ambrosia 170
Ann's Wild Rice and Chicken Salad 175
Broccoli and White Bean Salad 180
Chicken Salad 173
Chicken-Cranberry Salad 174
Colorful Rice Salad 179
Eggplant Salad 169
Fruit Heaven 170
Fried Chicken Salad 175
German Potato Salad 168
Grandmother's Mashed Potato Salad 168
Greek Salad 172
Green Salad with Apples and Cheese 170
Green Bean Salad 172
Guacamole and Shrimp Salad 176
Hearts of Palm Salad 169
Holiday Cranberry Salad 178
Hot Chicken Salad 174
Italian Vegetable Salad 180
Kolbs Salad 171
Layered Salad 167
Margaret's Shrimp Salad 177
Marinated Antipasto 178
Marinated Carrots (Copper Pennies) 179
Marinated Cherry Tomatoes 173
Shrimp Salad 176

Spinach Salad with Mango Chutney Dressing 167
To Make A Green Salad 164
Tomatoes Camille 181
Tuna and Potato Salad 168
Twenty-Four Hour Salad 171
Yellow Squash Salad 177

SAUCES (Also See Dessert Sauces)
Arnaud Like Rèmoulade Sauce 192
Asparagus Sauce 186
Avocado Sauce 186
Barbecue Sauce 192
Basting Sauce for Fish or Game 191
Bòarnaise Sauce 185
Cheese Wine Sauce 186
Chicken Marinade 190
Creole Seasoning 202
Cucumber Sauce for Fish 189
Double Cheese Sauce 190
Fresh Salsa 190
Golden Yogurt Sauce 189
Horseradish Sauce 185
Italian Spaghetti Sauce 187
Mornay Sauce 192
My Rendition of Tiger Horseradish Sauce 191
Pat's Greek Tomato Salsa 188
Pistou Sauce 184
Red Sauce (Milder Version) 191
Reverend Notar's Quick Tomato Sauce 188
Sherry Mustard Sauce 187
Spinach Pesto Sauce 184
Stir Fry Sauce 184
Sweet Mustard Sauce 185
Tujaque's Boiled Beef Sauce 191
White Sauce 188

SEAFOOD

Baked Snapper South Pacific 213
Cuban Fish 217
Crawfish Etouffee 211
Daddy's Lobster Newburg 214
Fish Filets Las Brisas 218
Fish, Mushrooms and Artichokes 216
Fish Stuffing from the Doggie Bag 216
Red Snapper, Excelsor, Maxim's Houston, Texas 213
Red Snapper, Tomato Sauce, Olives and Potatoes 214
Seafood Cheesecake 219
Seafood Mousse 220
Shellfish Crepes in Wine-Cheese Sauce 212
Stuffed Eggplant 218
Ye Olde College Inn Stuffing for Flounder Houston, Texas 215

SHRIMP (Also See Appetizers)

Barbecued Shrimp 201
Barbecued Shrimp in Wine 200
Cranberry Butterfly Shrimp 204
Gutsey Shrimp 202
Shrimp Brochettes 200
Shrimp Creole with Eggplant and Brown Garlic Rice 198
Shrimp Etouffee 201
Shrimp Fiorentina 199
Shrimp, Tomatoes, Wine and Feta Cheese 198
Spanish Shrimp Casserole 203
Shrimp Veracruz 204

SOUFFLE

Amaretto Souffle 87
Raspberry Souffle 88

SOUPS

Boola - Boola Soup 225
Chicken Soup 229
Cold Cream of Avocado 225

Crab Bisque 229
Cream of Spinach Soup 226
Gazpacho. 227
Lettuce Soup 227
Lobster Bisque 224
Mock Turtle Soup 226
Mushroom Soup 224
Seneglase. 228
Spanish Fish Soup 228
Zucchini Bisque. 224

SWEET POTATOES

Candied Yams 104
Fried Sweet Potatoes Remembered as a Little Girl 104
Sweet Potato Alexander 101

TABLES 256

VEAL

Boston Cutlets 138
Grillades. 141
Laurie's Veal Pockets 139
Veal Lasagna Like Mama Poli's 140
Veal Scallops 141

VEGETABLES

Artichoke Ring 250
Bleu Cheese Tomatoes 240
Barbecued Rice and Lima Beans 250
Broccoli with Tomato Sauce 241
Cabbage Casserole 254
Cabbage Rolls. 127
Carrot Pudding 253
Chili Black Eyed Peas 236
Confetti Vegetable Casserole 255
Creole Cabbage 254
Creole Onions 242
Danish Asparagus 251

Eggplant Pizza 248
Easy Asparagus 252
Easy Tomatoes 240
Fancy Peas 235
Greek Spinach Pie 234
Green Beans and Rice Provencale 245
Green Beans Like Mama Made 254
Hermena's Asparagus Casserole 252
Italian White Beans 238
Italian Spinach 234
Italian Vegetables with Pasta 248
Jeannine's Italian Vegetable Casserole 237
Lenten Spinach 233
Marinated Eggplant 247
Marinated Peas or Beans 237
Mariposa Vegetable Casserole 242
Mushrooms in Patty Shells 244
Mushrooms Newburg 244
Mushrooms Supreme 246
Onions That Don't Take Your Breath Away 243
Pineapple Squash Supreme 240
Puffed Broccoli 241
Ratatouille Savannah 246
Ratatouille Stuffed Mushrooms 245
Red Beans and Rice Paradise 238
Rice and Asparagus 251
Spicy Lima Bean Casserole 249
Spinach and Pine Nuts 234
Spinach Crepes 118
Spinach Dumplings 232
Spinach and Navy Beans 232
Spinach Nut Pie 233
Sunday Peas 236
Stuffed Onions 243
Summer Squash 255
Tomatoes Bombay 239
Tomatoes Stuffed with Squash 239

Reba Michels Hill, M.D.
6720 Bertner
Houston, Texas 77030
(713) 791-3184

Please send me _____ copies of
"A Doctor's Prescription for Gourmet Cooking" at $9.95 $_____
Postage & handling at $2.00 $_____
Texas Residents add 5% sales tax at $0.50 $_____
TOTAL ENCLOSED $_____

Name _____
Address _____
City _____ State _____ ZIP _____

Please make checks payable to *A Doctor's Prescription for Gourmet Cooking.* Proceeds from the sale of the cookbook support NEWBORN RESEARCH.